HIGH VELOCITY LEADERSHIP

HIGH

VELOCITY

LEADERSHIP

The Mars Pathfinder Approach
to Faster, Better, Cheaper

BRIAN K. MUIRHEAD and **WILLIAM L. SIMON**

HarperBusiness
A Division of HarperCollinsPublishers

A note to the reader: This book is supplemented by "VideoNotes™" video clips, enhancing descriptions in the text with visual depictions that can be screened on the Web. Places in the text that are supplemented by these video clips are marked with the symbol 💻

The Web site address is
www.HiVelocity.com

Kevlar® is a DuPont registered trademark.

Quotes from *Design News* magazine used by permission.

Photographs courtesy of NASA/JPL.

Art of entry/descent/landing by Steve Sharp, Sharp Ad and Design, San Diego.

HIGH VELOCITY LEADERSHIP. Copyright © 1999 by Brian K. Muirhead and William L. Simon. All rights reserved. Printed in the United States of America. No part of this book may be used or reproduced in any manner whatsoever without written permission except in the case of brief quotations embodied in critical articles and reviews. For information address HarperCollins Publishers, Inc., 10 East 53rd Street, New York, NY 10022.

HarperCollins books may be purchased for educational, business, or sales promotional use. For information please write: Special Markets Department, HarperCollins Publishers, Inc., 10 East 53rd Street, New York, NY 10022.

FIRST EDITION

Designed by Laura Lindgren

Library of Congress Cataloging-in-Publication Data
Muirhead, Brian.
    High velocity leadership : the Mars Pathfinder approach to faster, better, cheaper / Brian Muirhead and William Simon.—1st ed.
      p. cm.
    Includes index.
    ISBN 0-88730-974-7
    1. Leadership. 2. Industrial management. 3. Industrial efficiency. I. Simon, William L., 1930–. II. Title.
    HD57.7.M84 1999
    658.4'09—dc21   99-11400

99 00 01 02 03 ❖/RRD 10 9 8 7 6 5 4 3 2 1

For my daughters, Alicia and Jenna,
who grew up with Pathfinder,
and to Leslie, who shared the wonder of the experience
                                        —Brian K. Muirhead

For Arynne, Victoria and Sheldon
                                        —William L. Simon

We look around us now at other planets. . . . Someday we may sail among new enchanted archipela-
goes with . . . seeds clinging to our boots.

—Jonathan Weiner,
in *The Beak of the Finch*

CONTENTS

Photographs and illustrations to follow page 114.

by Price Pritchett, Chairman,
Pritchett & Associates

I first met Brian Muirhead at the IMAX Theater on Broadway in New York City, where I was attending a conference on cutting-edge work being done in technology, education and design. On day two of the program, those of us in the audience watched a stirring documentary film about the Pathfinder mission to Mars. Then Brian and three others from the Jet Propulsion Laboratory's Mars Pathfinder team walked onstage to a standing ovation. Over the next hour or so they shared their remarkable story with us. And they stole the show.

A couple of months later we invited Brian and three others from the Pathfinder team to speak at a conference we were holding in Dallas for Pritchett & Associates clients. Once again, they captivated the audience, and again finished to a standing ovation.

Our firm wanted to publish a piece about Faster, Better, Cheaper in action, and the Mars Pathfinder project looked like the perfect example. It offered hard proof of how a small group of committed people, operating under significant constraints and limitations, innovated their way to spectacular results. Together Brian and I coauthored a handbook on the mission.

But there was another big and important message inside Brian Muirhead that we couldn't cover in a short handbook. It's a story about leadership. And it's captured here in the pages of this book by Brian and Bill Simon. Their message will fascinate you. And you'll put the book down with a deeper understanding of the key role leadership played in the magic of Pathfinder.

Brian Muirhead—flight system manager for the Pathfinder project—is a most likable and impressive individual. Approachable, unpretentious and optimistic, he's also intense and relentless in his search for solutions. This is a purposeful man, one who consistently focuses forward and whose efforts are well aimed. Brian has a high energy level, as well as a keen sense of how to manage the energy of an organization. As a result of these characteristics, he covers a lot of ground. He truly is a high velocity leader.

Velocity, in the vocabulary of physics, is about both *speed* and *direction*. These two elements are critically important to consider in the context of leadership.

A person could be a strong leader yet a bad one, simply by setting the wrong course for an organization. Certainly there are many misguided groups that exist, proving that powerful leadership pointed the wrong way can be downright dangerous. High velocity leadership, however, is well directed—it means leading toward the right targets . . . taking dead aim at the appropriate objectives.

Then there's the matter of speed. In today's world of intense competition and frenzied change, the quality of a person's leadership skills also depends heavily on how fast he or she can move the organization forward. Obviously, it's not enough merely to be pointed in the right direction. The organization must be led such that it reaches its objectives quickly, meeting or beating aggressive schedules. Better still, the overall effort also should cost less and deliver better outcomes than before. *That* is what high velocity leadership is really all about. And it's precisely what Brian Muirhead brought to the Pathfinder project.

But Brian is quick to point out that this book is not just about leadership in the usual sense: not just leadership as exhibited by people at the top of an organization, but leadership exhibited throughout, which is an intrinsic ingredient for success. "The Mars Pathfinder mission team," he says, "had many leaders. Some carried 'manager' in their titles, others did not; leadership is a personality strength that transcends titles."

You might be wondering how these lessons from Pathfinder will be of value to you. Obviously, building a spacecraft to land on Mars is very different from the challenges most of us face in everyday business. What you'll find here are piercing insights into what works in today's pursuit of Faster, Better, Cheaper. This is a story that sheds light on the kind of leadership that work groups want and need when they're stretching to achieve very ambitious goals, yet having to operate under severe constraints. *High Velocity Leadership* will show you how to build a strong team . . . how to pull your people past the paralysis of uncertainty and heavy-duty change . . . how to overcome limitations, actually using them to drive innovation and achieve spectacular breakthroughs.

This is an invaluable management message for the demanding world we'll face in the twenty-first century. Whether you're leading a group that's exploring the mysteries of deep space, or venturing into the blurry and volatile business world of tomorrow, you'll need to provide your people high velocity leadership.

1. Faster, Better, Cheaper to the Surface of Mars

Any sufficiently advanced technology
is indistinguishable from magic.
—Arthur C. Clarke

The Martian dust hadn't been stirred by a craft from Earth in twenty-one years. This time the challenge had come with nearly impossible constraints: go there at a fraction of the cost, do it in a fraction of the time, take risks but don't fail. We were working on a budget less than it would later cost to produce the movie *Titanic*, but unlike the movie we would need to provide a happy ending.

Our effort, the Mars Pathfinder mission, has come to define the management style of "Faster, Better, Cheaper."

At the heart of any great achievement lies a set of incomparable lessons revealed to those who look for them. The story of Mars Pathfinder has been called a stirring highlight of late-twentieth-century technology. Yet the most valuable lessons may not after all lie in the realm of technology but in the areas of business, management and leadership. To me, Faster, Better, Cheaper is first and foremost about new ways of doing business, and the leadership skills required to make those new ways work.

On the Fourth of July, 1997, as Americans woke up looking forward to their Independence Day parades and picnics, some fifty of us were waiting anxiously in a small, windowless control room on the grounds of NASA's Jet Propulsion Laboratory—JPL—in Pasadena, just north of Los Angeles. The spacecraft we had begun to dream of in 1993 was nearing the time to start its perilous plunge toward Mars.

Focused intently at his control panel was the flight director who had been responsible for operating the spacecraft in its seven-month, 300-million-mile cruise through interplanetary space. Richard Cook, probably the youngest person ever to hold such a crucial job, had the task of flying the spacecraft, similar to flying an airplane except that the pilot is sitting on the ground and doesn't know until minutes later how the craft has responded to his commands.

Nearby, the Pathfinder navigators couldn't be blamed for fidgeting. We had chosen to risk an approach that demanded a degree of navigation accuracy never before attempted. Pathfinder would come screaming out of space at a blazing speed and careen directly into the thin Martian atmosphere. Not for us those usual orbits for slowing to a more manageable speed. Our approach, dictated by our budget constraints, came with a demanding downside. The angle of entry has to be incredibly exacting, accurate to within only one degree. Too shallow, and the spacecraft will skip back out into space like a rock skipping across a pond, to be lost forever into orbit around the sun. Too steep, and it will become a fireball hurtling to the Martian surface.

It was now 8:30 A.M. California time. The operations team crowded into the increasingly stuffy mission control room knew that touchdown was only an hour and a half away. At this point the spacecraft's onboard software was in complete control. Nothing for us on the ground to do except watch our progeny carry out its mission, responsible for its own fate.

As its first independent action, Pathfinder would expel into space the Freon gas that had been circulating as in a car's air conditioner to keep the onboard electronics from getting too hot. We watched anxiously to see if the venting would disturb the spacecraft's flight. A sigh of relief: no problem. It worked perfectly; everyone was feeling great.

Then two latch valves in the propulsion system didn't close on schedule. This wouldn't affect the landing but raised a major concern. Richard turned to flight director Guy Beutelschies and asked, "Are we sure the new load of software is on board and running?" Five weeks ago we had uploaded the final software instructions for the landing sequence; if the spacecraft wasn't using the new software, our chances of successfully reaching Mars had just plummeted.

Richard looked at the monitor displaying the latest spacecraft status information. It showed Pathfinder was running software version R051097—meaning the revision of 5/10/97, the date the new code was completed and compiled. That was the right software. So what was going on?

Voices were gaining the sharp cold edge of doubt and fear. "Could the version number be wrong?" "How can we be sure the spacecraft is running the latest software?" If not, we would have to reset the computer immediately—a scary idea, akin to stopping and restarting the engines of an airplane while on approach for landing.

Richard checked with Glenn Reeves, the lead software engineer. Together they went off to pore through the electronic files of recent communications with the spacecraft. To fill blank spaces, software programmers insert their names or zany messages like "Elvis lives." They hoped to find the name of Jordan Kaplan—the team's tribute to one of its members who a few months earlier had died after the engine of his antique King Air plane caught fire in flight.

Soon they were back, running. "It's there!" "Jordan's name is there!" So the spacecraft *was* running the correct version of the software. People visibly relaxed, the built-up tension draining away. Our first crisis of the day had been put to rest.

9:32 A.M. Suddenly the signal is gone. But not unexpected—the spacecraft is going through its planned metamorphosis, shedding its cruise stage skin like a molting crab.

(VideoNotes: www.HiVelocity.com, "Shedding cruise stage.")

Seconds later the signal reappears. In thirty minutes Pathfinder will face the most critical part of the entire mission, the incredibly complex sequence of forty-two events for slowing, shedding the protective outer pieces and safely landing. Hard to believe that this

---

*This book is supplemented by "VideoNotes™" video clips on the Web, enhancing descriptions in the text with visual depictions. Places in the text that are supplemented by video clips are marked with the symbol 🖳

The Web site is address is www.HiVelocity.com

entire make-or-break sequence that has been the focus of so much of our efforts will play itself out in a brief four and a half minutes.

10:02. The spacecraft pierces the Martian atmosphere, glowing like a meteor as it decelerates from 16,600 miles an hour. A control room readout displaying the frequency shift of the radio signal, the Doppler, shows we're decelerating at the proper rate. So far all is well.

The deceleration force reaches about 20 g's, triggering an improbable series of Independence Day pyrotechnics. A mortar fires, shooting out a 35-foot parachute that must safely deploy though the spacecraft is still hurtling at supersonic speed. More fireworks, and the fiery heat shield, glowing but charred, is shoved clear.

(VideoNotes: www.HiVelocity.com, "Entry, descent and landing animation.")

The lander, which must somehow be a safe distance from rockets that will fire in a moment, now rappels like a mountaineer down a bridle—a thick, braided Kevlar rope—then dangles 65 feet below.

At 1,000 feet above the surface four shock-absorbing airbags inflate, enveloping the lander in something like a ridiculous beach ball for a giant, 19 feet across. Deceleration rockets fire with such jolting force that descent is momentarily halted. The comical beach ball hangs in midair.

More fireworks, and the beach ball falls free the final hundred feet through the cold, black Martian sky.

If all is going as planned, the beach ball and its precious cargo have now careened to the Martian surface, hitting at close to 65 miles an hour, bouncing wildly on the red hardscrabble of an area called Ares Vallis.

If there were any Martians watching, we joked, then our explosions and rockets and bouncing ball have just scared the hell out of them.

10:07 A.M. Whatever happened had taken place eleven minutes ago. Hearts pounding, we breathlessly wait for a radio signal that will mean our cut-rate spacecraft has survived.

Over his headset, telecommunications lead engineer Gordon Wood commands the receiving station near Madrid, Spain, "Keep your eyes glued and let us know if you see anything at all, please." Its antenna, nearly the size of a football field, listens for a tiny signal from Mars out of the noisy emptiness of space. The voice of Sami Asmar comes back from the station in Spain, "I have eight sets of eyes watching. We don't see it."

10:10 A.M. Dead or alive, Pathfinder is on the frigid surface of Mars. Three minutes after our last signal. I'm trying not to think of all the ways our craft could have turned into a pile of space junk that we would never be hearing from again.

The image of the control room activities is being beamed by CNN to television viewers worldwide. Those watching don't see the lavish, spacious facility familiar from man-on-the-moon days, operated by serious-looking gentlemen in suits and ties, but instead guys and gals wearing their everyday jeans and T-shirts.

For the television audience, spacecraft chief engineer Rob Manning attempts to describe events he can see only in his mind's eye, offering details of what he thinks and hopes is happening more than 100 million miles away. It's so frustrating to us all not to know for certain.

By now the bouncing should have stopped . . . the lander should have rolled to rest . . . and an antenna should be exposed so that Pathfinder can let us know it has landed and is functioning.

Still no signal. Time to start worrying. Tony Spear, my boss, is standing, holding on to a bookcase for dear life, visions of a streaming parachute, unignited rockets and torn airbags whirling through his head.

The voice over the speakers from the station in Spain: "A weak signal is coming in and out of the spectrum."

Rob Manning announces over the net, "A very good sign, everybody." "Yes, yes!" someone exclaims. There are smiles and a little relieved laughter. But we all know this is wishful thinking. We still don't have anything definitive.

Then suddenly the flat data line on the monitors springs alive with a beautiful little peak, like a steep solitary mountain. And then the voice from Spain: "We have a confirmed signal."

That is the news we've been waiting for. The room erupts. Hugs and backslaps, hugs and handshakes, cheers and whoops, euphoric laughter mixed with unembarrassed tears, relief tinged with joy.

(VideoNotes: www.HiVelocity.com, "Control room.")

None of us had seriously thought we'd see a signal this early—
the odds were too high against it. First everything had to survive the
landing, then the lander had to stop rolling in just the right position,
and finally our antenna in Spain had to locate the faint transmission. Luck has been with us: the lander has bounced around the
Martian terrain for only about a minute and rolled to a stop in a
position that has left the descent antenna, no bigger than my thumb,
standing upright and transmitting its tiny signal, half the power of a
night-light, to us, 150 million miles away. Our extraterrestrial has
phoned home.

According to the original goals set by NASA, just getting the
spacecraft to Mars and landing in one piece means we have already
succeeded. But we hope to achieve so much more—photographs,
data collection about the conditions on Mars, proof that an untethered, free-roaming rover vehicle can travel the surface under its own
power gathering scientific data even in so frigid and hostile a place.

The team of Pathfinder scientists gathered in another room anxiously awaits the next events. Outside a flock of reporters and cam-
eramen, far more than we had anticipated, is counting on us to give
them a story worth telling.

The time at Ares Vallis, Mars, is 3 A.M. Our spacecraft, in darkness, unable to use power from its solar cells until sunrise, has been
programmed to perform some few essentials on battery power. With
the airbags deflated and retracted, it should be checking to see
which of its four faces is on the surface, and should then perform a
bit of ingeniously clever acrobatics to flip itself onto its base.

Then, like a flower unfolding, the three petals that make up the
exterior surface of the lander should open to the ground.

*(VideoNotes: www.HiVelocity.com, "Airbags retracting, petals
unfolding.")*

If the operation is successful, the solar cells will then be ready to
catch the sun's rays and start recharging the nearly depleted batteries. And the little toy-wagon-sized rover will be in position, ready
for its eventual drive off the lander, onto the surface. But all this
must wait till Martian sunrise, still four hours away. Patience. We
have all put out such a high-pitched, nonstop effort to reach this
point, now we must be patient. There is so little to do but watch for

the brief signals from the lander that tell us it is diligently carrying out its programmed instructions, one by one.

I take advantage of the break to walk across to the JPL cafeteria, which has been equipped with television sets so Lab employees can share the event together, as an extended family. My older daughter Alicia, age nine, spots me and I run to her, lifting her into my arms, hugging and hugging, as enormous tears well up and stream down my cheeks. She can't quite understand my incredible feelings of joy. Next to the elation of seeing each of my two daughters take their first breaths, there has never been a happier moment in my life.

When I return to the control room, little has changed. The flight director for our first operational day on Mars, Jennifer Harris, tosses me a smile as I walk in, but I know her heart must be in her mouth. So much responsibility for someone not yet thirty years old.

I take my accustomed place behind the telecommunications system engineer, waiting to see the spacecraft signal pop out of the background noise of empty space. And right on time, there it is!

Again the team lets loose a wild round of cheers. But then everyone quickly turns to their computer screens to look for the data that will tell us whether Pathfinder is as healthy as we hope. Jennifer sits at her terminal, headset on, watching data scroll across her screen. The image of this intent young woman leading the Pathfinder team will become famous.

We're getting lots of bits from Mars but no complete message. Then columns of words and numbers that had remained unchanged for over five and a half hours suddenly come alive. "We have data!" Jennifer shouts, jumping out of her seat and hugging the nearest person. Everyone starts poring over the screens, trying to make sense of the numbers.

I look over the shoulder of temperature control engineer Keith Novak. Lander temperatures are reporting just right. Power engineer Dale Burger checks for voltage readings from the solar arrays which, even on Earth, have never seen the sun. But they're working perfectly, producing power under the weak Martian sunlight.

At the rover station, Art Thompson knows it's early for rover data but seems a little worried as with trembling finger he points to a corner of his screen to show me what number should change when the rover starts sending. Just as his finger touches the screen, the number changes. I can't help yelling out, "We have rover data!"

Jennifer calls the roll. Each of the spacecraft engineers down the line reports loud and clear: All subsystems operational. And the rover is healthy, ready to go to work.

Jennifer now takes a poll of the team and everyone agrees: we're Go to proceed. She directs flight controller Cindy Oda, handling communications over the deep space network, to transmit the command that will launch the next critical sequence of events. The camera swings into action and locates the sun, and the computer uses sun position to calculate the location of Earth, then commands the high-gain antenna to point in our direction. How accurately it points has been an issue we've plotted over, sweated over, struggled with, tested and retested. We're hoping to be aimed within about three degrees, which would give us the ability to transmit a digital photograph every two to three minutes.

I've scheduled a special press conference at 2:30 P.M., a solo performance at which I would provide a brief mission status and answer just a few questions. But there is an unspoken, secret reason for this session: if there had been no signal of any kind by this time, we would be in trouble, possibly dead. I would be trying to explain to the world what had gone wrong, so the reporters wouldn't start calling their "other sources" or relying on their guesses. My job would be to offer a short, well-crafted sound bite, a "don't give up yet" message. I never found time to prepare one; now, thankfully, I won't need it.

4:30 P.M. If the unfolding operation has been successful, the high-gain antenna should be coming on line. My stomach is churning. All eyes in the control room are focused on a single console. Waiting.

And then, in a blink, bang, there it is—a signal is coming through, the first image beginning to form. "Mars," Jennifer yells. Pathfinder is sending back the first black-and-white photo of its landing area, and it is one of the most beautiful, thrilling sights any of us have ever seen.

(VideoNotes: www.HiVelocity.com, "First Mars photo.")

As further images come down, we gradually see a more complete picture—a rough, irregular landscape, rocks strewn in every direction, a few larger boulders, two peaks in the distance. The ancient floodplain of Ares Vallis. This rock garden is just what project scientist Matt Golombek has been hoping for. We have managed to put our spacecraft down within 10 miles of the spot we had selected. Navigator Robin Vaughn calls this "like a hole-in-one shot from L.A. to Houston." And it has sent us a picture postcard, "Wish you were here!"

In the science team's room, the shouts of triumph over this first picture drown out the Beatles' "Twist and Shout" booming from a speaker.

One of the local restaurants had sent over some wonderfully tempting dishes with a note of congratulations. From some anonymous donor, an appropriate gift of a case of Mars bars mysteriously appears. Still high from a massive overdose of adrenaline, I try unsuccessfully to eat and in the end just grab a soda.

The men and women of JPL's image processing lab under Bill Green have developed new state-of-the-art software tools that allow them to assemble a series of images, taken through three separate color filters, into a very wide, panoramic color mosaic, in a fraction of the time it used to take. We had long been talking about the first color panorama as the "mission success pan" since we thought, maybe naively, that even if we received only a single good image, the court of public opinion would still declare Pathfinder a success.

In less than an hour the image processing team has created our first panorama.

🖥 *(VideoNotes: www.HiVelocity.com, "First panoramic photo.")*

This historic photo, which *Newsweek* will later call "the ultimate Kodak moment," shows the lander resting on a dull-colored terrain under a flat, salmon-colored sky. The rover sits, stowed on its petal, overlooking a field of rocks of many irregular shapes and sizes, with two peaks in the distance. From the way the rocks are laid out and tilted over in one direction, it's easy to imagine the savage flood that Matt believes had roared through here more than three and a half billion years ago.

The photo is thrilling but also chilling: it reveals that one of the airbags has not fully retracted and is blocking a ramp, one of the two routes we've provided for the rover to drive down to reach the surface.

This is a contingency we had anticipated, planned for and practiced. While I prepare for another scheduled press conference, the team goes about the process of commanding the lander to raise the petal, retract the airbag once again, and put the petal back in place.

The scientist responsible for the lander camera, Peter Smith, a big, friendly, gregarious man with black and gray goatee, faces another standing-room-only crowd. When he brings the first picture up on the large TV screen, the reporters burst into applause.

There would be problems ahead, but none we could not surmount. Pathfinder and the rover would be front-page news stories around the globe for the next several days, and our Web site would, in a single day, receive a staggering 46 *million* "hits," an Internet record. In the first month alone, the number of hits would reach almost half a billion.

The instruments on Pathfinder and the rover would send back enough data over the following three months on the Martian composition, environment and geologic history to keep the scientists busy for a long time to come.

In its cover story about the Pathfinder achievement, *Time* magazine would write, "Space is a harsh and unforgiving place, where Murphy's Law is paramount." Surely Providence had dealt us a kingly serving of luck. Yet luck is the one thing you can't·buy, a thing you pay for with effort.

And life is not about luck, after all, but about the things we make happen. In a little over three and a half years, we had made Mars Pathfinder happen, along the way devising, revising, testing and applying the leadership principles of Faster, Better, Cheaper that made it possible. In that sense this is more than a story of a space mission, more than a history of a project done in half the time and for one-twentieth the cost of the previous Mars landers; it's a story that says, "These are the principles we used, these the practices we followed, here is the way you can put Faster, Better, Cheaper to work in your own organization or team."

This is a journey not just to Mars but to the new high velocity leadership style of tomorrow.

2. Risk Without Failure:
Deciding to Do Things Differently

You miss 100 percent of the shots you never take.

—Wayne Gretzky,
hockey player

Some of us prefer the tempo of a life with nonstop challenges. In April 1993, I walked into a meeting room at the Jet Propulsion Lab where the challenge was all too clear before a word was spoken. Here were thirty professionals looking at me expectantly, a clear and serious doubt in each pair of unblinking eyes, a single question hovering in the air: "What do you want us to do?"

At age forty-one, I had agreed to take on the job of flight system manager for the Pathfinder mission to Mars.

Some of my peers thought I was crazy. A joke I began to hear too often was "What did you do *wrong* to land that assignment?" Even those who didn't directly needle me with the question seemed to be thinking it.

But from deep within, a gut-level confidence assured me we would find a way to meet the impossible challenges if I could assemble the right management and technical team.

Would I have accepted the Pathfinder assignment if some prescient dream had revealed the unending months of hard days, long nights, and emotional roller coasters of colossal proportions? My answer, in a millisecond, is an emphatic Yes. I love the "mission impossible" challenge.

In my student days, a professor of mine at the University of New Mexico, Albuquerque, a former Jet Propulsion Lab research engineer, warned me against joining the Lab. The work sounded intriguing, and his negative advice was all the push I needed. I was about to receive a degree in mechanical engineering and would still have many years ahead to try other challenges if this one didn't work out.

JPL has always been successful in recruiting the pick-of-the-litter graduates from schools like Caltech, Stanford and MIT. But the man who hired me, Gary Coyle, was on the lookout for somebody with real-world hardware experience, not just another 4.0 student who was merely a skilled manipulator of mathematical equations. So it wasn't my grade point average from the University of New Mexico that got me in the door—it was my precollege jobs repairing motorcycles and, later, Mercedes-Benz cars.

Twelve fascinating years later I was head of the Mechanical System Integration Section, the same section where I had started. During those years I had worked on Galileo, now in orbit around Jupiter, and on smaller projects like MSTI, a satellite for the "Star Wars" Strategic Defense Initiative, and SIR-C, an advanced-technology radar system that first flew on the space shuttle *Endeavor*. JPL had made me stretch by giving me extraordinary assignments for which I wasn't quite ready.

Few things in life remain stable for long. In 1992, winds of change were sweeping across America and through the halls of NASA and JPL. Budgets were being cut throughout government.

In that climate, with space exploration being seriously questioned, it wasn't a surprise when Vice President Dan Quayle recruited a pragmatist like Daniel Goldin from TRW to be the new administrator of NASA, the National Aeronautics and Space Administration. Goldin's charter: replace the "grow 15 percent a year" mentality with a strong focus on budgetary responsibility.

And what were the NASA flight mission centers up to? The ones involved with manned flight, like the Johnson Space Center, in Houston, had recovered from the *Challenger* disaster and were hard at work on the space station *Freedom*. At JPL, many of the people and much of the resources were channeled to a single project: the eight-year, $1.5 billion Cassini mission to Saturn.

The new NASA administrator, determined that the United States must continue to do space science missions despite the government-wide belt tightening that had squeezed the NASA budget, began talking about "Faster, Better, Cheaper." The catchphrase summed up a philosophy that was right in step with the new administration's practical thinking. It also seemed to describe a way of doing business that JPL, which had evolved in an aerospace culture of large, "succeed at any cost" projects, just might not be capable of adapting to. The Lab had an unparalleled reputation for "doing the big ones." Would it be able to function in a Faster, Better, Cheaper mode? And if JPL people couldn't learn to succeed in this new style of doing business, then what would become of the place when the huge projects dried up?

NASA's Associate Administrator for Space Science, Dr. Wesley Huntress, had already been moving in this direction and had proposed a daring new series of science missions, the Discovery program, which has since become a mainstay of the small space-science projects. NASA would start Discovery with two challenging missions. One, using proven technology, would attempt to rendezvous with a near-Earth asteroid.

The other, a bold plan to put a spacecraft on Mars, would need to stretch way beyond current technologies. This was Pathfinder, soon to become my dream and my nightmare.

For JPL to succeed on the pared-down, speeded-up parameters of Faster, Better, Cheaper would require breakthroughs, a lot of breakthroughs. But when success was ours, it would silence the critics who said JPL couldn't make the adjustment to small-scale efforts. Success would ensure that the Jet Propulsion Lab would continue to have a future.

GOALS THAT MAKE PEOPLE STRETCH

Pathfinder had started in 1992 as part of a JPL study effort into the idea of landing as many as sixteen stations all over the surface of Mars. What came out of the pipeline instead was a much-reduced mission to Mars with a daunting set of requirements: Do it in three years. Do it for $150 million.

As a frame of reference, the last NASA mission to land on Mars had reached there on a budget, adjusted for inflation, of $3 *billion*, and had taken about six years. Now JPL was being challenged to find a way of doing the job in half the time, for something like one-twentieth of the dollars.

There were other goals as well: Demonstrate to Congress that the space agency is truly committed to low-cost planetary missions. And demonstrate to the nation that NASA is capable of valuable space science even in an era of budget-cutting and belt-tightening.

NASA's Office of Space Science was resolute in this rethinking of planetary exploration. With billion-dollar missions, any one that fails leaves a very large and very visible hole in the agency's reputation. With smaller, less costly missions, it wouldn't matter as much if a spacecraft were lost now and then. . . .

But we would soon painfully discover that this attitude didn't apply to Pathfinder. As the highly visible first project in the Faster, Better, Cheaper mode, Pathfinder was just what its name implied: a pathfinder for a new way of doing business. From NASA's perspective, it *could not* fail. It *must not* fail.

So those became our marching orders. We were chartered to prove that Faster, Better, Cheaper would work even for something as difficult as a deep space planetary mission. And failure would not be acceptable.

In the business world, fear of failure prevents people from taking risks. Many go through their work lives locked into a mode of avoiding risks. Often that's wisely self-protective and therefore understandable. But the behavior becomes self-limiting.

Wise leaders should ask how a company can encourage people to accept long-term stretch goals and still deliver on short-term results. How will your people produce revenue today while at the same time pursuing stretch goals that can serve the future? How does a company discover the truly innovative products, services, strategies, while at the same time pursuing goals that lay the foundation for tomorrow? How does a company come out with truly innovative products and services while at the same time improving on efficiency and cost control?

The secret in beginning to set stretch goals lies in knowing where you want to end. The key lies in pointing your organization, your people, toward a *dramatic destination*.

In the case of Pathfinder, the overall destination was clearly dramatic: the surface of Mars. A goal easy to identify and easy for the team to connect with. But at the working levels, every Pathfinder manager needed to create goals that would incite his or her team toward this outcome; these team goals, covering more mundane items like building electric wiring cables, weren't anything nearly so sexy.

What's more, organizations usually start with a high-level strategic goal, which they then translate into a series of tactical goals. Before long those tactical goals take on a life of their own, and people forget the forest for the trees.

A key element of good leadership is to make sure that while working on the intermediate goals, the team continues to focus on the final destination. Each manager must find a way to articulate how the tactical goals support the dramatic goal of the organization or project, and how it represents an essential step toward Faster, Better, Cheaper.

CHOOSING TO DO THINGS DIFFERENTLY

In 1992 I had been working on the Shuttle Imaging Radar-C (SIR-C) mission and functioning as manager of my section while watching the startup Pathfinder project from a distance but with curiosity and no little interest. Still, my hands were full.

At home I had the delight of viewing the emerging personalities of my two captivating daughters—Alicia, then four, and Jenna, age two. Otherwise life at home was giving me less to smile about. Cathy, my wife of six years, who has a master's in mechanical engineering from Berkeley, was also working at the Lab. Our marriage looked on the surface like an ideal relationship, but it had come unglued. Following a pattern familiar in too many modern households, we could not manage a marriage of equals. The divorce was amicable, we remain friendly, we share the children gratefully in our love for them and in custody.

In the winter of '92, Pathfinder project manager Tony Spear wanted to start building a team with some flight project experience, and took me aside to say he was going to advertise for the position of Pathfinder flight system manager and wanted me to apply. Though the project was still in an exploratory stage, a long way from being approved and funded, the person chosen for the job would in time be responsible for the design and building of the entire spacecraft, and for figuring out how to do the job on the minuscule budget and compressed timetable.

It would mean a tough transition. I'd be leaving a stable management job for a project that might never get an official start. I'd been down that bumpy road once before, in the mid-eighties, when I worked with a team that was trying to obtain funding for a mission called the Comet Rendezvous Asteroid Flyby. We tried for four years running, and every year NASA said No; we were the law school graduates who keep taking the bar exam and keep failing. Not fun, and hell on one's self-esteem.

I consulted with some people at JPL whose opinion I value—a mentor, spacecraft genius Bill Layman; Larry Dumas, the deputy director of JPL; and Charles Elachi, JPL's director of Earth and Space Science. They all offered the same advice, which Bill Layman summed up in a single phrase: "Go for it." Though Elachi agreed, he suggested not rushing into a decision. In the end my answer to Tony was that I wanted to wait until the '93 NASA budget was submitted to Congress, so I could at least be sure that NASA and the congressional budget office, OMB, supported Pathfinder's funding.

April came. Funding for the overall Discovery concept was in the budget, but there wasn't a detailed breakdown of Discovery projects. Translation: it still wasn't certain that Pathfinder would be funded. But my decision couldn't be put off any longer—Tony was growing understandably impatient. His message was curt: "Fish or cut bait."

I sat down and actually wrote out a list of pros and cons about taking the job. In the pro column, Pathfinder would be an extraordinary learning opportunity. And while I didn't want a straight management job, this one would combine the technical with the managerial.

In the con column, the underlying question was: Could I do this, did I really have what it would take? Usually not lacking in the self-confidence department, about this one I had some doubts—it would be a big stretch. My biggest project to date, SIR-C, involved a $12 million budget and about 25 people. Pathfinder would involve managing over 250 people and a budget of at least $130 million—ten times the scope and maybe fifty times the challenge.

Faster, Better, Cheaper was so far little more than a great-sounding concept. Could anybody really put a spacecraft on Mars on this kind of budget? Managers and engineers around the Lab weren't too optimistic about the odds. The assignment looked impossible, the chance of failure all too likely. To many, it had the earmarks of a career-destroying project. Yet I was being drawn toward the job *because* it looked so risky.

The con list looked prominently longer than the pro and yet somehow, from I don't know where, came a sense of confidence: I could do this. Perhaps because every big assignment I had taken on at JPL had looked damned daunting at the beginning. Perhaps from the accumulated experiences as a youngster on my own from an early age. So far in life I had managed to rise to every challenge. The Peter Principle talks about the danger in being advanced to the level of your incompetence; as yet I hadn't reached that level. Would Pathfinder be the fateful step?

The risk-taker in me couldn't refuse. When my appointment as flight system manager on Pathfinder became official in April 1993, I was, for the first time after fifteen years at JPL, no longer in the Mechanical System Integration Section.

At that first meeting after taking the job, facing that question of "What do you want us to do?" I knew that the short answer was "Do things differently." Only bold solutions would get us to Mars, in one piece, on time and on budget.

The Pathfinder team invented an extraordinary number of ways for putting "Do things differently" into practice, including some that represented basic management approaches on how we did business. For example, we based the project scope on a capability-driven design instead of a requirements-driven one. This meant the designs, rather than being framed around a set of predetermined requirements, were strongly driven by already available hardware and already proven capabilities.

Yet the management challenge we were presented—"Take risks but don't fail"—was unequaled.

Most people who heard that instruction simply laughed and assumed it was a joke. Okay, yes—it's an oxymoron, on the surface it appears ridiculous. But NASA wasn't joking. We could only succeed by taking risks, yet our project would be the proof of Faster,

Better, Cheaper, the proof that planetary space efforts still had a place in the new Washington thinking about controls on government spending. NASA couldn't afford to let us fail. They would be dogging our footsteps, reviewing our decisions, and challenging our assumptions, our data, our test results.

We were committed to Faster, Better, Cheaper . . . without truly knowing what it would mean, whether it was even possible.

Any business manager who wants to undertake Faster, Better, Cheaper needs to start at the same place we did: making the commitment to do things differently. It's inevitable in any organization, with the exception of the newest startup company, that as experience is acquired, as layers of organization are added, as some bright new ideas lead to success and others that seemed just as bright lead to failure, the company puts into place the Books of Dos and Don'ts, the Books of Musts and Must Nots—those managerial guidelines that come in every form from one-paragraph memos to manuals as thick as a phone book, and series of those manuals filling shelves. Every large organization after a while begins to codify ways of doing things. And as important to the success of the venture as each one of these edicts individually may be—or may, at least, have seemed at the time it was issued—the sum of them is too familiar to every manager who ever had an original idea. They tend to stifle ingenuity, dampen enthusiasm, and channel everyone into sticking with the safe but narrow path of routine thinking.

Not long ago my brother Scott came to me for advice on whether to move forward with a new business he wanted to launch. Like most oldest brothers, I assumed he hadn't done his homework and was heading for problems.

From my own experiences of what makes a spacecraft project work, I quizzed him to see whether he had a grasp of what it would take to get his project off the ground. Those questions make a good set for any manager.

Do you have the basic instincts for this project or field?
Have you done good planning, with attention to detail?
Did you ask and consider the advice of more-experienced people in deciding how much of each resource (money, talent, tools of the trade, etc.) you will need?

Do you have access to all the resources indicated?

How much have you lined up in the way of additional
resources, to allow for mistakes and for your own inexperi-
ence?

Do you have ways of dealing with the uncertainties, the problems that will inevitably appear?

Do you have a market already lined up?

Do you have an organization appropriately tailored to this specific effort?

How much confidence do you have about succeeding? You'll
always have some doubts, but if they're strong enough to
undercut your momentum, you'll end up dead in the water.

What a pleasure to discover he'd researched, thought and
planned. He had solid answers to my questions, he'd done enough
background work to line up some jobs, he had a good business plan
and a way of easing into the new business, and I could tell he was
reasonably confident about his own ability to do the job and to make
it work. And he wasn't burning any bridges behind him as he
moved into it—he had a fallback plan of how to stay on his feet if
the venture failed.

It turned out that he didn't need my advice or any instruction
from me. He had figured out "doing things differently" on his own
and needed only a small bit of reassurance from his older brother.
(For the record, confirming the conclusion I came to based on his
answers to my questions, my brother is doing very well with his
new business.)

EXPERT ADVICE IS AVAILABLE; USE IT

From the first I pushed the team, and pushed myself, to develop an
implementation plan—including a detailed cost estimate and integrated schedule. Trying to anticipate the problems we would most
likely encounter and how we'd go about solving them, we put as
much of that as we could into our plan.

The estimates would be essential for going in front of a formal
NASA review board with the power to recommend the much-cov-
eted approval to proceed that would give us status as a real project.

That review session was three months away when I officially took on my new post. Which may sound like more than ample time ... except that this was too important to leave to the last minute. Getting everybody ready was one of the high-priority items on my list, and I announced a full-fledged in-house review session as a kind of dress rehearsal and to drive everyone toward framing a firm system design.

We held that review as a two-day session starting on May 17, 1993, with a group of about fifteen highly experienced engineers and managers sitting as the review board. One of my major concerns was whether the presenters—mostly engineers and engineering managers—could stay at the right level of detail, or would instead become so bogged down in the nitty-gritty that we'd run out of time before covering all the material during the two days we'd have with NASA in July.

A simple expedient for handling that problem occurred to me. I informed the team that I would be sitting at the overhead projector and changing their charts myself. Not a task that most managers or team leaders would accept, much less consign themselves to; in fact, I had never heard of anybody else doing this. But—whatever it takes.

If somebody was moving too slowly, I simply looked ahead and pulled out material that was too detailed or non-controversial. Tough on the presenters, but they began to grasp how hands-on their leader was going to be.

As the July review approached, I was troubled about two still-unresolved biggies. The team had decided early on, before I came aboard, that Pathfinder could get to Mars within budget only if we attempted a "direct entry," meaning our spacecraft would not go into orbit around the planet in order to slow down, as Viking and Apollo man-on-the-moon spacecraft had done. Theirs was the sensible approach, the proven approach, but for us would require the spacecraft to carry a full propulsion module for a big burn to enter orbit, and another burn to leave orbit for the surface. And that would take a lot of additional hardware. Which would require a bigger launch vehicle. And so on. Far too expensive for a Faster, Better, Cheaper project.

So we'd have to head straight for the planet. This had rarely been attempted before in any space mission, by the United States or anybody else. And for very good reasons. Space navigation may someday be an exact science; it wasn't in 1993, it still isn't today. Yet we had to be able to convince ourselves, and JPL management, *and* a highly skeptical NASA review board, that we would be able to enter the Mars atmosphere at just the right angle, with so little margin for error.

So we were forced into a direct entry by budget. Now, how to make it work. We would have to slow the spacecraft from its 16,600 miles an hour interplanetary speed, to a low enough speed that the giant airbags protecting the lander could handle the impact with the cold, rocky Martian surface. We would be using a large parachute . . . but would it be enough?

The idea had been floating around of adding "deceleration rockets"—a rocket pack that would fire at the right moment to slow the descent before hitting the surface. But that posed a big question mark. On the plus side, it would free the spacecraft from the chute in the late stage of the descent—avoiding the danger of the chute draping over the craft once on the surface and preventing the lander from opening or the camera from ever seeing the Martian landscape. Which would be tremendously embarrassing, tremendously difficult to explain to the press, NASA, Congress, and the public.

But—and it was a big "but"—we worried about whether we could afford the added mass and volume for the rockets. The dimensions of the equipment we could put into the shroud of our launch vehicle were fixed; no fiddling with numbers would help—there would be only so much space, and we would have to fit all our equipment into it, period.

Mass—what non-technical people refer to as "weight"—is one of the zero-tolerance issues in spacecraft design: whatever launch vehicle you will be using can lift only so much from the surface of the Earth. No matter how carefully you plan and sweat at the front end of a project, you know that mass will grow. There are always things you forget or need more of. More computer memory. Or the flight structures will prove to need more strength, more stiffness. Almost every change translates into dollars and mass. The spacecraft that leaves the launch pad always ends up using every bit of available mass.

In our case mass would be even more critical. The heavier the spacecraft that reached Mars, the stronger the Martian gravity would tug at it, and the faster it would plummet toward the surface. Too fast, and even the comparatively thin Martian atmosphere would reduce it to a fiery shower of debris.

So we plan for this. We start with a design that calls for less than the maximum possible mass, knowing the figure will inch upward all along the way. "Inch" upward—that was the hitch. Adding a rocket deceleration system would be no small item.

Until test data could give us better numbers, we were estimating the airbags might work at a maximum descent velocity of about 80 miles an hour. Dara Sabahi, the chief mechanical engineer for this part of the project, came in and leaned on me with his view of the predicament: "This mass will grow to the point where the airbags won't be enough. In fact, they won't work at all." He figured we might eventually be coming down as fast as 140 mph.

And then there was the added risk to worry about—would the rockets work the way they were supposed to, would they all fire at exactly the same instant so the thrust wouldn't be unbalanced? How would we trigger them to fire at precisely the correct height above the ground?

This was an example of what I refer to as a problem that can't be finessed but has to be killed. The only weapon for killing it was a deceleration rocket system. We faced a choice, on the one hand, of a high added cost in dollars, mass, and volume, plus the added risk of another must-work subsystem; on the other, of a danger that the lander would become so heavy that the airbags wouldn't work and the lander would be destroyed on impact. A very tough call. But in May I went with Dara's recommendation: we would add a rocket pack.

On July 20, we faced the review we had so carefully prepared for, which would be our first go/no-go challenge. Executives from NASA headquarters flew in from Washington and were joined by other review board members—JPL management and various technical consultants. All together, a rather unwieldy board of twenty-five people. As leader of the group we had Jim Martin, formerly NASA, by then retired but still active, and well respected by Space Agency management. Jim is a big, stern-faced man with white hair cropped in a regulation flat top, whose image and style are a mirror of the great NASA managers of the sixties and seventies, stamped from the same mold as Christopher Columbus "Chris" Kraft, Jr., and Eugene

F. Kranz of the Apollo program. As project manager of Viking seventeen years earlier, Jim was the only man on Earth who had successfully landed a spacecraft on Mars.

Now he would be reviewing our plans and hopes to repeat the achievement of his Viking landers. We were keenly aware that Viking had been the most expensive planetary mission ever. Jim was very much from the old school of unlimited budgets and gold-plated everything, and we feared he might have trouble thinking in the Faster, Better, Cheaper vein that had to become our lifeblood. To say the least, he was skeptical. I believe he thought we didn't have a chance in hell. But he would listen to what we had to say and, I was confident, render an honest evaluation.

The group assembled in the large director's conference room at JPL, with portraits of the past Lab directors peering down from the walls as if in judgment of our efforts.

By this time we not only had schedule, cost estimates and a full implementation plan, we also had two volumes of paper describing the design—much of which was to remain unchanged throughout.

The review panel is a hard-bound, formal process within NASA for the approval of new projects, with the project team presenting its plans to a group of hopefully unbiased experts and high-level management, who then decide whether they're convinced that the plan is feasible, achievable within the constraints, and provides a worthy return on the taxpayers' investment.

The decision of this board is critical; a thumbs-down could mean the end of the project. On trial is not just the plan but the people. The presenters must sell ideas that are often, at this stage, half-baked, to people who doubtless feel they'll share some of the blame if they say Yes to the project and it subsequently fails. The quality of the presenters, their ability to communicate complex ideas and sway this critical audience, is key to success. So this is not a low-stress situation. We would need to do what Tony Spear liked to call "one hell of a job."

The routine is daunting. The members of the board sit at a horseshoe-shaped table, the chairman in the middle. A team member stands up in front of them and launches into his presentation. Or hers. (At that time only one of our senior engineer-managers was a woman; the number would grow to eight within a year.) It usually isn't very long before one of the review board members interrupts the presenter with a question—rather like an attorney presenting oral argument before the Supreme Court. The skeptical expressions, the intense looks, the scowls and smiles, are giveaways. And, just as at the Supreme Court, the questions are generally polite, occasionally harsh, but all with a clear aim of probing for the truth. Are the ideas we're proposing technically sound, realizable in the time and budget we have, and most important, do we believe in them ourselves?

We had four days of being raked over the coals.

This was the review board's introduction to our novel, highly complex lander design, a pyramid-shaped structure made so it could open flat. To grasp the idea, imagine a sheet of metal shaped like a flat triangle, lying on the ground. Now imagine three other sheets, or petals, the same size and shape, each attached along one side of the triangle that's lying on the ground, and free to pivot. These three can fold up so that they meet to form an elongated pyramid.

📺 (VideoNotes: www.HiVelocity.com, "Petals.")

The review panel scrutinized our design and examined our constraints. They worried about whether we could really do the job within the restrictions of volume and mass, and even more important, whether we could really make all this happen within our extremely limited budget and schedule.

Especially they did not like adding the deceleration rockets. What they saw was extra mass, and the additional risks of one more subsystem that might fail and ruin the mission. I argued back that the technology was well known, and besides—this seemed to me the most telling point—"Adding this subsystem will in fact increase reliability and make the overall design more robust."

I had a distinct feeling that some of the board were not convinced.

Their challenges were just as pointed on another design issue: our two computers. And rightly so. I had been afraid Jim and company would be stuck in old-school thinking, but on this *we* were the ones guilty of the mistake.

Spacecraft, like military and transport aircraft, have always been built with a high degree of redundancy. In an airplane, if a computer or hydraulic system fails, there's at least one backup system immediately available. On spacecraft, following the same idea, it's been traditional to provide two of every active electronic component, all continually monitored by the on-board computer or some kind of "watchdog" device. If something starts going wrong, the watchdog switches to the backup. (For craft that carry humans, like the space shuttle, the designers provide additional tiers of redundancy; the shuttle actually uses *five* computers, and a complex voting logic that polls all five before making any important decision.)

But the review board members picked up on our plans for a backup computer and grumbled at me, "The computer's probably the most reliable piece of hardware you've got." Their advice: "You're basically single string already—don't half-ass it, go all the way." *Single string*: using only one of everything wherever possible, making an exception only where we couldn't build in enough margin or demonstrate high reliability through testing.

This was an idea I had been struggling with for some time. The review board was saying, "You need to be really radical in your design," and the idea of single string for planetary spacecraft was very radical, indeed. It would of course mean we would have to be damned well sure everything was going to work. There's no repair station on the way to Mars. Everything works right the whole time or the entire mission is a bust.

The board that I thought might not be in tune with our attempts to do things differently was instead critical because we weren't thinking differently enough. Deep down one part of me was cheering for their forward-looking attitude, another part was quaking that they lacked confidence we could plan a mission that would be low cost but still successful. Was it possible that some board members were thinking about voting us out of business? We would know soon enough.

Meanwhile I knew that single string wasn't a totally insane idea. It's not like driving across the Sahara desert with no extra gas or spare tire. We felt we could make the approach work if we did an extraordinary job of testing, and single string could prove to be a strong incentive for making sure everybody tested the hell out of their system. Without the backups, we would have to be a great deal more thorough, a great deal more demanding of ourselves, a great deal more certain we tested for every possible flaw.

The board was giving us good advice, and we would accept and follow it.

In business, the idea of tapping available expertise and available knowledge seems to be one that a lot of people aren't ready for. Many companies—it would probably be more accurate to say "most," but nobody as far as I know has actually gone out and done the research—do a rotten job of getting advice from people who have "been there, done that."

Apple Computer, considered one of the most innovative of companies, even in high-tech where innovation is the name of the game, for years (until Steve Jobs returned, bringing a different approach) did a lousy job of using their in-house expertise. Whether they were designing a new piece of operating system software, or building a new component for the next-generation computer, or gathering customer data for the design of a new marketing program, Apple employees had a habit of starting from scratch. The corporate databases might be crammed with highly valuable information on what worked and what failed in previous design efforts, the results of earlier customer surveys, or other painfully acquired corporate wisdom . . . but people simply didn't look. They just started over.

At the end of our four-day marathon review, board chairman Jim Martin summed up the board's findings. We had won the only prize that mattered to us just then: the panel had agreed to recommend that the Pathfinder mission be approved and funded. It would still take months to receive the formal okay from NASA and for the first funding to show up, but we were en route to graduating from being a study program to becoming an official NASA and JPL project.

We were being allowed into the starting gate. We were on our way.

3. Think "Implementation": Establishing the Initial Conditions

The dream of yesterday is the hope of today
and the reality of tomorrow.

—Robert Goddard,
"the father of modern rocketry"

COUNTDOWN: 3 YEARS, 6 MONTHS TO LAUNCH

In the space business, the basic ticket of admission to any of the great assignments is another of those Catch-22s: you need to have experience designing hardware that has actually been flown in space—you won't be trusted to design space hardware unless you've already done it successfully in the past. But you can't get to do it unless they'll let you have one of those coveted jobs, for which you are not considered qualified.

Human resources departments too often search for a candidate who, on paper, best fits the written requirements for the position. We didn't follow that practice. Wisely, since some of our best people were hired without any traditional evidence they could handle the assignment. One of those was a young man named Tommasso Rivellini, who had never designed flight hardware, never even held a flight hardware engineering job, but showed the kind of ingenuity and energy the project was looking for.

Tom and the people who joined his team were given the task of figuring out how to cushion the lander in its head-on collision with the rock-strewn face of Mars at a speed of 60 or 80 or maybe even 140 miles an hour—a problem for which there were no existing solutions, calling for some eccentric, off-the-wall thinking. The team discussions were filled with "What if . . ." questions and "Just suppose . . ." suggestions. They had to think outside their comfort zones. And one of the most radical ideas of the bunch was "Think balloons. Think *airbags.*"

The idea of using airbags to cushion the impact of the lander hitting the surface of Mars was zany. Clearly eccentric. Sure, the automobile version works, does what it was designed to do—save lives. The auto airbag is tiny compared to what we would need. And it had taken many years to develop and perfect.

The team guessed that airbags for our Mars lander would probably have to be about 20 feet in diameter. And they would have to cushion not just once, like the auto version, but repeatedly, as the lander bounced and bounced until it finally used up its kinetic energy.

Nobody had any idea what kind of design might work—one large bag surrounding the lander? Several, attached at points along the lander's surface? A cocoon of bags completely enveloping the lander? There was no precedent, no one to call and say, "What did yours look like?" It had never been done before.

Another highly eccentric aspect: the bags would have to be constructed out of some kind of fabric. But what kind? This would be another first, another question for which no one on the planet had any experience to help with an answer.

Early in the project, well before we had received a go-ahead and funding, we asked for aid from the Sandia National Labs, outside Albuquerque, to include modeling the airbags using a high-powered analytical program running on one of their Cray supercomputers.

The effort brought the Cray to its knees. It cost us four days of Cray time to get a video about ten seconds long . . . which showed us nothing worthwhile except that an analytical approach wasn't likely to help.

So Tom and his team set to work pondering an airbag concept through a process jokingly called "hammer to fit." The designers don't sit at their computers for months working through mathematical equations, or produce carefully detailed fabrication drawings. Instead they try an idea, sketch a design, build it, test it, figure out what went wrong, modify the design ... and keep repeating the process until they succeed.

We did that with a variety of component elements; for the bags in particular, there wasn't any other choice.

The airbags would prove to be one of the most innovative concepts of Pathfinder, but also one of the most frustrating. Nobody promised it was going to be easy. But there would be dark moments when Tom was ready to call the idea a failure and start looking for a completely different approach. There would be moments when I was almost ready to let him.

THE CLOCK IS TICKING

The project time line we had presented at the July NASA review had been a focus of attention for a compelling reason: because of the orbital relationship between Earth and Mars, an opportunity for launch occurs only once every twenty-six months. And the launch window lasts only thirty days, at most. The first possible date would occur in just three and a half years, with the window opening on December 2, 1996. That would be our target for launch.

Backdating from there, we had calculated that system-level assembly and testing of the spacecraft would need to begin on June 15, 1995. But we still didn't have a firm commitment to proceed on the project, our staff consisted of only fifty people, and we were counting the pennies on a meager "pre-project" budget while trying to make decisions about what we could build in-house, what we might be able to obtain free as leftover hardware from completed missions, and what we would have to contract out.

June '95 was still some two years away, yet I knew we would all need aggressive reminders that we had to use time as an ally or it would fast become an adversary. Not a single day could be wasted. We either made progress every day, or we didn't get to Mars.

Product managers in every business face a similar challenge in pushing the team to have the product ready for market before the competition. Except, for us, there was no wiggle room: thirty-one days late, and we'd miss the launch window. Miss the launch window, and NASA would almost certainly cancel the project. I couldn't afford to let anyone forget.

I'd found from my previous experience that teams can work at a high pitch when there's no wiggle room. Instead of being demotivated by the pressure, most people will rise to the challenge and perform at their best. Once the date has been set, the role of leadership is to motivate and guide the team to the target. The high velocity leader is the guidance system on a "missile" that must launch on schedule.

ORGANIZING FOR SUCCESS

"Organization is the key to success," my sixth-grade teacher repeatedly told me. At the time I thought he was referring to organizing my room. It took a while, but once the message sunk in, I became a believer.

One of my first efforts in building an organization for the Pathfinder mission was a hunt to find the best electronics and software person in all of JPL, and the name Rob Manning kept coming up. "He'd be great," I heard, "but there's no way he'd leave his job on Cassini." Designed to send a spacecraft to Saturn, the high-profile Cassini project was JPL's flagship mission, and many of the first-tier employees, the cream of the crop, were working on it.

Never one to shy away from a challenge, I invited Rob to lunch and sat down in the JPL cafeteria with a man who turned out to be a burly, bearded young Scotsman with a deceptively jovial smile. He listened to my description of the goals we had been given on Pathfinder, thought we must be a sandwich short of a picnic, and said so. Repeatedly. Airbags, rockets, landing on Mars for one-twentieth the cost of Viking and do it in three years? "You guys must be crazy." And he'd shake his head at me as if to say, "You've really lost it."

Even so, kindred spirits tracing back to the Scottish highlands, and fellow Caltech grads, we must have hit it off. Three days later I got a call.

"Brian, is that job on Pathfinder still open?"

"Yes, Rob."

"Can I have it?"

"You bet!"

The arrangement promised to be good for both of us. His easygoing manner would balance my management style—which has been politely described as "somewhat demanding." His areas of expertise—including software and digital electronics, especially computers—brought strength of technical leadership in areas I knew relatively little about. Rob's newfound excitement, overcoming his initial reaction, would be a strong, positive influence on the entire team. And he came with the reputation of being an exceptional hands-on engineer—perfect for any groundbreaking development effort.

For Rob, this would represent a major challenge. On Cassini he had the cachet of being part of a high-prestige project, but was working at a detailed level that demanded too little of his maverick spirit and creative energy. On Pathfinder, as chief engineer, he would complement my talents in many ways. I would have much difficult recruiting still to come, but no one I hired would work out any better than Rob Manning.

Meanwhile the problem loomed about what kind of structure the Pathfinder flight system organization should have. Certainly not the classic "waterfall" structure—the familiar one with the boss at the top of the organization chart, a row of managers, and then more and more boxes on each subsequent row. Usually there are other boxes off to the sides, for the people sometimes referred to as "stem-winders"—the quality folks, and purchasing, and all those others who perform important functions but whose relationship to your organization remains tangential, even cloudy. Especially because of the way heads of organizations customarily draw this chart: they depict the stem-winders as being at a higher level than the workers—creating the image that they outrank everyone but themselves.

This arrangement of an organization chart is designed to obliterate the drawback of a structure based on hierarchy, which sends everyone the implicit message that there's always somebody above you to depend on, somebody who carries the real responsibility. Instead it conveys a message of "we're in this together"; it suggests there's going to be a constant give-and-take between the players.

PATHFINDER ORGANIZATION CHART

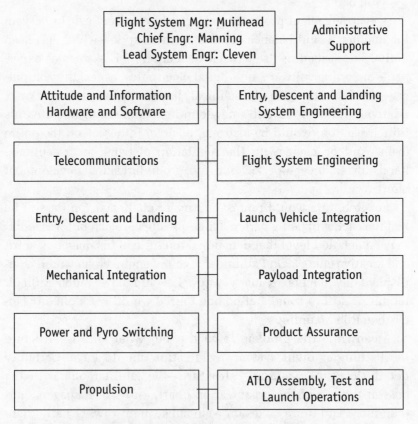

My chart depicts a different kind of organization, which you might say "eschews hierarchy," which in plain talk means it doesn't give the workers the message that they're at the bottom of a waterfall with everybody above pouring things down on them. On the left the chart shows all those groups responsible for the functional elements of hardware and software. On the right it shows the systems functions—the people responsible for gluing the systems together.

Most people don't bother to analyze an "org chart," yet it's definitely a clue to the culture and leadership of any organization, and so an important subject for the organization's leader to consider. I never expected that the people on my team would bother with it—which proved correct: everybody got the idea of the organization, nobody looked at the chart. But that's exactly the way it should be in any Faster, Better, Cheaper organization.

Even more striking about this org chart, of course, is what's at the top. Despite all the current popularity of the "flat" organization, nobody puts anything in the box at the top other than himself or herself. So what's this "troika" arrangement with three people seemingly in charge?

The answer is simple: few bosses have the insight, experience, strength and leadership to make wise decisions in every aspect of the work they're responsible for. I'm strong in the area of mechanical design and know about a lot of the subsystems. But I also knew I didn't have enough of what it would take to lead the technical efforts on the computers and electronics, or the radios, or the software, or the flight testing. So I went out to find people who would be strong in those areas.

Leaders should have a level of confidence which transcends the fear that by admitting some lack of knowledge or expertise, they'll weaken their position and authority. Those who don't have this confidence try to fake it, pretend, cover up. They may do this well enough to convince themselves, but they rarely fool their workers for long.

The cocky, know-all attitude is likely left over from the days, not so very long ago, when bosses were the only folks privy to information about what was going on, and the workers, those people slaving away in the data darkness, were just supposed to obey orders. Hoarded information was the coin of the realm, separating one class from the other.

Today we see that attitude for what it is: not just old-fashioned, but nonproductive, counterproductive, and enough to cost an organization its competitive edge.

DEMAND ROBUST SOLUTIONS

When I first heard the word *robust* to mean something other than vigorous and healthy, it was in the context of robot technology. I wondered if it was a play on words or a new acronym. But I came to grasp the idea as an intensely rich and powerful concept.

Customers these days, more than ever before, have high expectations. Sure, there's an incredible desire to own what nobody else yet has. But no one is very forgiving about a product that doesn't work or doesn't live up to its billing. People want to take quality for granted, and they don't want an expanded feature set so much as they want *robustness*—the confidence that the product will work as expected no matter what the circumstances.

Leaders must achieve robustness by nurturing engineers and designers into the frame of mind where they constantly challenge themselves—"Can I make this even more reliable, more certain?"— no matter how many tests they've already done.

For Pathfinder, that attitude promised to bring us a confidence in our hardware we couldn't come by any other way, given our limited time and budget. But as in the rest of human affairs, nothing about the relationship between desire and result is etched in stone—just reaching for robustness doesn't automatically guarantee that everything will proceed smoothly. A case in point: the spacecraft computer and its software.

Computer technology had been advancing so quickly that the machine in the dorm room of the typical 1993 college student was more powerful than anything ever used in space. I talked this over a number of times with Rob Manning and with the leader of our software group, Glenn Reeves. The three of us agreed it made sense to try moving up to a modern computer, one able to process the data fast enough to keep up with monitoring and controlling the spacecraft during the fast-paced sequence of events at landing. Another compelling reason: a modern computer would mean the programmers would for the first time be able to write their code in the powerful programming language called C, instead of having to write in an older, more arcane language or with the strings of zeros and ones that the computer understands, the "machine code" that is extremely difficult to use and even harder to debug.

But I was sure this decision wouldn't sell readily to our review boards. A space project is continually under pressure to choose hardware that has already been proven on earlier missions. A certain mystique has grown up about this; the program manager knows he's going to be asked, "Has that hardware flown before?"

And if the answer is No, people will frown, and squint, and wonder if you really know what you're doing.

Yet I saw this as a robustness issue. Experience told me that the software would grow in size throughout the project. The classic situation a program manager faces late in the design phase is running out of computing power. If we started with a computer that wasn't powerful enough, we were likely to find ourselves making all kinds of compromises later on—giving up tasks we really needed the computer to do, simply because we had already given it too many other tasks.

We put out a request for proposals asking for ideas on a computer solution that would suit our needs, which narrowed down to conversations with IBM, and led to a contract. It wouldn't come cheap: $2.3 million for one computer and a backup, to be created around a version of their R-6000 processor chip. Though the R-6000 wasn't by the standards of the day very impressive in computing power—the equivalent of an Intel 486 machine running at 33 megahertz, a snail compared with today's desktops that run at 300 and 400 megahertz—yet it was at least five times more powerful than anything that had flown in space. (Though it had superb potential: a later generation would run the computer nicknamed "Deep Blue" that in May 1996 defeated world chess champion Garry Kasparov, an incredible feat that many people had said would never happen.)

Even more significant, the version we had our eyes on, called the RAD-6000, had been radiation hardened, meaning it was designed to withstand the intense radiation of space. But it came with a big drawback: the RAD-6000 was still just a chip—it had not yet been built into a computer, with input and output functions, memory, and so on.

As on virtually all our contracts with outside suppliers, we insisted this deal be for a fixed price. Maybe that's taken for granted in other industries, but with flight hardware for space, it's never been the norm. The attitude in the past had always been, "We don't know how much effort it's going to take to meet our requirements, you don't know either, and we'll probably want to keep improving our designs as we go, so we'll pay you based on what you spend, plus a reasonable markup for overhead and profit"—the familiar "cost-plus" formula.

For a fixed-budget Faster, Better, Cheaper project, that wasn't an option. As with most of our other contractors, IBM's people would have to agree to do the job for a fixed price. They did. Yet we always ran the risk that if the effort became too expensive, contractors would simply back out.

Some of the wise old hands thought that in depending on an unproven computer, we were playing an extremely risky game. It just wasn't done. There would be times when I wished I had listened to that advice.

SOFT PROJECTIZATION

Along with all the technical innovations we would have to develop, we were also pioneering a new relationship within the structure of the Jet Propulsion Lab—a different kind of relationship between the existing line organizations, and the separate organizations formed to carry out each major project. The new approach, called "soft projectization" (surely someone could have come up with a better name), expanded on the arrangement I had used on my two previous, smaller-scale spacecraft efforts. But for the much larger scale of a full planetary mission, the arrangement would still clearly be an experiment, one that might prove a significant enhancement, or might turn out to be another obstacle to our already challenging job.

In the typical line-and-project structure, the project organizations look to the line departments to furnish the people, be responsible for them, and provide them with leadership. But this sets up a rigid perception of the line being exclusively the people side of the business and the project being only the product side. In such organizations, every project depends on the line organization to be responsible for the people doing the work. However, line organization managers have many other duties and institutional responsibilities—so the needs of the project people get only a fraction of their mindshare.

Instead, so people would have no doubt where their allegiances lay, we took our workers from the line organizations and put them onto our project, under managers who, while still part of their own line organizations, reported directly to the project leadership, making it unmistakably clear whom they worked for: the project. The flight system manager.

On Pathfinder, the top managers were on a first-name basis with nearly every member of their team, even for the largest teams. From the project manager on down, open and honest communication was always strongly encouraged. Key decisions could be made quickly because the managers, keeping in very close, daily touch with their people, knew the status, the problems, the ramifications of the problems. They were in position to know that the person working on a particular issue was the right person to come up with the solution. All team members had access to all project data, as well as all decisions, the state of the budget and the level of reserves. Our flat organization fostered a feeling of trust between management and other team members.

There was, though, a downside to soft projectization for some of our managers. It kept them away from the line organization that provided their reviews and their salary increases. As the old adage says, "Out of sight, out of mind." Throughout Pathfinder and ever since, I've been fighting the battle to correct that.

WHEN YOU CAN'T ELIMINATE RISK, *MANAGE* IT

Neil Armstrong was the first man to walk on the moon; Buzz Aldrin lays claim to being "the first man to piss his pants on the moon." No one involved with a space mission of any kind can blithely dismiss the subject of risk.

All space exploration carries huge risk, but a mission designed to land on the surface of a planet ratchets up the risk much higher than a flyby or orbiter. Pretty much since the beginning of the space age, loading a spacecraft with backups and extra systems to boost reliability has been the standard practice defining the commonsense approach. This thinking is based on what might be called the concept of *reducing* risk.

In the case of Pathfinder, since we didn't have the mass, we didn't have the dollars, and most important we didn't have any place to put a lot of extra hardware, we had to take the approach of *managing* risk—a subject I'll return to more than once in these pages.

We worked hard to identify the factors that posed the greatest threat of failure so we could pour enough effort into managing those specific risk elements. To do this, we examined every element of the spacecraft, asking two questions: What's the probability of failure? And what's the likelihood that a failure would result in losing the mission?

The method isn't new, but many people simplistically assign numbers to this analysis—implying a degree of accuracy that has no connection with reality. We evolved a rating system simplified to just three values, Low, Medium, and High. Anything that rated Medium/High or High/High in answer to both of the questions became a focus of our attention. The rocket system that would fire shortly before landing rated a Low, High (Low because the technology was so well established, High because a failure would mean crashing to the surface), so it didn't merit an increased level of attention. The power amplifier for the radio was rated High, High, a red flag meaning we would have to do our damnedest to make it more robust.

The radio would need to send out a signal so strong it could be detected on Earth after traveling 120 million miles through space. We didn't have enough room to carry the traveling-wave tube system that many earlier planetary mission had relied on. The leading alternative used "S-band" radio waves, which would have restricted us to grainy, poor-quality photos, probably in black and white, and a low transmission rate for the scientific data.

Instead we chose X-band radio technology, operating at 8 gigahertz and promising to deliver many times the amount of data. But like every other new technology we set our sights on, the effort to develop this hardware would bear close watching. "New" meant it might not work, it might not be ready in time, it might turn out to be too large or have too great a mass, it might not be able to survive the vibration of launch or the chill of deep space . . . and on, and on.

But I also realized from the outset that the risks in Pathfinder—as in projects of just about any kind—didn't all fall into the technical category. There are risks as well in the programmatic areas. Especially schedule and budget.

If we went over budget, NASA and JPL would red-stamp us a failure and pull the plug—a fact of life that the powers-that-be reminded us of, over and over again.

How would we communicate this down to the working-level engineers, who rarely, if ever, had been asked to think about dollars? Their entire work experience in the space program had been "If you need more money, speak up and your boss will get it for you." We wanted people to think twice over even a few hundred dollars. We wanted them continually asking, "Can I do this cheaper, can I do it faster?" That's a major change in culture, which generally turned out to be easier for the younger guys than the older hands (though there were plenty of exceptions). Getting every engineer to consider the technical tradeoffs of budget and schedule proved a continual challenge for the managers.

But in this effort, leaders need to make sure everyone understands that management isn't going to chip away at the expenses until product quality and performance have been disastrously eroded. Leaders have to reassure their people that they share the same goals for the final product.

There's another aspect to financial risk that I think is too little recognized. A corollary to how much money you'll get is the timetable of when you'll get it. On Pathfinder—and, I suspect, on most projects of whatever kind—you face bigger expenses during the first one-third or so of the work. Dollar needs tend to be weighted toward the front end. But too often the funding profile, dictated by political or other considerations, is biased toward the back end—it's always easier to find funds in the "out" years of a project. This profile may make good sense from the bean-counter's perspective, but not from the project manager's. Fortunately we had the experience to anticipate the problem, and NASA kept its commitment to provide the funding on the profile we needed.

Valuable projects are killed all the time because they appear to have run over budget; sometimes the truth is different: the money was there, but allocated too late in the development cycle. The wise project manager analyzes his or her funding needs at the outset, and makes sure that the funding profile matches the anticipated need.

DON'T BE RESERVED ABOUT SETTING UP RESERVES

I look at the problem of setting reserves from two perspectives simultaneously. One asks, "Where are the risks, what problems do we know from experience we're likely to face?" This is the analytical approach. Early in the project, I created a "what if" list, assigning each item a specific probability and a specific amount of reserves I anticipated we might need.

The other approach asks, "How much of the reserves are we likely to need at each stage of the project?" This is a gut-level way of looking at the problem, and I approach the question from the *end* of the project, moving forward: How much reserves are we likely to need when the spacecraft leaves for the launch site at Cape Canaveral? (Some, but not a huge amount.) How much when we start the "flight build," beginning to fabricate the subsystems of the spacecraft? (A hefty amount—the number of people on the payroll would be at a maximum, and any delays—a design not ready on time, errors in the interface or documentation—could mean a lot of people standing around unproductively.)

I balance these two approaches against each other, making sure the decisions look sensible from both perspectives. When it comes to making presentations to management and our review boards, though, the analytical approach is the one I rely on—it's easier to justify and defend.

My performance reviews have always said I needed to do a better job of delegating. Maybe it's true that I keep my hands on too many things, but my own view of the matter is different: my list of items that I consider essential, too important to leave in someone else's hands, just has more items on it than other managers have on theirs. With Pathfinder, I personally handled three items of reserves that I viewed as absolutely critical for success: budget, schedule, and mass.

Mass, because the lander would burn up descending through the Martian atmosphere if it was too heavy. Budget, for the reason I've already indicated: NASA had made it clear, "Do it within budget or don't do it."

And schedule, because I saw it as key to making the budget. If I lost control of the schedule—if the deliverables weren't coming in on time, if hardware wasn't being finished on time, if tests weren't being completed on time—it meant we were taking too long and wouldn't be able to finish without more money. Or we'd increase the risk of failure because there wouldn't be enough time to test the systems thoroughly.

In each of these three areas, we established a reserve fund. For budget, a hefty $40 million, representing nearly 30 percent of the total. Even first-time project managers usually know to set up a dollar reserve (though a reserve of this size would usually be justified only for a high-risk or cutting-edge-of-technology project), but the other categories are less obvious. For anyone who hasn't encountered this idea before, it may at first sound like a head-scratcher. A reserve fund for schedule???

Exactly. To keep from being sunk by those unexpected but inevitable delays, we budgeted a reserve of working weeks for each phase of the project, based on the degree of perceived schedule risk. The thirty-seven months of design, building and testing carried a total reserve of approximately twenty weeks of working time. What business guru was it who used to say that "Work expands to fill the available time"? If we hadn't budgeted schedule reserves, I'm convinced we would not have been ready to launch within the brief available window.

TAKING RESERVES OUT OF YOUR POCKET

Setting up the reserves is only the first step; the catch lies in how you dole them out. How do you decide when some part of the effort is in sufficient hot water that it justifies taking a portion of reserve out of your pocket and handing it over for use? Let them go too early, and you won't have them when they're most needed. Let them out too slowly, and you stifle progress and increase risk, and end up with leftover reserves that could have been put to good use.

My guideline: set hard limits of how much you'll let go of in each period throughout the project, and *stick* to it. With schedule, for example, we were determined not to allow any of the reserves to be used until after the start of system assembly and test, almost exactly halfway through the project.

Something has to give to maintain the timetable. Knowing there couldn't be any leeway in schedule, I made up my mind early on that we would commit budget reserves as needed to help any manager in trouble keep from falling behind schedule. This tradeoff would be different on another type of project; in the face of a thirty-day launch window, schedule is king.

This meant holding the subsystem managers' feet to the fire on when they would deliver their goods to the test facility; we demanded they stick to the original delivery schedule. But I had reason to be nervous: having picked several people who had never built flight hardware before, could I really be confident that they would really be able to come through on time?

. . .

On August 21, 1993, JPL had the painful duty of reporting to NASA and the world that the billion-dollar Mars Observer probe, which was to have gone into orbit around the planet and sent back scientific data, had been lost in space.

The problem may have been a propulsion system failure, or a massive short in the power system, or something else quite different. Failures of big-ticket projects had been plaguing the United States space effort—the blurred vision of the Hubble Space Telescope had been an ongoing story in the press—and the Observer loss cast a pall over the laboratory.

A senior JPL manager had once told me, quite emphatically, "JPL is one failure away from extinction." Some of us thought the loss of Mars Observer might have been that failure. *Time* magazine described the consequences of the loss in dramatic terms: "Gone . . . is another chunk of NASA's eroding reputation for technological brilliance," and went on to point out that the agency in 1993 alone slipped thirteen deadlines in space shuttle programs.

A dark day. Yet—how selfish could I get?—my concern was for my own mission. The hardware spares from the lost spacecraft were embargoed by NASA headquarters, meaning that they were put on hold against the possibility of building a new Observer. These were spares that would have been leftovers, available for another purpose once Observer had successfully arrived at its destination and gone into orbit around Mars.

We had already contracted for those spares. We were counting on them, had written them into our plans and budgets. In the end, the Observer failure proved extremely costly for Pathfinder. Building and buying replacement hardware would burn up more than $7 million worth of our precious reserves, 15 percent of the total gone in a stroke.

Still, the need to overcome problems like this would create an even more intense determination on the Pathfinder team; we had chosen the right kind of people.

4. Glue and Grease: Leadership at the Fourth Level of Change

A mind stretched by an idea can never
go back to its original dimensions.
—Oliver Wendell Holmes

Successful organizations teach
leadership at every level.
—Noel Tichy

COUNTDOWN: 3 YEARS, 3 MONTHS TO LAUNCH

Sounding like some kind of management oxymoron, "glue and grease" symbolizes to me the quintessential roles of a leader. Glue: melding the people of the organization together into a team, keeping the system together and the team together, providing the strength of vision needed to reach the goal. Grease: smoothing the skids to make sure the team can move ahead and succeed, knocking down the barriers and roadblocks that would otherwise hinder their progress.

In the glue role, skillful leaders recognize that their people, each working on one part of the whole, have only a partial, hazy grasp of the overall picture. Immersed in the day-to-day, they can't reasonably be expected to appreciate how their own efforts and goals tie into the grand destination—that destination sometimes referred to as "over the horizon" but in the case of Pathfinder more aptly called "in the heavens." It's an essential role of the leader to create the atmosphere, set the tone of focus and commitment. These essentials generate in all team members a willingness to put aside the internal competitiveness and office politics that rule many workplaces, and replace them with an attitude of people supporting people, an attitude of "we're all in this together."

This was a theme emphasized repeatedly with my core leadership team: "We're the glue, the systems guys, we have to have the overall picture, and we constantly need to work to make sure this very complex system hangs together."

All leaders apply grease with their people, usually without thinking about it as a separate function. But operating in this mode only incidentally, occasionally, doesn't cut it in a Faster, Better, Cheaper effort. Removing roadblocks and greasing the way needs to become an ingrained, almost unconscious, pattern of behavior. My message on this one to the key Pathfinder managers: "Your job is to facilitate your workers and see that they have what they need, so they can stay focused on making their piece work successfully."

For me personally, I'll do whatever it takes to get the job done. Wherever there's a hole, a vacuum, I look to the leadership and systems team to fill it, whether the situation demands finding the right talent or doing it yourself. To the dismay of some people, I wasn't afraid to pick up a screwdriver or a soldering iron if I was on hand and saw a need. There's even a picture of me, wrench in hand, assisting one of the guys working on a mechanical system. But most important, my willingness to pitch in communicated to the team how far I'd go to help them accomplish the job. If someone needed priority in the machine shop, I'd make a call and nab the priority. If someone was late in delivering a component to system test and it was holding up the team, I'd go find out what the problem was and shuffle that component into the lab as quickly as I could.

A caveat worth noting here: there's a fine line between the very desirable hands-on management, and the similar but very undesirable micro-management (an issue I address later on). The distinction is one that depends on the particular circumstances and the particular group of people.

Practice the art of "grease" in small ways, and when the big ones come along—as they always do—you'll have the right mind-set for tackling them ... always checking yourself to be sure that your actions qualify as the hands-on kind of managing, not the micro kind.

Listen to your team—they'll tell you whether you're on the right side of that fine line.

THE FOUR LEVELS OF CHANGE

So much talk of "change" has flooded the management landscape over recent years that many executives, given the choice, would likely say the change they most want to see is a reduction in the talk about change. This is offered as a caveat, as I leap into the fray myself—offering what has for me proven a valuable insight into a leadership perspective of today's workplace, based on the work of management consultant Price Pritchett.

Pritchett has observed an evolution in the way organizations deal with change that he traces back to the mid-1980s. In that period, which he labels the First Level of Change, the operative word was *cope.* Companies beginning to feel the dank breath of competition started taking radical steps to streamline their operations, leading to a shift in the prevailing attitude toward employees, which became "We must help our people cope with change." The pressures on employees were seen as something temporary; many leaders sounded as if they were apologizing, as they promised that things would soon "get back to normal."

But "normal" wasn't coming back. A steady march of decline was beginning in the trust between employers and their employees. New phrases began to creep into the corporate lingo, phrases like *stress management.* Pritchett sees this period as characterized by a *victim* mentality. "Management," he writes, "somehow felt personally responsible for the problems and guilty for not being able to protect their employees from the changes nobody really understood."

By the end of the eighties, this mind-set gave way as the Second Level of Change brought a new key word: *adapt.* Organizations, no longer apologetic, no longer willing to accept blame for change, shifted the burden to employees: "adapt or else." The voice of the

CEO could be heard in the land with stern warnings to "get on board." Gone were the promises about a return to normal as the notion sank in that change was the new standard of normal, bringing the demand that workers and managers alike become comfortable with what Pritchett terms "the *adjustment* mentality." Employees trotted off to management classes on dealing with change while secretly hoping that the more relaxed pace of earlier times might really still return.

The early 1990s brought the Third Level of Change, characterized by the word *exploit.* Management now looked for employees who could adapt to change, respond to it, and even benefit from it. Pritchett describes this as a period when management speeches were peppered with lines like "change is full of opportunity," and "within every change is a challenge." As companies began to turn their backs on the age-old, unwritten covenant of permanent employment, workers discovered they had to take responsibility for their own careers. Downsizing and budget tightening forced everyone to do more with less.

Some companies tried to cope by adopting technology solutions from firms like SAP and PeopleSoft, but, observes Pritchett, this just forced companies to "change their business to fit the new software." Change, taking on an *advantage* mentality, was still being viewed with suspicion by workers, who saw it as something imposed by external forces, threatening, to be avoided if possible. Yet change was clearly the permanent whitewater of business, here to stay. And, it was already clear, threatening to accelerate rapidly.

The mid-1990s saw the beginning of a transition to the Fourth Level of Change, the one we are in today. The operative word has become one that represents a quantum leap: *create.*

Create. The perception has shifted. We no longer see change so much as a threat that we need to respond to defensively, but more as a tool to be used offensively for gaining strategic advantage. As Pritchett sees it, "Organizations and individuals that have evolved to the Fourth Level don't wait for change to be imposed on them. They drive change from within, using it for competitive gain, creating new markets, and forcing their competitors to play catch-up.

"Work is more often being done by cross-functional teams. Organizations and individuals are being asked to play an entirely different game—team-based, as in soccer, rather than dependent on a single heroic leader like the football quarterback of the past. More often requiring teams of players to move the ball down the field together, passing from player to player . . . operating from a general plan but relying more on instincts and natural talent than on strict rules. The game is faster and looser. And everyone on the team is responsible for success."

This description of Fourth Level management fascinated me when I first encountered it, because it so closely matches what we did on Pathfinder. I felt as if Pritchett could have been looking over my shoulder, describing how the Pathfinder team instinctively prepared for the challenge of Faster, Better, Cheaper. While I wouldn't exactly call our management style "seat of the pants," there was going to be a lot of "dead reckoning" in our flight plan as we navigated from concept to the launch pad. But the responsibility to create our own path was clearly there. We were "pathfinders" pure and simple.

SETTING THE TONE

The SIR-C project I had been on before Pathfinder turned out to be a good warm-up for me. My boss there, Mike Sander, refused to let his subsystem managers become adversarial. From Mike I gained a powerful sense of how a project manager sets the tone for his organization. And that tone permeates the organization to every level, all the way to the shop floor.

Many times through my career I've seen episodes like this: the department/group/project has been spending faster than planned, they're in hot water on the budget, and the manager needs to do something quickly. He calls his people together and says, "Cut your budget 10 percent, give me your new plan by the end of the week."

Friday comes. Some of the group have struggled and scraped, and found ways of complying. And probably there are one or two who tell the boss they did their best, but simply couldn't find any area with give. The boss adds up the numbers, and, surprise, he's still short of making the budget numbers come out right. So he tells everybody to go back to it and cut another few percent.

The ones who did what they were told the first time now realize they're being penalized for cooperating—they have to give up even more to make up for those who balked. The good guys lose, the bad guys win. And all the good guys, and gals, make a point of remembering the experience. Next time, they'll pad their own figures. People in this position are effectively being forced to lie to protect their resources so they can follow through on the commitments they've made.

I saw Mike Sander carefully avoiding this unsettling behavior on SIR-C, in spite of enormous budget problems that almost cost us the mission. But with other managers on other projects, I had had it happened to me a few times, and promised myself, "If I'm ever in position to lead a project team, I'll never do that to my people." When we landed in budget trouble on Pathfinder, which we did several times, I asked my team what specific things we could reduce, what we could do for less money and still meet our goals. We'd talk through the options, I'd make the decisions, everyone would groan, but then they'd go back to work and make it happen.

The team members were willing to put all their cards on the table because they learned that when they were in trouble, they wouldn't be just told to swallow the overrun but would receive help from me in overcoming the problem. If the situation justified dipping into the budget reserves, I'd fork over the money they needed.

I'm convinced that people arrive at work prepared to do their jobs to the best of their abilities. To get the most out of people in today's environment, to get the more-than-a-hundred-percent needed to operate at the Fourth Level of Change, management must set the right tone. Trust and openness between employees and management are essential ingredients. Without them, you don't have a chance.

FACTS VERSUS INSTINCTS

Most people—perhaps it would be more accurate, even if not politically appropriate, to say most *men*—are rotten at being guided by their instincts. As educated people, as professionals, as businesspeople, we're trained to gather facts, pore over them, and then choose a course based on them. But I've learned that there are areas where I make better decisions if I open up enough to trust my gut instincts. Finding out how and when to trust instinct comes from experience.

A team member is presenting a report or making a recommendation. You ask standard question number one: "What's your data, what are you basing that on?" Once you've heard the data, try going on to question number two: "What does your gut tell you about this?" Often they'll give you something quite different. If you then ask why the head is telling them one thing while the gut is telling them something else, they can usually reconcile it. "I'm worried about this and this and this."

Now try asking, "Which do you trust more right now, your gut or your head?" You may find yourself saying, "Good—then go with your gut, because you don't have enough data to make this decision."

When things are vague, we pick up on small nuances that weigh in on our thinking process. These nuances aren't substantive enough to become a hard analytical piece of the picture . . . but they are nonetheless *there.* Some people pick up on these nuances; others, less intuitive, don't sense them.

In mid-1993, five months before the project officially started, we were struggling with basic choices about the most difficult phase of the Pathfinder voyage—the entry, descent and landing. The navigators had given us reason to be fairly confident about the direct entry into the Martian atmosphere, and nothing had happened to undermine that confidence. The parachute and deceleration rocket decisions, too, were holding firm for the moment.

Those were looking solid, but something else was troubling me: the question of how we would determine when to fire the rockets to halt the descent. At the May review we had run into a good deal of skepticism over the method, which only built the anxiety I was already feeling. We had proposed dangling a plumb bob under the lander. When it hit the surface, a contact switch would close, passing a signal that would tell the system to fire the rockets.

The more we thought about it, the more ways it seemed that idea could go wrong. Maybe the plumb bob would be trailing so far behind that it would be over a valley, not finding anything solid, while the lander was about to hit the edge of a cliff. Kaboom! Not good.

If not a plumb bob, what else could we use for giving the trigger signal? The most obvious choices were a laser or a radar altimeter. Deciding to go with a radar would be a highly risky choice, in some ways perhaps even more risky than the plumb bob. No one had flown this kind of radar altimeter on Mars; it might simply not work there.

High velocity leaders don't have the luxury of doing a Scarlett O'Hara "I'll think about it tomorrow." When you have the facts, when you've gathered the views of your lieutenants and peers—and, for the really tough ones, consulted with your most trusted advisors or outside experts—then you make the decision and move ahead.

Risky or not, both the facts and my instincts said the radar altimeter was the best of the choices. I would have liked the choice more if I could have counted on putting a backup unit on board. But the single-string concept and the problem of space in the launch capsule both said No. So we would go with radar, a single radar altimeter.

The job of getting us a radar system went to an unlikely candidate. Our institute's name, Jet Propulsion Laboratory, was a heritage from its early days of developing propulsion systems for the Army in the 1940s and '50s, among them solid-fuel rockets. JPL, and technology, have changed a lot since then. Of some 3,000 technical employees at the Lab today, only a handful still deal with propulsion and a still smaller number with solid propellant rockets.

Les Compton, a mechanical engineer with a Ph.D., was among that latter group, and was, as well, the kind of hands-on guy who had actually mixed and poured his own propellant. Though he had worked most of his career as a research scientist, he was looking for a new challenge. Just the kind of not-stuck-behind-a-desk person we were looking for, just the man to develop our deceleration rockets.

Later, when we started talking about a radar system, he saw the need and came to speak with me. He thought this had the makings of a fascinating challenge and wanted to take it on in addition to what he was already responsible for. Though he had no experience with radar, his enthusiasm won me over and I went with the instinct.

Les soon brought me his proposed solution, a military radar altimeter from Honeywell that had been used on cruise missiles but never in space. He had found a great answer to the need, and the Honeywell unit would eventually be built into the lander. But not before some harrowing and discouraging tests in the desert.

FACING UP TO MISTAKES

This chronicle would be less than honest if it left the impression that my seat-of-the-pants, trust-your-instincts decisions were all shining examples of managerial wisdom. An example of the reality: the parachute fiasco.

Our parachute design effort was in the hands of an avid young parachute jumper with impressive enthusiasm, whom I'll call "Don." Despite his lack of experience in developing parachute designs (he was a software developer by trade), his experience as a skydiver and his confidence that he could handle the job had been infectious.

He started well, contracting with a parachute manufacturer and hiring the firm of experimental aircraft designer Burt Ruttan to build a half-scale model of the aeroshell out of fiberglass for a drop test.

With the drop test approaching, Don's zealous behavior sent the message that he intended to bail out of the airplane in company with the aeroshell. Then I learned that he had arranged with a parachuting buddy to jump with him, and film Don and the aeroshell on their way down. JPL carries no insurance to cover such plans. I was not pleased, and made him sign a memo stating that he would not jump except in a true emergency.

One problem averted, but the trouble wasn't over. He went off to run the test, and came back to report that the aeroshell had begun to tumble as soon as it left the airplane, so the chute couldn't open. Aeroshell, chute and all had splattered on impact on the ground.

He had a video showing the whole business. I couldn't help but laugh as hard as everybody else who saw it. When they pushed the rig out of the airplane, instead of dropping as designed, it flipped, broke the cord needed to pull the parachute *out* and began tumbling. And tumbling faster and faster as it went down. The whole business looked like some hilarious engineering version of Amateur Hour.

This despite my questioning of him before the test, when I had specifically asked, "Is this aerodynamically stable?" He had assured me it was. Absolutely.

Now I asked to see the calculations. To my surprise, he hadn't done any. His assurances had been based on arrogance, not on analysis.

Part of the glue that holds a team together is trust. What do you do when faced with someone in a key role whom you no longer trust?

One thing you *don't* do is nothing: you don't overlook it, you don't wait to see if it happens again, you don't put a memo in the record and go on to other matters.

I clearly needed to take action but didn't want to lose his knowledge, creativity and enthusiasm that would continue to be a benefit if we could dampen his lapses of judgment, so I made plans to put a more experienced manager over him. Trust had been breached; I needed someone who could guide his creative energies and mentor him in the more practical sides of engineering.

He said that wasn't acceptable, and quit—probably more out of pride than anything else.

In the long run we'd be better off without him, yet his departure left a big gap. Nowhere in all of JPL was there anyone who had experience with parachutes. The problem was solved when engineer Ann Mauritz, from JPL's Structural Analysis Group, became available. Despite being as much in the dark about parachutes as the rest of us, she grabbed hold and did an extraordinary job, first learning what she needed to know, then going out to industry for the expertise to make it all happen. Providing her own grease, Ann developed close, effective working connections with our parachute contractor, Pioneer Aerospace, as well as with her Pathfinder teammates.

The toughest problems a manager faces are people problems. When someone on a team isn't working out, the leader's first role lies in providing the grease to smooth the way. If direct guidance doesn't work, or, worse, you reach the point where you no longer trust the person, then the role of the grease is to "slide" him out and someone else in.

"MANAGING UP"

The principle of providing the glue and grease that make a team or organization become powerfully effective can, surprisingly, work in the other direction as well. These less obvious, and less practiced, techniques are what management consultant Dr. Arynne Simon calls "managing up"—meaning supporting your manager (and, when necessary, *managing* your manager).

I had a lot of respect for Tony Spear, my boss on Pathfinder, despite dramatically different management styles—Tony much more of a people manager than what Richard Cook calls an "issue manager." He trusted and supported me and we had an effective working relationship. Still, Tony occasionally treated my reports to him with the same healthy skepticism that my own management team sometimes received from me.

Of the five key managers reporting to Tony, as flight system manager I had responsibility for by far the largest part of the project, the spacecraft itself. John Wellman, the payload manager, had charge of the scientific instruments that would take the photos and sample the Martian atmosphere and soil. Allan Sacks, ground data systems manager, was responsible for all the hardware and software on Earth that would send and receive the signals from the spacecraft. Mission manager Richard Cook planned and led the team that would actually operate the spacecraft in flight. And Donna Shirley was the manager responsible for developing the rover vehicle.

Tony was the Mr. Outside—working the interfaces with upper management of JPL, with NASA, and with our senior review boards. On the inside, he set the tone of the project and set the priorities.

If I learned a bit late to be skeptical of what people told me, Tony was already well versed in the attitude, apparently something that came naturally to him. When I'd bring in what sounded on its face like a wild or crazy idea, he'd look me in the eye to judge whether I believed in what I was saying. He'd ask some questions, and when he found the confidence he was looking for, he'd roll his eyes and tell me, "You'd better be right"—which was Tony's form of "Okay." And then—a great quality in any leader—he would back me up if it didn't work out, or in any other controversy. When I went into a battle with the JPL hierarchy, as happened a number of times, Tony was behind me all the way.

It's possible to be the type of leader who immerses him/herself in the details, and still not interfere in the day-to-day decision-making. That's the balance I strive for in my own management style. *Design News* magazine quoted Rob Manning's description of me as "not a micro-manager, not fanatical, but certainly a stickler about wanting to know what the hell is going on, who's doing what and how it works, right down to the bottom of the box." He called me "very high in the curiosity department because he needs to know."

But given Tony's reputation, I could see there might be an ongoing series of battles royal. Making allowances for the style of the boss should be part of everybody's regular work practices . . . but what do you do with a boss who sometimes wanted to be involved on too detailed a level?

My answer was to address the issue in the open, right up front. I sent him at the outset a "memo of understanding" between us, describing what I saw as my role, what I needed, and what I expected to have from him. Part of that was directly intended to head off any micro-managing:

> The Project Manager will use the Flight System Manager as the principal conduit for communication to the flight system team. Requests for detailed briefings will be channeled through the Flight System Manager.

In other words: If you want something from my people, go through me.

It worked. Tony did not get in my knickers, and I honored his hands-off stance by doing my best to keep him well informed of everything we were doing.

Well, *almost* everything. Tony's penchant for honesty had a rather annoying side effect: the instant we had any kind of problem, he'd want to advise NASA headquarters—leaving us to face the time-consuming chore of providing reassurances and smoothing feathers with headquarters people over what were often really quite minor items and short-lived problems.

In time I realized I needed to put a little "impedance" in the system. When a problem showed up, we took a little breather to make a first-order assessment and develop an initial approach toward resolving it. We were then in position to do what most managers prefer—including me: deliver a report about a problem and a proposed *solution* at the same time.

Would a "memo saying how I want us to behave" approach provide glue with every boss, or just cause trouble? The answer is obvious: judge the individual and the relationship between the two of you before putting something like this in writing.

GLUE AND GREASE WITH PEERS

When I joined the Pathfinder project, the decision had already been made to carry a rover vehicle that could wander the Martian surface gathering scientific data. Donna Shirley, who was at the time head of the rover project, had waged a battle against people who thought adding a rover to Pathfinder would reduce our chances for a successful landing. But she stood her ground, and won.

Now, in late '93, I was beginning to appreciate just how great the challenges were in trying to "glue" the rover into our compact spacecraft. The two design teams, working together, had seen a way to load the rover sitting flat on one of the lander's side panels, securing it in place with cords that would be cut after landing. Though it weighed only 25 pounds, we would have to figure out how to mount it securely enough so it wouldn't be damaged by the vibration and g forces of launch and landing. At the same time, we had to worry about protecting the items around it—too much flexing and the rover might bend enough to hit the lander petal, insulation, the precious camera, or vital solar cells that would be needed to supply power. We would have to provide stiff bracing in the lander petal design.

Rover would be creating heat problems as well. To fight off the chill of Mars while roaming the surface, the little vehicle was being equipped with heater units; they would generate a minuscule three watts of heat, but it would be *continuous*. Such a small amount of warming, yet getting rid of it so the rover's well-insulated belly wouldn't overheat and burn up all the electronics would be one more challenge we hadn't initially recognized.

Though I didn't see her much because her team was located in another building on the other side of the JPL grounds, Donna's office was just two doors down from me. It was inevitable, I suppose, that the two of us would have occasional minor skirmishes over finances. Both on Faster, Better, Cheaper budgets, neither wanted to pay for any items that belonged to the other.

My commitment to the concepts of glue and grease said it made more sense just to accept the costs of integrating the rover rather than argue about equality, which would waste valuable time and pit two teams against each other. Besides, I had been a fan of the rover from early on, more for its public relations value than its scientific promise—the idea of a little vehicle chugging around the surface of a planet for the first time in man's history was, some figured, likely to bring us more public attention than the rest of the project put together.

For her part, Donna had always firmly believed that a planetary rover, even a very small one, could do good science. Her foresight would in the end prove valid.

COLLOCATE: BRINGING THE TEAM TOGETHER AT ONE LOCATION

In this era of high-tech communications, the conventional wisdom says that with reliable overnight delivery, e-mail, the not-quite-prime-time desktop video conferencing, and especially intranets and the Internet, a project team can smoothly integrate members in other buildings, other cities, other countries—what we might call "virtual collocation." For projects on which it's not a problem if people don't rub shoulders, that looks like a great idea.

But when it comes to Faster, Better, Cheaper, I maintain that virtual can't compete with the real thing.

One of the smartest decisions the Pathfinder team made right up front was to push for enough space to collocate. At the Jet Propulsion Lab, a facility that's more root-bound than a ten-year-old philodendron, it's next to impossible to find enough space to put a full team together. But our boss Tony Spear, who had previously been project manager of the enormously successful Magellan mission that had mapped the searing surface of Venus, knew that Magellan was closing down and vacating a sizable work area. He maneuvered to move as much of the Pathfinder team as possible into this space.

No project at JPL had ever tried collocating this much of its workforce. We had no idea how enormous the dividends would be. Eventually some one hundred engineers would be at work in one building, on a single floor. This provided the capability to gather together and work problems quickly, without the delay of scheduling formal meetings. It also helped create a personal connection among co-workers from different areas of expertise, providing glue that contributed significantly to team spirit. In a setting like that, interdisciplinary creativity can blossom.

One good architectural call I made early went beyond collocating. I wanted a place where we could bring hardware and software together—all the engineers near at hand. Since the building had no labs, we simply picked an area where there was 1,000 square feet of space available. Some team members argued that we should use their test space in another, existing facility, but I held my ground. The JPL facilities department was told, "We want the Pathfinder test bed constructed *here*."

It was, I still think, one of my best decisions—not just for the synergy of exchanging ideas and the time-saving when people needed to get together, but for how readily my leadership team and I could find out directly how things were going. The memories were still vivid from when I was a young hardware engineer working on the Galileo mission to Jupiter—the surge of excitement on finding project manager John Casani, whom I admired greatly, coming in, addressing us by name, and talking details with us about our work.

Lesson learned—I had done a lot of walking around on my previous two spacecraft projects, and continued on Pathfinder. People who stopped into my Pathfinder office to see me would occasionally find written on my whiteboard, "GONE WALKABOUT"—my way of designating that I had carved an hour or two out of my schedule and gone visiting.

I'd go to any lab or shop, put on a white coat, look over the shoulders and ask, "What's going on?" The first couple of times brought stunned looks growing out of fear—"What did I do wrong to have the flight system manager show up in my lab!" But as soon as they realized it wasn't *that* kind of visit, they would enthusiastically show their hardware, describe how it was working, and talk about improvements the next version would have, like proud parents showing off a child.

This practice pays off royally in glue and grease. The boss gets an opportunity to see where grease is needed through gaining a first-hand sense of what's really happening, and the workers get the glue of feeling part of a cohesive, well-knit team, a morale boost that sparks their energy and keeps them willing to put in the extra effort so necessary to a Faster, Better, Cheaper project. Everybody benefits. (Yes, of course, it naturally has to be done so you aren't stepping on the toes of the worker's direct manager. With a little sensitivity to the dangers, that's not hard to arrange.)

Locating everyone together also makes it practical for managers to be on hand for highlight events without having to go on an excursion to take part. I attended one of these in December '93, when the engineering teams ran the first "end-to-end" or "functional loop" tests, demonstrating how a signal would one day be sent from Earth to the lander on Mars, and from there to the rover, and back.

Usually a spacecraft project runs its first functional loop tests much later in the development cycle. We were able to do this test so early because we had inherited a ground system from the huge efforts on previous missions. Al Sacks, our ground system manager, had had the radical idea of actually using software and hardware left over from earlier projects and gluing the pieces together into an efficient but very low cost system. That may seem obvious, but was a break with precedent at JPL and saved the project millions.

The end-to-end test took place only a few paces from my office. I watched as one computer generated a software command intended to tell the rover, "Turn wheels ten degrees right." The message went from the ground computer to a computer representing the lander. That computer then relayed the message through a modem to the rover computer, which accepted the instruction and relayed back through the same chain a message confirming the action.

The team smiled, patted one another on the back, shook hands. Though a relatively small achievement, it marked a significant milestone. We had some actual software, some actual hardware, and had made something happen. The engineers made their notes of work to be done. Beyond that, as a demonstration that we were moving down the road, the test provided a morale and confidence builder . . . and also raised a flag for the value of testing, a theme that we continued to drum on throughout the project.

. . . So how do you move an organization to the Fourth Level of Change, creating an atmosphere that embraces change at every level? It doesn't happen by learning a set of leadership gimmicks but by creating the kind of environment that encourages people to be creative. And, like every powerful leadership approach that is more than just a slogan or fad, it has to be nurtured constantly by the leadership, starting with the person at the top of the organization.

Leadership that provides glue and grease is the essence of the Fourth Level of Change.

5. Hands-on Management

My greatest strength . . .
is to be ignorant and ask a few questions.

—Peter Drucker

COUNTDOWN: 2 YEARS, 8 MONTHS TO LAUNCH

Who designed this piece of shit?" I heard a machinist complain, mostly to himself. The drawing he was gaping at was one of my own, for a part I had designed. Tail tucked firmly between my legs, I made my presence known and listened as he explained why the design would be almost impossible to machine. I made the changes and never forgot the incident, a personal lesson in the value of direct, hands-on experience.

Working directly with hardware early in my career ratcheted up my judgment skills and gave me an awareness of what can actually be created in the real world.

As manager of this complex spacecraft, I knew the leadership team would need to identify problems very early, recognize real ones from passing nuisances, and—as rapidly as possible—make solid decisions. We would need to call on our experience and trust our judgment as the rapid succession of problems confronted us.

And I've come to appreciate the benefit of hands-on experience in others, measuring whether a manager has a calibrated judgment engine with the ability to prize his or her instinct but know when it's not working.

At an industry conference, the press cornered me for a statement and one reporter asked what I considered the single most important factor in the success of Pathfinder. From my gut I rapidly shot back, "After the people on the team, it was the hands-on leadership." I said it without thinking; after time to consider, my answer is the same: the team and hands-on leadership, in that order.

Hands-on leadership demands that the leader know the *details* of what his people are doing, what challenges they face, what decisions they're struggling with at any given time.

"MICRO-UNDERSTANDING"

The first airbag test did not go well.

Tom Rivellini and I were trying to do the small-talk act as if we weren't both apprehensive over the test about to take place in the desert at the Sandia National Labs. Even at an impact speed that was tame compared to what the lander would face on reaching Mars, this first test would tell us if we were on the right track.

Tom had originally contacted Sandia because of its expertise in working for the Department of Defense on high-speed reentry systems and parachutes, areas we didn't have much experience with. The Sandia organization had people who could actually sew up a parachute from scratch in a couple of days and have it ready to fly. They're skilled at handling what in that business is called "soft goods"—fabric materials like nylon and Kevlar. Best of all, they stocked materials that seemed to be right for making our airbags.

To give us a crude approximation of the way the bags would behave on impact with the Martian surface, Tom, Don Waye and the rest of the crew designed bags for an initial test at three-eighths scale, since the Mars gravity is three-eighths of Earth's. These first bags, fabricated after the pattern of Tom's initial concept, were made using a single nylon inner layer with an outer layer of Kevlar.

Besides being handy with soft goods, the Sandia folks brought another set of credentials that suited our testing needs: to develop safe ways of transporting nuclear materials, they had for years been running tests like slamming railroad trains into concrete walls. Compared to much of what the Sandia people do, our test specifications ranged on the easy end of the scale. It should be a piece of cake.

But today's efforts had begun with a problem. The gas-powered winch that was supposed to haul the test object up to its drop height wouldn't start. Three different people had struggled over it without success. The test was about to be canceled over this really dumb problem.

So I joined the group to see if I could lend a hand. I'd spent a couple of years working as a mechanic (coincidentally, partly right there in Albuquerque), and figured I might be able to help. The technicians looked at me as if I had just stepped off a flying saucer, but they gave me the chance to have a go at it. In fact the problem was easy to see: a flooded carburetor, due to a broken choke mechanism. A minor repair, easily diagnosed and quickly fixed.

I had the experience, the know-how, and just because you're a manager doesn't mean you can't do useful work. And, damn it, I needed to see this test run. From my point of view, this was nothing more than experienced management facilitating the workers.

I rejoin Tom to watch as the test object is hauled up to 100 feet above the desert floor. On the call to clear the test area, we move behind an imposing concrete wall. We hear the countdown, and it's followed by a loud BANG as the bag is released.

Tom barks in annoyance that a strong wind is causing the bag to rotate. It hits at about 40 miles an hour, bounces once, and plops to the ground. The deflated bag lies there in a heap, green fabric showing through the yellow flak-jacket outer skin of Kevlar. "Shit!" Tom shouts. "That's the inner liner coming through that hole—it's a huge hole."

A closer look gave us the information we needed to understand the problem. The force of the wind had caused the airbag to land on an unreinforced side, something we had not expected, predicted, or designed for. Back to the drawing board.

But this test did offer one silver lining: the onboard instrumentation recorded g-loads at an acceptably low level. The design concept had proven more robust than we'd expected. So though it was a "failed" test, it in fact offered an unexpected bit of confidence in the airbag concept. Despite the failure, it looked as if maybe this offbeat bag idea wasn't so crazy after all.

Years ago, before I became a JPL manager, I learned that you can't be a successful manager (or parent) with glue on the seat of your pants. It doesn't work from behind a desk or from a couch. So an 800-mile trip to watch an object fall to the ground seemed perfectly reasonable to me. When managers issue directives from their air-conditioned offices, spend days on the phone or at a computer terminal, or attend meetings from beginning to end of every week, they're sitting on their organizations, not leading them. Manage an organization in this sedentary style and the only view you'll get is the one your people *want* you to get.

Much more powerful is an eyes-on, hands-on approach we call "micro-understanding," a term coined by Rob Manning, which we enthusiastically adopted to describe the level of involvement the Pathfinder managers would have: in-depth knowledge of what their team is up to, how things are going, what the problems are, and what hazards lie ahead.

Hands-on management that is not micro-managing may seem impossible to attain. The difference is simple: hands-on is about *facilitating*, doing what needs to be done to help the team succeed in their jobs. That may occasionally involve doing a calculation or tightening a bolt. Micro-managing, which aims to control everything, is damaging to the workers' drive and self-respect. The practice of "micro-understanding" allows the managers to be hands-on and the workers to feel that the success is their own.

DEVELOPING THE "FEEL"

Colonizing the planets is more likely to succeed than finding a predictable, surefire way to bring up responsible children with a strong sense of independence and self-reliance. I wish I knew just exactly how I acquired those qualities so I could be confident of passing them along to my own children.

My father worked in space but in a much different sense than the career I would later pursue: as a space salesman for *Fortune* magazine, meaning he sold advertising pages. Illinois was Dad's base of operations, Evanston was where I was born. We later moved to a tiny house in nearby Park Ridge, and later still to Detroit.

My self-starting genes seemed to have kicked in early. I'd found a way by age fifteen to set up and run the golf-course restaurant at a posh country club catering mostly to executives of General Motors, a considerably more lucrative job than the gardening service I had established at age twelve. The country club work may have revealed my willingness to bend the rules slightly to advance in the direction I'm headed: I was driving a car around the club grounds, and serving beer to the diners, even though not legally old enough to do either. They didn't ask, I didn't tell.

But my home life at this stage was less than ideal. For my senior year in high school, I moved into a small house on a lake with three guys already out of school and in the workforce. My housemates came home every afternoon and partied till late at night in the small family room. Since that was also my study room, with a couch that served as my bed, I couldn't start on homework until they wore themselves out and hit the pillows.

Somehow, despite the distractions, I managed to finish school, even graduating near the top of my class, good enough that I was accepted by the University of Michigan. Instead I went on a motorcycle tour of eastern Canada, followed by a long overdue visit with my grandparents in their small Kansas farming town of Jennings, population two hundred. King and Gladys were not judgmental except for my ponytail, which irked them; certainly it was a topic of town conversation in rural Kansas.

Granddad, who had been a banker in the town during the Depression, was a highly popular man because he had helped so many people keep their farms and hold their lives together during tough times. The smaller the town, the longer the memories for kind acts (and, I suppose, cruel ones as well). He had often loaned money to hard-pressed folks with no collateral, basing the decision just on his instincts. From him I learned an important lesson about the willingness to trust people, which has worked well for me many times in my career.

From Kansas I went back to start college but after two terms at Michigan State again felt the travel lust. I met a captivating young lady who joined me on my motorcycle tour through the western United States and then on to Europe in the summer of 1972. We eventually landed in Greece where I talked my way into a job repairing motorcycles.

After nearly a year in Europe, with money running out, we came back to start college again—she to the University of Wisconsin, me narrowing down to a choice between Berkeley and the University of New Mexico, Albuquerque. Albuquerque won out, probably because it suited the pleasure I find in smaller towns and mountains.

And once again I landed myself a mechanic's job, this time at a Mercedes-Benz shop, though I didn't even know how to open the hood of an MB. Two months later the man I was apprenticing under, a German mechanic who had been trained at the Mercedes factory, announced he was leaving. The owner offered me the job as head mechanic; I accepted without qualms. As on the motorcycle repair job, I didn't feel I was cheating anyone—I learned as I went, got the work done, and satisfied both boss and customers.

Looking back I realize that talking my way into mechanic's jobs I probably wasn't quite qualified for must have taken a lot of chutzpah—especially the one in Greece, working at times on bikes I'd never touched before, in a country where I didn't speak the language. The answer must come from those early experiences of earning my own money, finding a healthy way to overcome the problems at home, making my own decisions from my early teens.

But the success of those experiences confirms my attitude expressed earlier about selecting employees: experience is usually less important than other qualities, as long as people have the ability and the willingness to tackle new things and learn as they go.

What I call the "feel" of a manager is the instinct for making valid decisions, even when all the facts aren't available, for picking a team of rising stars. That instinct comes in part from the elements that shape us as we grow, but they come as well from how open we are to learn the emotional truths of the experiences we encounter as adults.

STRETCHING YOURSELF

One of my first and smartest acts as flight system manager had been hiring Rob Manning to be my flight system chief engineer. Besides being as friendly and easygoing as the dogs he loves, he's also an absolute wizard with digital electronics and software.

After we had been looking for months for someone capable enough to oversee entry/descent/landing (EDL), Rob breezed into my office one day and said, "I'm the chief engineer of the flight system. The EDL portion of that is the most critical thing we have to do. *I'm* the guy who should be doing that job."

"Are you nuts?"

It was a selfish response to a noble offer: As one-third of the flight system leadership troika, Rob was a critical leg of the stool supporting the spacecraft design. He was already overloaded. And I couldn't face the idea of losing my chief engineer, allowing a man who is sensational at electronics and software to go off and do a different job that has a huge *mechanical* component.

Yet his instinct was right—entry/descent/landing would prove to be the hardest part of Pathfinder. The manager would have to be someone who could understand both software and simulations, plus the mechanical side, and in addition would not be cowed trying to guide a wildly disparate team of mavericks. He or she would need to run the development and see through the harrowing job of testing to prove, as best we could on Earth, that our formula for the intricate series of events making up this crucial aspect of the mission would work on Mars the way we expected it to.

Rob and I talked about it on and off for a whole day, and he convinced me when he asked, "It's my job as chief engineer to make entry/descent/landing work—so why not make it official?"

We whipped up a plan in which Rob and I would swap some responsibilities. I took more of the oversight for electronic hardware, relieving the load on his plate so he could continue to serve as chief engineer and at the same time take ownership of the entry/descent/landing effort. There was a whole new class of problems that we hadn't faced yet or foreseen, for which Rob's instincts and experience would be absolutely essential. The job would stretch his technical and leadership skills to the limit and force him to grow from the experience. Rob was quite clear about what his new role would demand in time, mental turmoil, and risk; he was determined and confident he could pull it off.

When a team is led by people who are sparked by challenge, others working near them are ignited and perform at their very best as well. A few great people provide the heat, the inspiration for a whole team of people warming up to the adventure, who, because of the warmth, exceed their own expectations.

THE HANDS-ON MANAGER IS *YOU*

We had planned to keep the radio, battery and digital avionics at a comfortable temperature while on Mars by putting the gear inside a special enclosure, a well-insulated thermos bottle that I called our "million-dollar beer cooler." It was to be made of a custom graphite composite assembly, with 4 inches of a state-of-the-art insulating material called eccofoam. This thermos bottle would be nestled inside the lander. And until the spacecraft reached Mars, outside the lander would be two more layers—the lander's petal structure with the airbags, and the aeroshell, that graphic composite exterior being built by Lockheed Martin Astronautics, which on its outer surface had yet another type of insulation, called a special lightweight ablater. Altogether this made up our own version of the Russian wooden doll that has a smaller wooden doll inside it, which in turn has a still smaller one, which in turn . . .

Our Russian doll insulation solved one problem but turned out to be creating another. On its seven-month journey to Mars, Pathfinder's electronics, though throwing off no more heat than a hundred-watt bulb, would become hot—much too hot.

We had to figure out a way to handle these conflicting requirements—getting rid of the heat when it was building up, and letting the insulation do its work during the cold times. Searching for a solution, the team tried thermal straps, heat pipes, and radiative coatings. None worked well enough.

To rid the spacecraft of this heat we would have to attach a heat conductor—assuming we could find a feasible one—to Pathfinder's heat shield, from where it could radiate out into space. But then, during the descent phase, we'd have to cut the conductor so the lander could separate from the cruise stage, which would mean building into the spacecraft a number of large guillotine-like devices we call "megacutters."

We went down that road for a while and finally realized that we were heading for one helluva mess.

There had been some talk about a system that would put a refrigerant fluid through the spacecraft, but the idea hadn't been pursued. One night I went home, sat down at my computer, built a spreadsheet and started doing calculations. I wanted to see if such a system was feasible, how heavy it would have to be, how much power it would need. Called a "heat-rejection system," it would pump liquid Freon from the cruise stage into the lander, through the structure that supported the electronics to pick up the heat, and back out again to a radiator. Simply put, I needed to know if we could "push" the heat out into space the way a home refrigerator gets rid of the heat when leftover roast beef and potatoes are stored while still hot.

It was clearly a radical idea—no one had ever flown an active cooling system in deep space. But my conclusion was, Yes, it had a good chance of working.

At almost the same time, Pathfinder staff engineer Pradip Bandari was doing similar calculations and reaching the same conclusion. After talking with him, I was even more convinced the theory was sound. Would it work in practice? We certainly didn't have any better option. Pradip took on the assignment as the designer of the new system, and along with Gaj Birur turned theory into exactly what we had been looking for. Pradip's design worked in space (and during testing on Earth, which, surprisingly, is in some ways an even tougher challenge).

We couldn't afford to keep studying heat-handling options for months. From my own "back of the envelope" calculations, which then agreed with Pradip's, I was able to decide overnight to start the team moving together in that new direction. There are times when a manager must confidently reach into a project to move it forward; it helps to have the experience and confidence in your own analysis to guide you.

Besides, it sure felt great to clear away some of the cobwebs and practice the art of engineering again, if only for an evening.

WORK THE CRITICAL WEAK SPOTS, *YOURSELF*

There are those projects so important to an organization that they're funded from deep pockets—almost whatever the project manager can show is needed will be forthcoming. The Apollo man-on-the-moon effort was such a project. You and I may never again see another. Today we work instead in a terrain that requires dealing and negotiating within difficult practical limitations.

One of these limitations has to do with a specific aspect of the manager's time: deciding which activities are worthy of some day-to-day attention, and which others are so dynamically critical that you damned well better handle them *yourself*.

Every project has a vast number of make-or-break items that are routinely handled at some working level in the organization—handled that way because it's always been done like that, or because it's on the desk of somebody who had specialized in a narrow function and has more experience with it than anybody else around. That's often the way most responsibility is passed out. But when an item is identified as make-or-break, the project manager should bring it under his own very close observation . . . or even handle it herself.

I came to this insight by way of a back road. On Pathfinder, we knew that money and schedule, volume, mass, and power were all crucial issues, and I was watching each of these regularly. But one in particular presented serious concerns throughout: mass.

One day something pushed my mind back to the time when I was on the Galileo project, building hardware that has since gone into orbit around Jupiter. I remembered the job of keeping track of spacecraft mass was the bailiwick of one particular engineer. He'd regularly obtain the numbers for each subsystem, and send the list and total up the line to the flight system manager.

But how reliable were those data? The engineer was gaining those numbers by calling each of the hardware engineers and saying, "Give me an update on your mass."

They all knew they needed to report their numbers. But this guy was little more than a bookkeeper. Though the engineers took the request seriously, the number somebody gave might be accurate, or it might have been accurate last month, or it might be an honest guesstimate by a well-intentioned engineer who at the moment has six balls in the air, three of which have "crisis" labels on them. Just give a number and get back to your work—that's how it was sometimes done. And since the man gathering the data wasn't a hardware engineer himself, he really couldn't evaluate the quality of the figures he was being given.

So the total mass number that went to project management might sometimes not be very closely related to reality. Which on a mass-critical mission can be a disaster waiting to happen.

My Pathfinder team had a major board review looming that—if everything went well—would be the formal point at which the project would receive an okay to begin building hardware (although we already had in the pipeline a few crucial items like the computer). As we began pulling data together in advance of the review, I was stunned by a huge jump in mass, a sudden increase of 50 kilograms, some 110 pounds, over the previous number I had been given, which made me intensely nervous. At this rate of change, it was threatening to go through the roof.

The navigation team members had sharpened their pencils more than once and found a way of raising the limit, but now we were at the end of our rope. The entry mass could not exceed 1,330 pounds, period.

If everything had to stop while we tackled an excess-mass problem, then our chance of making the launch would be significantly reduced. And the cost of fixing a mass problem this late in the game or later could be highly expensive. (On Galileo, the project manager was willing to pay as much as $100,000 per kilogram saved—which at today's prices comes out to about ten times the value of gold. At that rate, I could afford very few kilograms.)

To control this critical resource, that I knew from experience could eat budget and schedule reserves like a starving jackal, I decided on a course no other spacecraft manager I know of had ever done: I would take over the job of managing the mass myself.

Bill Layman calls this a task that can keep two people busy full-time, and others thought it far too detailed an item for the flight system manager to concern himself with. My answer was that losing control of the growth in mass could kill the project. I called at least monthly to gather as accurate a figure as possible from each of the hardware engineers.

But even when the flight system manager personally calls to ask for the current mass numbers, you aren't always given information that's as reliable as you hope. So I asked not just for the numbers but for the "pedigrees" as well—what was the state of the design, was the number based on hand calculations or a computer model, how much confidence did they have in the numbers.

I kept track of three separate values for each subsystem: the current best estimate based on the number provided by the engineer; a figure that included an uncertainty factor I generated myself, based on the engineer's confidence in the number plus my own judgment about the estimate; and my own personal estimate of how high the number for that element might eventually go in a worst-case scenario. The key to this game was to end up with the lowest-risk spacecraft while staying just under the maximum mass.

Sure, this kind of hands-on, do-the-dirty-work-yourself approach can quickly swamp a project leader. A big part of the challenge lies in figuring out which items are important enough to justify your taking them on, and then going right to the source for the facts you need.

An even bigger part lies in the initial step of deciding that actually becoming involved in the nitty-gritty is necessary. In most organizations, it will collide with tradition and irritate the hell out of many people. On the other hand, it just might save your project and be what it takes to hit your target. I found that managing something as pedestrian as the mass kept me closely in touch with the technical action and allowed me to be much more effective when it came time to mete out the other key resources, money and schedule.

PLAY FAIR WITHOUT LEANING OVER BACKWARD

Even if you're not a worrier by nature, there's always something to worry about—a condition that becomes magnified severalfold when you're doing a Faster, Better, Cheaper project.

Among the problems cluttering my platter in early 1994, one in particular looked as if it wasn't going to go away any time soon: designing the "high-gain antenna" that would transmit data from the surface of Mars back to Earth. The engineers of JPL's Avionic Systems organization were working on the design—logical enough, since the effort basically calls for creating a device able to rotate in three axes and point *very* precisely to an antenna on the surface of planet Earth.

But what they were coming up with didn't look to me as if it would do the job. Not that this was an easy assignment: the system would have to operate continuously despite conditions on Mars that would be dirty, thick with dust, and often as cold as minus 150 degrees Fahrenheit.

The avionics organization had argued that the job belonged in their bailiwick because it involved precision pointing. But they had never before tackled a design job for a device that would need to operate in such a hostile climate, and the challenge was compounded for them by what seemed an uncommonly tight budget and schedule. Instead of stretching to the demands of the job, they seemed to be tackling the problem with their everyday bag of tricks. I tried leaning on them, and then leaning harder; I was growing frustrated with their lack of progress and their apparent inability to come up with a concept for a device rugged enough to meet the challenge within the constraints.

What choices did I have? One would be to pull the job and ask outside contractors to bid. But I felt certain this would only add to the costs. Instead I checked to see if I could get some mindshare of Doug Packard, mechanisms wizard in Mechanic Systems, the section I had formerly run. Luckily Doug was available, and I asked him to come up with an alternative design of his own.

But now I had a problem. I would shortly have designs from two separate organizations that had been competing forever in the area of precision mechanisms—both of them organizations we needed for doing a variety of other Pathfinder jobs. How to decide without alienating either one? A delicate situation, made more so by the fact that if I awarded it to Doug and the Mechanical Systems section, it was bound to look like I was playing favorites, a perception I couldn't afford.

The solution I came up with: use a shootout. This just isn't done within JPL, but seemed the best of the choices. I announced a competition in which each of the two organizations would have a month to come up with its best design concept, documented to show how its design would do the job and that it could meet all the requirements of pointing, volume, mass, budget, power consumption, and so on.

When the designs were ready, I and the project element managers from the two organizations sat as judges. We all agreed that Doug Packard's design, from the mechanical organization, would meet all the requirements and be lighter, and what's more could most likely be built within budget. I gave the job to Mechanical Systems. There would be injured pride in the avionics organization, of course—but at least they knew that the decision had been made in a fair competition . . . and so did everyone else. To their credit, the avionics people acknowledged that the other design was superior.

The temptation is to lean over backward to avoid any appearance of playing favorites, and we've all seen managers lean so far backward that they make a lousy choice just so they won't seem biased. It's human and understandable . . . but wrongheaded. When the chips are down, you need to forget what decision is best for the politics, or for your image, and make a decision that's best for the project. Just do it openly, and do it fairly.

EVERYBODY NEEDS TO THINK HANDS-ON

It makes good sense that cost-plus is the standard contract type in the space business. Since you're inventing with practically every step, no established company will be eager to work for you unless it can be covered for all its expenses, plus reasonable charges for overhead and profit. Perfectly understandable.

It's also perfectly understandable that people who design things that fly want to build in as much guarantee against failure as they can. So the builders keep improving their designs. Which is why the cost of airplanes and spacecraft keeps going up.

Okay, cost-plus is standard, but cost-plus can be a blank check—hardly acceptable for a Faster, Better, Cheaper venture. Doing as much as possible fixed-price looked like the only way to go—not just with IBM for the computer, but with all our vendors.

That decision was a good one, but I was soon to discover we couldn't be inflexible about it. Tom Rivellini came in to tell me that our contracts people had been leaning on him over the deal we were making with his airbag vendor.

"My design is a long way from anything that's working," he said. "And contracts is telling me if we give the vendor a fixed-price contract, every time we need them to try something we didn't spell out up front, they're going to have to write a proposal for the change, you're going to have to review it and approve it, and then contracts will have to generate the paperwork."

That didn't sound anything like the "faster" we had in mind.

"It's probably gonna take weeks of red tape every time we decide to try something different," he said. "What do I do?"

We talked about options. There seemed to be only one. "Tell contracts to make it cost-plus," I said. And the contracting criteria became: Go fixed-price unless neither we nor the vendors have a clear idea of how to build the item; only then consider cost-plus.

But to Tom I emphasized the responsibility that went with this: he would have to be a very hands-on manager, deeply involved with the contractor every step of the way. Even though we knew the solid reputation of the contractor, ILC Dover, the company was famous for making space suits and didn't know anything more about how to fashion the kind of giant airbags our lander would need than we did ourselves.

Tom, all of twenty-five and quite young for the job, had never done a multimillion-dollar contract before. But, the quintessential engineer, he lived up to the responsibility, staying right in there shoulder to shoulder with the folks at ILC, innovating and inventing all the way while watching the dollars at the same time. His challenge would prove to be among the toughest on Pathfinder.

A Faster, Better, Cheaper project depends on people—not just managers, but at the working levels and with the contractors as well—who will take hands-on responsibility.

It's no small added benefit that people blossom under these circumstances. They become invigorated, and invigorating to work around. The get-in-there-and-do-it attitude helps keep up the enthusiasm level that makes everyone willing to cope with the challenges and frustrations.

The bottom line: a hands-on attitude is the most important characteristic of the high velocity leader.

6. Physics of Leadership, Part I: Developing and Controlling Momentum

If we did all the things we are capable of doing,
we would astound ourselves.

—Thomas Edison

COUNTDOWN: 2 YEARS, 4 MONTHS TO LAUNCH

If you can't afford the time or the money to build with the goal of perfection, as many of JPL's previous deep space craft had been built, then the next best thing is to test the hell out of every piece of hardware and software—beginning as early as you can lay your hands on anything to test.

Which is why a pack of sweaty migrants from JPL and other locations around the country were gathered at a small patch of desert, in the middle of the summer, at a place doing its best to live up to its well-earned name, Death Valley. We always headed for the particular spot known as Mars Hill, the label bestowed by the famous United States Geological Survey scientist Henry Moore, who probably knew more about the landscape of Mars than any other human; he had selected Mars Hill as being very much like the surface of the red planet. (Henry's death in September 1998 would come as a real shock. A man whose energy had seemed unflappable, he was a great friend to Pathfinder and loved the little rover vehicle as much as we loved him.)

The rover fielded for the tests, nicknamed "Rocky," was assembled out of preliminary versions of the hardware, and looked about as sleek and sophisticated as a baby rhinoceros. With oversized computer boards that shadowed the rover, and flat cables wrapped between boards and chassis, the whole Rube Goldberg thingamajig looked, in Donna's words, "like a woman with fat curlers in her hair."

The test would be an attempt to control the rover with signals relayed as if from the Pathfinder control room on planet Earth. Unlike earlier tests, though, this one aimed at actually driving and steering the rover around the rock-strewn landscape.

Tony was especially nervous about the radio modems that would relay the signals to and from Rocky. In keeping with the principles of Faster, Better, Cheaper, the rover team had chosen not to contract for expensive new hardware, but instead had selected $150 commercial modem radios from Motorola. The joke going around was that "Motorola told us if we take the radios to Mars, they're out of warranty."

The test started. Signals were beamed to the rover, signals that we knew would bounce off the rocks, causing distortion, perhaps enough to garble the instructions. But after a moment the rover wheels jittered and shimmied, and then started to turn. Rocky inched over the landscape. On order, it backed up to press one of its scientific instruments against a rock. The jerky movements brought laughter but it was laughter of relief: everything was working—the rover's onboard computer, the modems, and the software issuing the steering commands, which was running on a laptop computer.

The frequency band being used for the radio signals works only for "line of sight"—the transmitting antenna must be able to "see" the receiving antenna on the rover. The team tried carrying Rocky to a spot about 150 feet from the transmitter. It worked fine. Then they took it ten times farther, nearly one-third of a mile, so far that a helper had to stand between the people handling the laptop and the rover, signaling back and forth between them. When everything was ready, the spotter waved his arms, a command was transmitted . . . and the rover received it.

Project manager Tony Spear had from the first held grave reservations about the free-ranging rover, pushing instead for a "tethered" rover that would receive its power and communications signals over hard wiring from the lander, which he much preferred because it meant far fewer uncertainties. But it would also mean the rover wouldn't be able to travel beyond a short distance—the extent of its tether. Or, rather too likely, far less if the tether hung up on the rough terrain. That would be frustrating to the scientists, who would doubtless be able to see a lot of fascinating objects beyond range that they couldn't gather any data on.

The test results seemed finally to satisfy Tony that an untethered rover could work. He clambered down the hill to congratulate Donna, wrapping her in what one observer described as "a big fatherly hug."

This exercise was just one of the many early steps that helped the team build momentum—making sure we were on the right course from the beginning rather than being surprised later and having to make major changes. Big changes late in the development of a Faster, Better, Cheaper project can sink the entire venture.

MAINTAINING MOMENTUM IS MORE IMPORTANT THAN ALWAYS BEING RIGHT

Maintaining momentum is a cornerstone of successful management. Especially in a Faster, Better, Cheaper effort.

While *momentum* is a word in everyday use, to the scientist and engineer it has a quite specific and precise meaning, defined as "the product of mass and velocity." Mass, like "weight," requires that there be some physical substance. And velocity, in physics, involves not just speed but direction; a car traveling 60 miles an hour going north has the same speed but not the same velocity as another going 60 miles an hour headed east.

The point here is worth the effort. Momentum requires velocity, so if you're pumping away on an exercise bike at the gym, you may be working up a great sweat, but your velocity is zero: you're not moving anywhere. Zero momentum.

Now, picture me out on my mountain bike, pedaling like mad, working just as hard as you were in the gym. The difference is that I have momentum. The mass is me, my clothes, bike, water bottle and energy bars, and since I'm covering ground, I also have velocity. Now I'm working hard and I'm getting somewhere.

Think about *changing* momentum; here's where it starts to become interesting. Newton told us in his First Law of Motion that a body in motion will tend to stay in motion unless acted upon by a force, and a body at rest will tend to stay at rest, ditto. To change a body's momentum requires applying some amount of force for some amount of time.

To bring about a change in momentum, I can pedal faster—applying force from my legs to accelerate the bike. The mass is unchanged except for a little body weight that I hope has gone off in sweat, but since I'm now moving at a higher speed, I have more momentum (which would make a difference if I ran into something).

If you're with me so far, you recognize there's another way I can change momentum: change my direction. I still have to apply a force, this time by a torque or twisting motion on the handlebars.

To manage the velocity of a spacecraft, we apply the same principles in a way that's actually quite straightforward. On board, the spacecraft carries a propulsion system that has thrusters. The ground-based navigators figure out where the spacecraft is; they know where we want it to go, so they can calculate in what direction it needs to be traveling. Based on the figures that they grind through their computers, we can use the thrusters to rotate the spacecraft in the right direction, and then turn on the thrusters to apply the calculated force for the determined period of time, giving the increment of velocity the navigators have said we need. The process is precise, mathematical and straightforward (even though, like most things in the real world, not 100 percent accurate).

Managing momentum in the business world—while unfortunately nowhere near as precise and straightforward, never mind "mathematical"—nonetheless follows the same logic.

In the process of developing a new product in business, you start with a requirement or idea; if it's at all complicated, you form a team. Firing up the team members and shepherding them toward a common goal is a problem in momentum. Your effort doesn't have momentum until you bring the people together and start the process of molding them into an effective working group.

Eventually, out of what in physics we refer to as the soup of Brownian motion—scattered, apparently random activity—concepts come together, drawings are sketched on paper or computer, specifications solidify, and performance parameters take shape. Soon the system elements work together and begin to make sense, and you start to see what the system might be capable of doing. The team has begun moving together as a unit toward the goal.

A real-world example: how the idea of momentum is applied in the case of one subsystem organization within Pathfinder—the attitude and information management team (the acronym is AIM—highly appropriate), which is responsible for building the avionics, the digital electronics that are basically the brains of the spacecraft.

They would have to create a full set of electronics and software plus a suite of test equipment, conduct the testing, correct the problems encountered, and deliver a space-worthy working package, all in about eighteen months from project start. Team leader David Lehman, a former submarine officer, never lost sight of the goal. To protect his delivery dates, he pushed his team to complete the designs two months early. Though this required greater momentum by pressing more people to work faster, it would prove to allow greater flexibility later, when the inevitable problems arose.

The biggest challenge for Lehman and his team was the budget, a fixed sum of $30 million. At the risk of sounding as if I'm using the same descriptive phrase too often, no JPL spacecraft avionics system had ever been built for deep space exploration on so minimal a sum. John Casani, who had led the Voyager and Galileo missions, was so sure we couldn't do the job for $30 million that he bet us two cases of "good" wine. Tongue in cheek I proposed Lafite Rothschild, and took the bet.

Moving quickly, you will make some mistakes—but experience shows it's much easier to reach a goal by building and maintaining momentum, and cranking in small corrections as needed. Managers who continually stop, assess the perfect direction and then get started again, will likely land well short of their goal.

In summary, I offer this thesis: Maintaining momentum is more important than always being right.

DECISION-MAKING ON THE RUN

The nugget of wisdom within the preceding adage warns against placing too much emphasis on always being right, and therein lies a primary secret to initiating momentum and continuing to build it in your team.

On occasion, any leader or manager may be forced to make an important decision based on imperfect, limited or even nonexistent information, and perhaps, as well, on very short notice. People who work in a Faster, Better, Cheaper setting may find this the rule rather than the exception. Certainly that was frequently true with Pathfinder. Stopping to study every problem in depth was neither an option nor our style; we had to keep moving, keep up the momentum, to meet that inflexible launch window.

Rob Manning has described my approach to problem solving under the pressures and demands of Pathfinder. I'd be walking down a corridor and, according to Rob, someone would come up to me and say, "We've got this problem." My approach, he says, is to solve it right that second, a method he describes as "Why screw around, if we can solve a problem in real time, let's *do* it."

Which on some occasions meant a snap judgment, a decision literally on the spot, but at other times meant walking with the team member into the office of somebody who could bring experience or additional knowledge to bear. Often it required sending the questioner back to gather more data or to find another alternative—but always within a clearly stated pocket of time. One way or another we had to quickly arrive at the best answer and then verify it.

A key to the success of this approach is having strong lieutenants, people who will tell you when they think you're off target or just plain wrong. If you're surrounded by "yes men," then you'd better be a damned-close-to-perfect decision-maker because you won't get the feedback you need to see a poor call until the damage has been done.

Leaders need to develop a fine instinct for knowing when there are enough facts to base a decision on. It takes experience and confidence to make fast decisions; it takes experience and confidence to know when to wait for better information. As a manager or leader, you probably didn't reach your position without experience, without plenty of opportunities to observe which of your decisions proved sound and which proved faulty or even flaky. And you've had time to analyze and learn, which is, after all, what "experience" is all about.

Managers who postpone decisions they should be making on the run, or make fast decisions when they know they should have more information, become the weak link in the leadership chain. Weak-link managers can turn a body in motion—their project—into a body at rest. Decisions unnecessarily delayed cause goals to be missed and projects to fail.

On Pathfinder we sometimes made dozens of decisions in a day—knowing full well that several of them would have to be watched carefully, and a few, more than likely, reversed. But we made the calls, and moved ahead. The decisions ranged from some as simple as whether to add a new command in the software or whether to hire additional talent, to others as complex as whether we needed to add yet another test, whether to revise a delivery schedule.

Managers sometimes become the weak link in other ways as well—such as taking on too many roles, or not delegating.

Don't be the weak link that slows down the project. Keep up the momentum by making decisions promptly. If there's a lot of uncertainty about the outcome, watch the progress closely and be prepared to crank in a change of course.

Because there's so much to do and so precious little time to do it on any Faster, Better, Cheaper project, when there are decisions to be made, managers and leaders must never falter. Cultivate the style in yourself and your managers of making decisions on the run whenever circumstances permit.

TEST YOUR CONCEPTS EARLY

In any project that's breaking new ground by using innovative processes or materials, or relying on invention and fresh thinking, the manager needs to identify high-risk elements and devise ways to put them to the test early in the project. The goal is to "retire the risk"—wring the risk out of the project—as early as possible.

Some leaders operate on what I call a "studies-type mentality," where people dream things, design them on paper, analyze them, and start manufacturing without testing them early. Faster, Better, Cheaper, though, with its demands for a high-momentum approach, means that you damned well better test your maverick concepts in the real world early enough to make sure they're likely to work.

In our initial thinking about the airbags, we had a mental image of a nice straight vertical drop. Then we began thinking seriously about winds during the descent, plus the effect of our deceleration rockets, which would also kick in a significant horizontal velocity.

This added great complexity to the bag design, and also meant the team would have to devise testing methods much more intricate than the simple "haul up to 100 feet and let go" we originally used.

We identified each of the Pathfinder concepts that belonged on a "Risk" list, and subjected each to rigorous testing that began early and continued through much of the life of the project. These tests gave us confidence that we were moving fast enough and along the right path, that we had the right momentum.

This process of discovery should have prepared me for a related challenge with one of my daughters—but didn't. Alicia came home from kindergarten with a science project her school runs every year: design a package that will protect an uncooked egg being dropped from the school roof. To me this was simply a momentum problem, quite similar to our lander-impact challenge. A clever solution occurred to me immediately, and I led her through a process that brought her to the answer herself: a milk carton with newspaper for padding.

She cut up the newspaper and stuffed it into the carton, then put the egg in a plastic bag and sat it on top of the loosely packed paper wadding. After a few test drops from our twelve-foot-high balcony, she found the right amount of paper and the egg survived.

But at school, when the kids and a few parents gathered for the Great Egg-Drop Challenge, the school principal tested the designs not by dropping them straight down but by *throwing* them to the ground in a big looping arc.

Her egg was smashed, Alicia was crushed, and I was devastated. The man building a spacecraft to fly 300 million miles and land on Mars couldn't help his daughter design a successful lander to protect an egg!

At work we had discovered the oversight of not having made provision for sidewise forces; for my daughter, I had completely overlooked that lesson. It was a valuable experience I would not forget. Instead of bringing JPL expertise to the kindergarten, I took kindergarten experience back to the Lab. Some valuable lessons are learned where least expected.

I had not understood the environment that Alicia's "product" would have to survive in, so the testing plan I had suggested wasn't rigorous enough; it was simply wrong. A test plan needs to assume the worst, and test for those worst-case conditions.

But testing is more than that; it's also a vital factor in the momentum of the project. Whether a spacecraft, marketing plan, airplane, word-processing software (or Egg-Drop Challenge), testing lets you find out whether you have the right velocity—the right speed in the right direction.

TEAM MOMENTUM

In July '94, we finally came to grips with a difficult decision that had been hanging over us unresolved for too long.

When we had contracted with the Federal Systems division of IBM for our flight computer, it seemed a no-brainer to buy along with it their operating system software—the massive set of instructions, equivalent to DOS or Windows, that tells the computer how to start up in the morning, how to retrieve instructions and data from memory, and all the other myriad functions it needs to operate. (As an indication of complexity, the Microsoft Windows 98 operating system contains 18 million lines of code.)

Contracting with IBM for the software turned out to be a unenlightened decision: the RAD-6000 computer chip came with a large array of perfectly good software, but not with a "real-time" operating system, one specifically designed to monitor a large number of parameters and events, process thousands of bits of data, and control many operations simultaneously—which is a wholly different requirement.

"No problem," IBM had assured us—the company needed a real-time operating system for the RAD-6000 anyway and was already at work on it. The software was made part of the contract.

Then, in January 1994, IBM sold the division making our computer to another company, Loral, but assured us it was still at work on our software.

In time we ruefully came to see that an IBM real-time operating system would be risky. This kind of software needs a great deal of testing; neither we nor IBM would be able to provide enough. The idea of flying a major element of software without adequate testing was asking for trouble, big trouble. Worse, software development projects are so notorious for missing schedules that it's almost an industry joke, even spawning its own descriptive noun, "vaporware." And if IBM were months late in delivering . . .

We asked a number of people highly experienced in software to assemble for a discussion of the situation and advise us on whether they thought we should be doing something different. After laying out all the facts and answering questions, I polled the group. Their advice: Don't leave ourselves in a position that problems with the IBM effort would strand us high and dry. Find a company with a well-established operating system, one already in widespread use. Then let the two companies work in parallel, and see who would deliver the best product. A very sound course of action.

Since we already had a fixed-price contract with IBM, the company would keep its software team working in any case. We decided not to let the IBM people know we were also looking elsewhere, figuring that if they caught on that we weren't 100 percent dependent on their effort, they might ease up, lose some impetus, even pull some people off the project.

For an alternative provider, the leading choice was a Silicon Valley firm called Wind River Systems, developers of the operating system "VxWorks." Widely used in labs throughout the United States and elsewhere, VxWorks was real-time software designed for uses like controlling laboratory experiments. Many JPL people had experience with the software and knew it well. In addition, there was a huge user community, people who had in effect put hundreds of thousands of hours of test time on the system.

VxWorks looked like a great solution, except for two things: it had never been flown in space, and it didn't run on our processor. Though already running on the IBM R-6000 chip, the radiation-hardened version we would be using, the RAD-6000, was sufficiently different that the software would have to be adapted, would have to be, in techie parlance, "ported," to make it run on our chip. Although this looked like a straightforward effort, it still entailed considerable risk. We simply couldn't be certain the company could do it successfully in the time available.

But the VxWorks executives were willing to try and felt highly confident they could meet our schedule.

I personally called the president of Wind River Systems to tell him of our decision and to stress the importance of the schedule. I also shared with him that this might open the door to VxWorks becoming the standard as *the* real-time operating system to use for space flight. (And in fact, that is exactly what eventually happened. The IBM software did not come through in time, we used VxWorks, it did the job for us and has since become widely used on other spacecraft missions.)

Sometimes one or another work group on a project is at risk of losing momentum and slowing down the whole team. That's what could happen to Pathfinder if the software had fallen behind—without a viable operating system, the whole project would be largely stymied.

Now, with a backup plan in place, one we felt could probably be counted on, the software team had new momentum and the momentum of the project would not be slowed.

In business as in physics, momentum is the sum of all the parts.

RIDING TO THE RESCUE

It was the summer of 1977 that I arrived in Los Angeles from New Mexico on my BMW motorcycle, seeing through a golden haze the singular city I had until then avoided like the plague. The road vibrations further blurred my vision as I bounced along westbound on Interstate 10. I was headed to the Jet Propulsion Lab for my first real engineering job as a student summer employee.

The young man who walked into JPL that day looked like a latter-day hippie, complete with ponytail, beard, sandals and a leather bag slung over the shoulder, presenting, I suspect, a rather startling image to the clean-cut, business-like engineers who passed in the hallways.

My new boss, Gary Coyle, took one look at me and blurted out "I don't know what I'll do with you this summer." I took this to mean he wasn't sure what work I'd be doing, but he may have been thinking more along the lines of "I wonder how quickly I can get rid of this guy."

Not long after arriving I met Bill Layman, whom I would come to recognize as a magician in engineer's clothing. He would guide and influence me for years to come and would one day join my team to support the mission to Mars.

Bill is the single most brilliant planetary spacecraft designer at JPL. And since JPL is the preeminent center for planetary spacecraft, that would make him the leading spacecraft designer on Earth, a man I would discover to be a master of "back of the envelope calculations," essential for quickly checking the sanity of an idea or verifying a computer analysis. He taught me what to look out for when building spacecraft hardware; he taught me to view the big picture, thinking in terms of the overall system. But most important, just watching him in action taught me how to work with and influence people—Dale Carnegie could have learned a thing or two from Bill Layman.

Over a span of more than twenty years, Bill had worked on every spacecraft JPL built, and was the project engineer for mechanical systems on Voyager, which has flown by every one of the outer planets except Pluto. Arguably the most impressive deep space mission ever accomplished, it led to a complete rewriting of the science texts.

On the Pathfinder mission, when I proposed that Bill take on the assignment as chief engineer on the rover, working with Donna Shirley, his technical abilities made Donna nervous. Though she would later refer to him in her book as "probably the best all-around engineer in the world," at the time she was afraid that with such a talent as her number two, when the project was finished she wouldn't get her card punched as someone who had developed flight hardware. As it turned out, his manner at their very first meeting reassured her that Bill would not look for ways to outmaneuver her. So Bill became the rover chief engineer.

Donna and Bill turned out to be an effective team, sharing duties smoothly, she handling the business end and interfacing with JPL and NASA management, he providing the technical leadership. Together they kept the highly challenging rover development on track.

Some months earlier I had chaired the Critical Design Review for the rover. Bill and his team were in very good shape, easily six months ahead of the lander. Now I approached Bill with the idea that he come over and help on the lander, arguing that Howard

Eisen and Henry Stone, the mechanical and electrical tigers of the rover, could carry the ball without him, whereas the Pathfinder spacecraft was in what I term "deep yogurt," and I needed his help desperately. Layman remembers that he "kind of swallowed hard because I already had more than a full-time job with the rover," but agreed the rover team was well enough along in their development and could manage without him.

So here was my old mentor riding to the rescue, agreeing to help out and take on a huge responsibility for me. Once Bill settled into his duties with Pathfinder, he looked around and gave me his appraisal of where we were: with the configuration so densely packed, he thought surviving launch and then landing without damage looked nearly impossible. Not encouraging, but knowing Bill to be the master of making the impossible possible, I could count on him to help find some answers.

Bill Layman enjoys his role as team coach, creating an atmosphere where less-experienced team members can test their wings and learn to solo. The quintessential technical leader, he has an uncanny ability to look at a problem some engineer has brought to him, ask just a few well-focused questions, and watch the engineer leave with a solution and sense of ownership from the feeling that he has arrived at the answer himself. A one-man graduate school, Bill tutors, teaches and cuts quickly and efficiently through the densest technical thickets.

Leaders lead people to be their very best; managers and supervisors tend to miss that essential.

PROJECT REVIEWS ARE LIKE A WEEK AT THE DENTIST . . . BUT ESSENTIAL

We were scheduled to face another make-or-break formal review in July '94 and another decision that could profoundly impact our future.

Formal project reviews come with a clear but unavoidable downside. Done well, the preparations can take an enormous amount of time for the team. Preparations for a formal board review could take too many of us—me and the project's top managers plus a number of the key managers and engineers at the next level down—off line for as much as *six weeks.* Necessary to the overall process but a significant distraction; and even worse, a significant loss of momentum.

It's notoriously difficult for even seasoned managers to be organized, succinct, and persuasive, and to exude sufficient levels of confidence when so much is at stake. So, despite the added time, I called for another of our in-house peer reviews, a kind of dress rehearsal.

This in-house review guided us in solidifying the issues we would need to focus on. We discovered progress had all but stalled in developing the vitally important mechanical interfaces, which describe how all the physical pieces will fit together; without a definition of interfaces, a whole slew of engineers would be stymied in trying to move ahead with their own designs.

The engineer responsible for the lander design was not getting the job done. The airbag design was only just starting to come together. On top of everything else, the mass was continuing to creep higher; everybody pointed fingers at the lander—we certainly couldn't afford to make the lander any less sturdy, but would need somehow to figure out a viable way of reducing its mass.

On top of all that, we were having people problems, unable to bring in additional designers. Pathfinder didn't rank as a top-dog project, and too many of the people we needed were working on the Saturn spacecraft, Cassini.

We had started months before to make several changes in key staff, placing major contracts, and launching the test program, but still had a long way to go. With the formal board presentations coming up fast, we had a lot to accomplish in a short time so we wouldn't go in without solid answers to key questions, inviting the threat of cancellation.

Yet facing the issues raised by our in-house review, I could sense the team's confidence and enthusiasm erode as clearly as wet sand under a riptide. Some Pathfinder people were beginning to feel that maybe we weren't going to make it after all. We were at a low point and many seemed to be questioning if we could really scale the heights of this mountain we were trying to climb.

UNDER TOUGH SCRUTINY

Stung by the list of areas where the project was in trouble, we managed to carve ourselves a little breathing space: the major board presentation, called a Critical Design Review, would be put off until September.

As the time neared, shortly before the session, I had the chance to attend a speech by NASA Administrator Dan Goldin, and brought along my project notebook to record his words of wisdom. He told the audience that "less is more," and that he wanted "revolution, not evolution." I was sure these messages came from his vision of Faster, Better, Cheaper missions, and it certainly applied to Pathfinder. But it turned out to be a prelude to something very different.

We hadn't anticipated the disconnect we would encounter at the hands of the review panel. The traditional spacecraft project of old might be two or three years into a six-year course before it faced the challenge of a major board review like this, where the team presents its designs and seeks permission to start fabricating the hardware. What's at stake is merely the future of the project: this is an all-or-nothing gate. Worse, Administrator Goldin had been saying that if a project looked as if it were going to run over budget by as little as 15 percent, it would be subject to cancellation.

On our compressed schedule, the parameters were different. We had received our funding only ten months before. But the board didn't see it that way; the members were expecting the same drill as with every other project in the past. They were expecting virtually complete designs. And no amount of fancy footwork could fool them—these are old hands, experienced and hardened.

We had gone in knowing we still had some holes but feeling confident about the shape we were in. We had repaired some problems; others remained but we knew what they were and how we were going to address them. In particular, the entry/descent/landing work was behind, still in proof-of-concept testing with the design phases barely started, but we also had lots of schedule margin and we were prepared to explain how we would proceed from here.

In addition to NASA and JPL managers, the panel for the two-day session included a few outside consultants like the retired Israel Taback, who had been spacecraft manager for the Viking mission. Altogether there was, once again, an intimidating crowd of twenty-five reviewers.

My notebook records that through the long hours, we heard comments like these: From NASA's Mark Saunders, "You seem to be enamored of new ways of doing business that may be hiding problems," along with the suggestion that we look for ways of creating more reserves.

Consultant Duncan McPherson thought our entry/descent/landing sequence of events "needed a good scrub by a paranoid mind." By which I assumed he meant somebody who would ask "What could go wrong?"—a practice we already planned to follow, and would do all the way to Mars.

John Casani, whom I looked up to as the most successful project leader at JPL, said, "Stop improving the performance. Reduce the cost." Certainly on target, and something we had been working on from the first. But comments like this carry a significant value: they reinforce the priorities and stiffen one's resolve.

My heart pounded at comments from former Viking project manager Jim Martin. He didn't think our presentation measured up and wanted a "Delta CDR." Translation: he thought we should be sent home to improve our planning, make more progress on our designs and test plans, and then come back at a later time to do it all over again. But without an official okay to move ahead with hardware fabrication now, we could have little hope of reaching the launch pad on time.

On the other side we heard from Mike Griffin, vice president at Orbital Sciences Corp., who voiced the view that "Basically you're doing well and you put up with a lot more kibitzing than I would have." He argued that Pathfinder wasn't being given enough priority at JPL and ominously added, "Six months from now, we'll know whether you guys make it or not."

The bottom line: the panel was not happy with us but didn't find the situation serious enough to call for a Cancellation Review, which could have been the death knell. So in essence we passed. In school terminology the grade may have been only a C, maybe even a D, but it was good enough. We had been promoted to the next class. We could move onward and upward. But we would have to overcome some difficult challenges if we hoped to graduate.

CHANGING THE MOMENTUM—APPLYING "DELTA V"

The corollary to making swift decisions is being ready to change your mind if the first approach isn't working. At this stage we still weren't completely sure how the spacecraft electronics, the avionics system, would work; we weren't even absolutely sure whether what we were building would be able to perform all the necessary functions.

To find out if we were on the right track, we did something that people talk about a lot but rarely do, and it turned out to be crucial: we tested the system *incrementally.* Instead of waiting until all the pieces were on hand, we dove right in and tested each element as it arrived—building up the system and verifying increased functionality as we went. And of course finding new problems . . . but that's just the point. While this isn't a radical notion, it was a break with "how it's always been done here," and required that somebody say, "Hey, why don't we . . ." and then somebody else says "It's never been done that way before, but that's a great idea, let's do it."

We had pushed hard to get a "breadboard" computer in the first six months after project start, which allowed us to begin testing our hardware and software ideas, discovering the shortcomings and the glitches in our thinking. The testing also gave me and my top managers a first opportunity to see how well our contractors were working with us and how well our designs were integrating with each other.

We were applying resources—dollars—to figure out where we were in the project, to see if this system would take us to where we needed to go, and we were doing this much earlier than spacecraft projects typically do. It was like taking our first sighting on Mars to see if we were on track.

We saw that we needed to boost momentum—applying what in physics is called Δv—"Delta v"—where v represents velocity, and the Greek letter Delta represents a change or increment. We had to pick up speed, which we did with additional team members who brought needed skills, as we managed to add more testers and more designers.

These changes increased the mass of the team. In the physical world that Newton's Laws deal with, as in a development project, simply adding mass doesn't increase momentum. Often, adding people even slows a job down at first, because the need to train them drains working time from the more experienced people, as suggested by the phrase about bringing new people "up to speed." You count on the new hands quickly gaining enough knowledge of what's going on so that their efforts result in speeding up the team's performance—adding back more momentum than was lost.

An intrinsic part of understanding Faster, Better, Cheaper lies in knowing when to bring on additional people. Managers can't afford to wait until a crisis has appeared and their team is in the cold clammy grip of panic. It's already too late when a manager reaches the point of saying, "We can't afford to let anybody take time out to show new people the ropes, we'll have to do the best we can with the people we've already got."

Learn to read the early signs that will tell you when a team is in trouble, when it needs more talent, more people, more experience. And when you spot the signs—take the leap: insist on bringing in enough people to do the job properly. As in sports, politics, investing and many other aspects of human endeavor, timing is everything.

I faced that situation on several occasions during the Pathfinder mission; one of the earliest grew out of ominous signs that emanated from the entry/descent/landing group.

WHEN YOU SEE YOU'RE GOING THE WRONG WAY, CHANGE DIRECTION

We had known going into the Critical Design Review that entry/descent/landing was in trouble, and didn't need to be told by the board to focus in it. They had told us anyway.

The whole Pathfinder team saw the basic problem: entry/descent/landing had evolved into a highly complex series of events. What would it take to integrate the individual events so the whole progression would run as smoothly as an operating room team performing open-heart surgery? And how would we be sure what seemed to be working in the entry/descent/landing tests would really work in the neighborhood of Mars?

The original idea had been to do some version of the comprehensive "end-to-end" testing. Eventually we had faced the hard reality that tests in Earth's gravity and atmosphere came with so many limitations that they wouldn't give us the assurance we needed about the performance in the neighborhood of Mars. And we couldn't afford them, anyway.

By 1994, the sequence we had decided on to provide our safe landing on Mars was already very close to what would become the final version.

📺 *(VideoNotes: www.HiVelocity.com, "Entry, descent and landing sequence.")*

It would start by jettisoning the cruise stage, like doffing a hat. A mortar would fire the parachute out like a cannon shell. Six explosive bolts would trigger and the heat shield, no longer needed after protecting the craft from the fiery entry into the Martian atmosphere, would be pushed away by a number of springs. The backshell, still holding the lander with its airbags, would probably be swinging under the chute like some first-time parachute jumper. Moments later, the lander would be freed to drop 60 feet below on a tether.

Now there would be this awkward string of parachute, backshell and lander, the swinging of each effecting the swinging of the others. The laws of physics could let us calculate the possible gyrations, but could only give us an approximate prediction of the attitude the lander would be in, seconds later, when the radar system signaled the moment that would trigger the final events: the airbags inflate, deceleration rockets ignite to stop the descent, the lander releases and falls the last distance to the surface.

And then, one more intricate stunt: the pyramid-shaped lander might come to rest on any of its four faces, but the rover would only be able to drive off if the lander was sitting on its base. How to flip it upright?

Mike O'Neal, mechanical systems engineer, had been, with Tom Rivellini, one of the originators of the airbag design. The same pair had come up with an intriguing way of righting the spacecraft. Each petal was provided with a powerful actuator, able to produce about three times the torque of a Porsche 911—enough to push against whichever petal lay on the ground, raising the lander farther and farther until it tilted so far that it would finally topple over onto its base.

📺 *(VideoNotes: www.HiVelocity.com, "Lander uprighting to its base.")*

Still so many unknowns. Would the parachute really deploy properly at twice the speed of sound? How radical would the swinging of the tethered lander be? If the system was swinging severely, would the radar be able to work properly? Would the rockets really stop the descent? Would the blast from the rockets damage the airbags? And hundreds more.

The Viking project team had spent probably hundreds of millions of dollars on their entry/descent/landing testing to answer questions like these—more than our total budget for the entire project.

We had been plowing ahead on a somewhat naive course, not appreciating what it would take to conduct tests of so complex a system, and now needed a change in direction of the effort. We needed to change our momentum. This was a management call that had to be made, and it had to work.

Rob Manning took the first step in defining a new path—the brilliant step of recruiting Sam Thurman out of our navigation team to become his right-hand man. Sam, tall and with the well-groomed aura of the Air Force officer he had once been, made quite a contrast to the shorter, bearded, slightly unkempt look of Rob. Their styles offered an even greater contrast: Rob laid-back, big-picture oriented; Sam precise and extremely analytical. But they were alike where it counted—in their commitment and technical prowess in attacking the full range of entry/descent/landing dilemmas.

It was Sam who proposed using a massive computer simulation that would rely on software and data from a large number of sources. NASA's Langley Research Center would provide the code and data on the entry dynamics and heating rates, the parachute manufacturer would send software describing the chute dynamics, a JPL engineer would create a computer program defining the behavior of the radio altimeter, to name just a few.

Our simulation would rely on weighing the probabilities of every possible situation that might be encountered—a natural enough approach for Sam, since the inexact business of space navigation all depends on calculating probabilities. This one would be what's called a Monte Carlo simulation, involving many variations of many variables, resulting in thousands upon thousands of simulated landing sequences.

Sam, Ken Smith and Chi-en Peng would bear the challenge of

receiving inputs from all the sources and marrying them into some cohesive whole. We began to talk about this project as "the mother of all simulations." At times it seemed like a mountain too high to climb. But it was our only choice.

Sam had proposed what seemed like a brilliant idea. Rob and I had to grease his way to success, mostly with money, but Sam and his team would have to make it succeed.

COPING WITH NEGATIVE MOMENTUM

In Washington, some unexpected changes were taking place. Support had been growing for an extended effort of exploring Mars, and NASA proposed a program for launching at a rate of one spacecraft every time the Mars launch window opened—every twenty-six months—on the same kind of Faster, Better, Cheaper budget as Pathfinder. NASA wanted JPL to create a Mars Program Office, which would require creating the new post of Mars program manager, held by the person who would become czar over the entire effort. Tony Spear applied for the position and looked like something close to a shoo-in.

The job went to Donna Shirley.

Donna, I think, was as shocked as anyone else, though she would later write in her book, "I felt as if this was the job I'd been preparing for all my life." At the time the Lab had no women in senior-engineering management positions. Donna had the great good fortune to be, as the cliché says, at the right place at the right time.

But her appointment in July 1994 provoked some uncomfortable side effects. Tony Spear was in the awkward situation of having a subordinate suddenly become his boss. Worse, Donna and Tony had never fully overcome a personality conflict that had led to some fierce shouting matches. And though I firmly believe that each held a certain respect for the other's abilities and contributions, that kind of acrimony can poison not only the relationship but the workplace environment. Tony saw Donna's promotion to a position above him as an insult and he felt she did not have the skills or experience for the job. Later Tony would tell me about how Donna had tried to get him removed from Pathfinder and very nearly did; the loss of his experience and leadership would have been devastating for the Mars Pathfinder project.

Donna's appointment was not a cause for celebration among the Pathfinder people, who were much surprised by the choice. She was a good talker, but could she effectively lead such an effort? Our best hope was that she would leave us alone.

Personally I thought things would work out okay as long as Donna didn't try to tell us how to run the project. She started down that road, but we figured she would soon find herself too busy with the management and marketing duties. Tony wasn't going to listen to her anyway.

Luckily for us, the battles did not last long. As I had anticipated, Donna soon became deeply involved in negotiations with NASA and high-level program planning. She had little time to pay us much attention.

The experience had provided a pointed lesson in dealing with *negative* momentum: forces pushing you directly opposite your desired direction.

Getting unwanted, unneeded or poor direction from above must be dealt with by the managers of a project. Being able to manage the conditions for success sometimes means fighting battles with your boss.

We live and do business in a world of limitations and constraints, where change is constant, where the role of the manager is being redefined, and where leadership is even more important than it has ever been in the past. Leaders need to learn how to manage momentum as a tool for achieving maximum productivity and mission success.

The elements of business momentum—direction, speed, and people—all need to be managed constantly to carry the project to its goal.

7. Physics of Leadership, Part II: Channeling People's Energy

> The boss says, "Go";
> the leader says, "Let's go."
> —H. G. Selfridge, British merchant

COUNTDOWN: 1 YEAR, 11 MONTHS TO LAUNCH

Like momentum, the concept of energy also has parallels that carry over from the arena of science to the arena of business.

In the physical world, energy comes in various guises: mechanical, as in the coils of a spring; chemical, as in a fuel or battery; electromagnetic, as in light from the sun; nuclear, as in the nucleus of an atom.

These energies exist in either of two forms: potential or kinetic. Potential energy is stored, ready to do work, like the gasoline in a fuel tank or the energy in the battery that powers the Energizer bunny. When potential energy is put to use in doing work, we call it kinetic energy. Throw the On switch, and the Energizer bunny starts marching across the floor and beating his drum, as potential energy from the battery is converted to a flow of electricity that drives the little rabbit's legs and arms. In the same way, gasoline is converted by a car's engine into the work of turning the wheels. When energy is used in this way, work is being done; it's a basic precept of physics that kinetic energy and work are equivalent.

If you want the bunny to go twice as fast, how much more energy will it take? Answer: Not twice as much, but four times. To triple the speed will take nine times.

In humans, our physiology is dominated by the conversion of chemical energy that the body has stored, which can be converted on demand to mechanical work in human muscle. Potential to kinetic.

Body chemicals like adrenaline control how and when we burn energy, and how much. The brain determines whether the bear outside your camp tent is real or not, and if it is, triggers the release of adrenaline, allowing you to beat a hasty retreat.

Besides physical energy, the human psyche houses other forms less answerable to the laws of physics: intellectual, spiritual, emotional. These, too, can be potential or kinetic. Emotional energy—excitement, or passion—can power us through a detailed, mundane task, as well as energize us in a moment of physical embrace.

But just as in the physical world, energy doesn't spontaneously convert from one form to another. There must be some sort of driving force to crank up the action or the reaction. Most of us are well familiar with that jump-start in the morning for the particular day's challenge ahead, something that drives us emotionally, something better even than three cups of coffee. Where does that spark come from, why do some regularly have it and some not?

Partly the answer lies within the personality of the individual, but partly it lies in the atmosphere. People who work in an intellectually or emotionally or spiritually exciting environment are much more likely to have that third-cup-of-coffee bounce, all day, even if they are not coffee drinkers.

In the case of Pathfinder, many of us had the emotional and the intellectual spark, some may even have had a spiritual spark, but almost all responded to the spark of the exciting environment and the challenge of "It'll never fly, Charlie," the taunt of the doubters. The challenge of the mission, redoubled by the challenge of proving the doubters wrong.

By the early months of 1995, coming off the low point of the September '94 design review, we were moving rapidly toward the peak of our effort, the time when we would have the maximum number of people at work and would be spending money at the fastest rate of the project.

HARD FUN: LIGHTING THE FIRE

The first version of our computer, when it arrived, wasn't the kind of metal or plastic box that sits on your desktop, but just an 8-by-9-inch electronic board with some silicon wafers, resistors and memory modules, which our avionics guys would plug into the chassis they had created. To the untrained eye it didn't look like much; to us, it represented a lot of things. Proof that Loral had worked through the usual engineering baggage of problems. Proof that it could meet the contract obligations for delivering hardware on time.

There's something special about receiving the computer board, even the first prototype. The overused cliché dubs the computer the "brains" of a system; to us it was that and much more, something approaching the soul. The health and well-being of a spacecraft's computer, both during development and during flight, is a barometer of how things are going. Running smoothly, it engenders a sense of confidence; showing problems, it's serious worry time.

When Dr. Frankenstein put in the brain, he rejoiced at bringing his creation to life. We were in a rejoicing mood as well. But our "brain" wouldn't have intelligence until our software team had loaded some programs and begun exercising our newborn. Until the testing was well under way, we would not know whether we had a lumbering creature or a spectacular "thinking machine."

The Wind River programmers had so far delivered only the first generation of the operating system. For the time being the test team members would have to content themselves with this, operating as best they could with it, along with early versions of our own software, to see how well the computer could "talk" with other systems of the spacecraft. This is tedious, often frustrating work, something like putting together a 3-D puzzle with pieces from many different sets and not knowing exactly what the final product should look like. And the pieces themselves keep changing.

Some people thrive on formidable challenges like this—a lot of the Pathfinder people did. On a Faster, Better, Cheaper project, the hours may be long and the hurdles may sometimes look insurmountable, but in one way this works to your advantage: the team members come to see themselves as a little like underdogs, which builds a feeling of rapport and closeness that can pay large dividends in enhanced communications, heightened commitment, and a determination to prove that it really can be made to fly, Charlie.

STIRRING UP CREATIVE JUICES IN YOUR PEOPLE

On the third Monday in April 1995, Tom Rivellini was in Cleveland, at a facility known as Plumbrook Station, where, he had found, NASA had what is probably the world's largest vacuum chamber. Originally developed to test the performance of nuclear rockets in the vacuum of deep space, the chamber is something like 100 feet in diameter by 120 feet high. Walking into it is like entering a giant vacuum bottle.

Tom, at times accompanied by Dara Sabahi, chief mechanical engineer for the entry/descent/landing team, had come to do the first drop tests with full-scale airbags of a new design. The ideal bag would have been an arrangement that created a perfectly spherical outer surface. How close could we come to a sphere? The bags had to be fastened to the exterior of an object the shape, size and mass of our lander—more or less a pyramid shape, a very awkward configuration to try to protect with oversized balloons.

The original design had used four largely spherical bags strapped to the four sides of the lander, forming a very lumpy outer surface. And just as the ancient knight was vulnerable where the plates of his armor met, so the airbags were weakest and most susceptible at the juncture lines where the separate bags met. If the structure landed so that a rock struck in a weak place, it would probably be lights out for our precious cargo.

Tom and his contractor, ILC Dover, had made two highly significant changes in the bags following the previous tests. Once it was clear that the deceleration rockets were really going to work, the effect of the rockets in momentarily stopping the descent meant the lander would be hitting the surface at a worst-case speed of about 60 miles per hour instead of the earlier-expected 75. Only a difference of some 15 mph, but a big reduction in the impact energy, in turn making possible some major improvements in the design. The airbags for this new series of tests were smaller, and also were inflated to a lower pressure. Both these changes contributed to making the bags less likely to tear.

More important, the bags now sported two outer abrasion layers, and were made entirely of Vectran, a material normally used for sails on racing boats and ropes for the Army. The ILC Dover people had never worked with Vectran before; they had to devise new methods for working with it, and new methods for sewing by their "seamstress," Eleanor Foraker, a lady who had been sewing space suits since the Apollo era and had come to be known as the Betsy Ross of the industry.

Tom was confident these changes would make the bags much more robust at impact. The contractor had put a huge amount of effort into the design and fabrication to reach this point, and everybody had great hopes for a successful test. If we could establish that this design would offer good protection to the lander, it would remove one of the great question marks still haunting us.

For the first in this new series of tests, Tom tried the simple vertical situation—having the bag hoisted 30 feet in the air, and released. Each time it bounced like a superball, back up almost to the full 30 feet. They then repeated the test, this time dropping from 70 feet, with the same excellent results. When the news reached JPL, we were all elated. I felt like jumping in the air.

But how would things fare under more realistic conditions?

Tom had faced the problem of how in the world you test for the airbag landing, not straight down, but with a component of motion along the ground. Build a giant rig on tracks at the top of the chamber, which would whip up to speed and drop the bag as it traveled? Figure out some oversized device that could shoot the bag out horizontally, with so much force that it would still be traveling sideways when it smacked the ground?

Instead of anything so complicated, he and his team hit upon a elegantly simple idea: they constructed a long ramp, and erected it at a 60-degree angle. The bag, falling vertically, hits the ramp at an angle like a parachutist landing with a stiff wind behind her.

 (VideoNotes: www.HiVelocity.com, "Airbag test.")

And one more step: to simulate the Martian landscape, they carted in rocks to place on the ramp. Not just any rocks, of course, but a size and distribution dictated by what we called "the Henry Moore model"—using data from that expert on Martian rock distribution to tell us what landscape conditions we might most likely encounter. We had decided to base the terrain on something similar to one of the sites where the Viking spacecraft had landed, but allowed for a margin of error by making the conditions somewhat more severe, just to be on the conservative side.

Adding to the playground look, each of the rocks was laboriously dusted with colored chalk, a different color for each, so the team would be able to tell which rock had hit where and caused what damage to the skin of the bag. And in the spirit of naming landmarks on the moon and the planets, the team concocted a name for each of the rocks. The one name that still sticks with me, two years later, is Fang—a highly appropriate choice, since that particular rock had quite an appetite for airbags, tearing them up as if it had sharp, pointed teeth.

Altogether it looked like some outlandish, oversized playground equipment, and represented a great example of lateral thinking— bringing the mountain to Mohammed.

The first tests with the ramp and rocks worked fine. But when we pushed to a more realistic speed, around 55 miles an hour, the bag that landed on the rock surface was torn to shreds, with a hole 6 feet in diameter. The group was totally depressed. Back to the drawing board.

But I sensed that Tom's dedication and energy wouldn't allow him to dwell on the failure. A hard worker and a clever, creative engineer, he had my confidence. If this job could be done, I believed he could do it. Yet the result was far from a foregone conclusion.

When a setback fills the air with a sense of doom—a situation that every complex project faces—energy flags and progress slows. This is the time when the alert manager recognizes the need for some kind of special action. A pat on the back (figuratively, when the physical action is inappropriate or not suitable to the manager's style) or a few morale-boosting words may suffice for the little everyday annoyance, but not when the clouds of doom have spread.

To pump the energy level back up at times like these, I remind people of other crises the project has faced and overcome. There's a feeling of "You're not alone, this team has struggled through and beaten big problems before" in these stories, an energy-building, confidence-building moral that you don't have to spell out. Tell the story, and let the listener piece the lesson together for himself.

Tom jumped right back into the fray with new determination. His next idea was to try different configurations of up to three layers with different thicknesses—trying to find the right combination that would make the bags tear-proof without pushing their mass through the roof. The team he was working with at ILC Dover, no less committed, kept rising to every challenge he threw at them.

Two months later, back at Plumbrook Station, Tom prepared to start the next round of tests. Because it took such an enormous amount of power to pump the air out of the chamber, we couldn't afford to begin the process until the Cleveland power rates dropped—at midnight. And even then, the cost of each test, including the bag itself, salaries at overtime for the Plumbrook crew, and the expense of the pumping, came to something like $75,000 for every drop.

It would be 1 or 2 A.M. before the chamber was pumped down to a Mars-like near-vacuum. The ball would be released, and the test itself would be over in seconds. Then another hour of waiting, while air was gradually released back into the chamber and the enormous, heavy doors swung open.

Each night, after he had examined the bag and ascertained the news, good or bad, Tom would call. This would be around 5 o'clock in the morning, California time. I could tell in the first moments of the call from the sound of Tom's voice whether he was jubilant or depressed, and would know the gist of his report just from the way he said, "Hi, it's Tom."

On one 5 A.M. phone call, when Tom's report was filled with gloom, I told him about how the electronics test team had struggled with a computer problem that only showed up under cold testing. We were glad we'd found the problem, it would have killed us in flight, but it was a bear to isolate and fix. I told him, "The Pathfinder team has been in a lot of tough spots and we've gotten out of every one."

One writer on the game of tennis advises his readers that as you go to hit the ball, you should not be thinking of the shot like this one that you botched a few minutes ago, but of the one that was a success and clinched the game. Keep the successes in front of you. A great lesson for any game.

Those early morning phone calls were part of business for me, because Tom was at the center of a maelstrom, and knew it. If his airbags couldn't be made to work, the entire mission was dead. Tom would have all the support I could give him, and just about as much of the project's resources as he needed—in morale, money, mass, or schedule.

Within reasonable limits. He was soon to conclude that even three layers of abrasive covering weren't sufficient for doing the job, no matter what the thickness. At any realistic velocity, the bags were still being gashed and ripped by the rocks. He would need more protective material, still another layer of the Vectran. But that would kick up the total mass of the airbags by another 25 kilograms to over 90 kilograms—nearly 200 pounds. Allowing Tom the increase he was asking for would leave me almost no reserve for the many other contingencies I had every reason to expect lay ahead.

EXCITEMENT COUNTS

The radios on the lander would provide our two-way link from Earth to Pathfinder, our only window into its lonely world in deep space. A spacecraft radio must be small, lightweight, and use very little power, yet still be able to communicate over vast distances. (As testimony to the skill of the JPL telecommunications group, the radio on the Voyager spacecraft, twenty years after launch, is still sending signals to Earth over a distance of more than 8 billion miles.)

In the perverse vortex of daily life, where problems you could not have anticipated become the crisis of the moment, I suddenly had a new one. The manager of our telecommunications team announced he was leaving for a "better" job; I assumed this meant "better paying."

We looked around and asked around for people at JPL qualified to take over, and came up with a very short list: a single name,

Leslie Livesay. She was the best candidate for the job, the only real candidate, and I had no doubts she could do it. But there was just this one little problem: Leslie and I had been dating for some months, and had become quite serious in our relationship.

She and I worried the dilemma back and forth. Both of us agreed that we could work together, even in this pressure-cooker environment, and not let it interfere with our personal relationship. We spoke discreetly to people we trusted, but they without exception emphatically urged that if we valued the relationship, she should not take the job. Still, we were sure that even if the personal relationship collapsed, the professional one would not be compromised. This said volumes for our dedication to professionalism and to Pathfinder, yet of course there could be no guarantee we wouldn't end up like so many other couples in spoiled office romances, vindictively trying to hurt each other, and hurting the organization in the process.

In some companies and work groups, a relationship like this can poison the atmosphere. Others in the organization become afraid that if they say anything to the junior member of the pair, or cross swords with that person, it will become pillow talk—which could result in pressure on them from the boss when they never had a chance to make their own case. As a result, people tend to steer clear of this person, who may end up eating lunch alone and having arm's-length dealings with coworkers.

At JPL, on the other hand, the atmosphere is different—people seem to be able to weather the ups and downs of relationships without unleashing an emotional spillover into their professional lives. Lots of personal involvements spring up among employees and there are many happy, successful couples at the Lab. A few of these connections are what most would consider unusual. Case in point: though Tony Spear asked me, "Are you *nuts!*" my ex-wife Cathy came to work for me on Pathfinder; later, when Leslie became manager of her own spacecraft project, Deep Space 1, Cathy went to work for *her*.

On a personal level, though, this one looked like a no-win situation. If Leslie took the job, our relationship was at risk, and if she didn't, my mission was at risk.

Together we bit the bullet and announced the decision. Leslie Livesay became the Pathfinder telecommunications system manager, responsible for building, testing and delivering all the radio hardware including the antennas.

And, as well, the telecommunications modulation unit, the device that converts digital data from the cameras and instruments into a so-called analog signal, a form that the radio can then pump out over the antenna to Earth. When Leslie looked into the state of the TMU development, she was alarmed, and red-flagged it. Just started on her new job, she was already saddled with a critical-path delivery item that was late and might hold up her subsystem and the entire project.

But as I anticipated, Leslie's leadership and talent, combined with the talent of her team, produced a miracle of a radio, which would fit into a large shoe box, weighed only about 17 pounds and used no more power than a reading light, about 90 watts. State-of-the-art in every way, it carried more new technology than any other subsystem on the spacecraft.

My boss Tony Spear became quite a fan, frequently commenting at management reviews, "Thank God for Leslie." The remark always brought a laugh.

A traditional leader, intellectual and analytical, coolly detached, may inspire obedience and even respect but does not get people excited. Leslie, in contrast, brought a great spark in her ability to translate her own energy and excitement to her team. She and two other engineers, Rocco Scaramastra and Gary Glass, brought together, tested, tuned and delivered the radio in only ten weeks, less than half the time anyone thought possible. Excitement counts.

A Faster, Better, Cheaper leader learns to stimulate emotional energy, galvanize, excite his people, her team. Out of this excitement comes the potential for spectacular accomplishment.

CELEBRATE SUCCESS

"Success" aptly describes the mood around Pathfinder in mid-June 1995 when, right on track with the schedule we had originally set, we began delivering flight electronics to begin the "Assembly, Test, Launch Operations" phase of the project. ATLO, as it's called (spoken as "AT-low"—we love acronyms), marks the time when elements of the spacecraft start being delivered to the test bay and built up into what, at last, begins to resemble the hardware that will be sent into space.

With the culmination of one huge effort and the beginning of another, we now began for the first time to see all the disparate elements we'd been working on come together, gradually taking shape as the spacecraft we'd seen only on paper and in our mind's eye for the past year and a half. An experience akin to your first solo flight or your first speed run on skis, this is something that engineers pretend to be blasé about, when deep down they're feeling exultant.

From an overall project standpoint, this is a peak, an emotional high point. Especially so on Pathfinder. After the nearly disastrous Critical Design Review the previous September, our low point in spirits and outlook, we were now at a place where we could see successes all around. Problems overcome, design work completed, components fabricated, assembly about to begin. This was an important moment psychologically for the team, and did much to quiet critics who still doubted we would succeed.

Sure, the airbag design was still uncertain, structural components were behind schedule and threatening to hold us up, and other problems still threatened. Despite these chasms not yet crossed, we had plenty to celebrate.

And we did. Taking short breaks from regular work schedules, we brought the teams one at a time into the test bay, where they arranged themselves around the components of Pathfinder hardware that they were responsible for while a JPL staff photographer took their pictures. We also invited all the Lab's top management and division managers to see the historic event and have their pictures taken. These photos become treasured items to the spacecraft builders. Copies are framed and hung in offices at JPL, and proudly added to photo collections at home.

John Casani had lost his bet that we couldn't build the avionics for the budgeted $30 million. Lehman's team had done it on budget, and John came through with the two cases of wine he had wagered. Not Lafite Rothschild, but while I had expected all along to win the bet, I never really expected anything so pricey for the payoff. The team extended the celebration by gathering one Saturday night for a party, where we polished off all the wine except for one bottle, held in reserve to be opened after a successful landing.

At this point, Curt Cleven, part of my management troika, took charge of the assembly operations. An experienced veteran of many missions, Curt is even-tempered and rarely abrasive (whereas some would say that compared to me, Attila the Hun might be considered soft-spoken). Throughout this phase of the project, Curt began the day with an 8:15 A.M. standup meeting for all lead engineers—dealing with what they would be doing for the day, what people would be needed, what test equipment, what procedures. He used these sessions to keep the work effort organized and focused, making sure that good communications would help keep the energy level high.

A GALVANIZED WORK GROUP CAN ACCOMPLISH GREATNESS

You've probably seen photographs of a clean room, like the ones where computer chips are fabricated. Visualize a gigantic clean room, a vast space wide enough and long enough to house half a football field, and tall as a four-story building. This is the assembly area at JPL called High Bay One, a place filled with an aura of the history of space, where many of JPL's spacecraft have been built up through the years, and where we were to do most of our assembly and much of our testing on Pathfinder.

By the time of the photography sessions, we had received the computer, radio with its antennas, individual slices of the electronics hardware, and the attitude control sensors that would guide Pathfinder through space and into the Martian atmosphere. We also had the physical elements that would provide the backbone for the assembly: the flight structure, the plate and support brackets that would hold the electronics, as well as the electronics chassis itself.

The Pathfinder effort had reached its peak. The workforce was at its maximum, the equivalent of about 250 full-time people (the Viking Mars project at its peak had employed about 600 at JPL and another 1,600 at Martin Marietta in Denver). Financially we were already past the peak, with most of our money, well over half the budget, already spent or committed. Yet we still had a long way to go.

As each member of the assembly crew arrived for work in the morning, he or she would have to go through the ritual of suiting up for the clean room. First an "air shower": you stand in a closet-sized chamber, press the button on the wall, and a huge fan draws a hurricane of air past you, pulling dust and particles off your clothing. Next you put on the clean-room garb of smock, hat and booties, and if you would be handling hardware, finished off with latex or cotton gloves. Then one more air shower, and you're ready to step into the High Bay work area, brightly lit as an operating room. At any one time there might be ten to twenty workers here, coping with the demanding tasks of assembling the spacecraft out of hundreds of components, which the mechanical interface documents said *should* fit together.

The man responsible for building the lander structure, Jim Baughman, called the spacecraft our "900-kilogram Swiss watch" because it was such a complex machine with so many intricate moving parts.

Mike Mangano, mechanical integration lead engineer for the assembly and test operation, had to guide his crew in building not just one spacecraft but two, including a preliminary that we call the dynamic test model—full-sized, and structurally identical to the hardware that would actually fly.

The usual practice had been for a separate team to build the dynamic test model. But because our spacecraft was so complex to assemble, Mike made the decision that having the flight team do both would let them gain the experience from a complete practice run before starting to handle the flight hardware. He was sure this would significantly reduce the risk of damage; it was unprecedented and would put a lot of extra pressure on Mike's team, yet made good sense. I agreed to the plan as soon as I heard his proposal. To keep himself from becoming the weak link in the operation, Mike created his own leadership team composed of Linda Robeck (who referred to herself as "the lander babe"), cruise stage engineer Brad Gibson and deployments engineer Kendra Short.

The challenge for Mangano's assembly team boiled down to a simple demand: cramming a great deal of equipment—including rover, lander, airbags and aeroshell—into the available space, 9 feet in diameter. Though some items had only a half inch of clearance from an adjacent piece of hardware, the whole works had to be so secure that vibration during launch and during entry to Mars would not cause items to bang or rub together.

And after arriving at Mars, most of this system also had to open up again. This was certainly the most demanding job of spacecraft assembly ever attempted at JPL, perhaps the most complex ever attempted anywhere.

A set of demands like this presents a challenge not just to the team but to its leaders. Successful leaders like Mike know how to produce emotional energy, energy that motivates their people to commit and outperform. Teams running on this energy can accomplish great things.

Some people, on the other hand, are well aware of their failings in this area but feel powerless to improve. One corporate manager recently told me she feels, and knows her people feel, that she hasn't managed the emotional energy of her group as well as she could, hasn't done some of the things she should have in terms of structuring her operation. Now traveling a great deal, she finds that "I can't be there to galvanize my group when they need it."

And when she's in the office but not exuding an aura of positive energy, she finds it acts like a wet blanket on her whole team. Some of her people start sidling up and asking "Can I do anything for you?" or "Do you need something to eat?" They can't quite put their finger on what's wrong, but sense that her downer is sapping energy from the whole group.

We can't, of course, measure corporate energy directly, but money and people provide two measures of energy being expended, and so offer a guide to the level of leadership called for. At the peak of effort, the demands for strong leadership also peak. You have so much talent at work, you've built up so much energy, now it's more important than at any other time to make certain you're moving in the right direction, that efforts are channeled correctly, so that this peak energy is being expended productively. Because, like a charge of explosive, if it isn't being channeled right when you're at the peak of staffing and spending, it can destroy you. Unless you're finding solutions to the problems and working through them quickly, one big difficulty can cause a great deal of energy to be wasted. The whole organization slows, waiting for the problem to be resolved or the decision to be made.

The most successful leaders have learned to channel their own emotional energy, focusing it to energize their people. Teams sparked this way run on the induced energy and accomplish great things with it. They are electrified by the energy and passion of their leaders. Teams focused like this can achieve greatness.

A SENSE OF WHAT IS POSSIBLE

Patrick Henry wrote that he was guided only by "the lamp of experience. I know of no way of judging the future but by the past."

If you were to follow that as a life dictum, you would probably not hazard out in the morning. It's certainly not a view that I share. Experience is important, but you really need a sense of what's possible and what you believe you're capable of doing in order to create the future.

Tom Rivellini's request for 25 kilograms more mass so he could add a fourth abrasion layer to the airbags continued to haunt us.

The issue came to a head at a brain trust meeting in my office, with all my top engineers agreeing the airbag design was highly risky without these added layers. The idea of eating so much of my reserves with sixteen months still to go was scary, yet the airbags had to do their job successfully or the entire mission would be a fizzle; giving Tom what he needed now would certainly reduce the risk to the overall mission.

With some of the hardware already in hand, we were able to weigh it and have a better idea of real mass instead of just relying on the numbers that the engineers had projected based on their designs. From this I judged I could give some additional mass to Tom without blowing the reserves. *Some* additional. But not all he was asking for.

It's a balancing act. If we ended up on the launch pad with mass to spare and the risk still high of the airbags surviving multiple bounces, I would have been failing in my responsibilities. On the other hand, give away too much now and I could be in deep trouble later on.

In August, I looked at my analysis curves, something akin to looking at a crystal ball, and told Tom, "I feel comfortable letting you have an additional 17 kilograms"—38 pounds instead of the requested 55.

He went back to the contractor with that number, and together they figured out a way to use the 17 kilograms effectively: rather than cover the bags entirely with the fourth layer, they would cover only those areas most likely to be damaged. Another example proving the dictum that when the energy level is high, a constraint doesn't look like a barrier but a challenge to be overcome by creativity.

Tom, who excelled at keeping the creative juices flowing, was so unflagging in his efforts that, despite long months of grueling work schedules, he would still be refining the airbag designs up until the final assembly a few months before launch.

Nowadays when times turn tough, I like to share stories of how Tom overcame the many hardships of the airbag development. A few workers like this can spark the energy levels for an entire organization.

8. It's the Team, Stupid!

I have yet to find the man, however exalted
his station, who did not do better work
and put forth greater effort under a spirit
of approval than under a spirit of criticism.

—Charles Schwab

COUNTDOWN: 1 YEAR, 6 MONTHS TO LAUNCH

The key to the success of Pathfinder—of *any* project or organization—is the people. Management thinkers have been saying this for years, most annual reports say it, most leaders mouth the words . . . but too often without follow-through.

Building a team means collecting talent, building trust, and nurturing dedication. When you provide those elements, amazing things can happen.

Just as the whole of the Pathfinder project succeeded in part because we were challenged by a difficult, stirring goal, so do individual teams sometimes come alive and "gel" as a group when faced with some hurdle or hazard so formidable that the prospect makes everyone question their sanity. When our software team delivered the first version of spacecraft software to the High Bay test team in June '95, it represented a dazzling achievement for team leader Glenn Reeves and his bantam-sized crew.

Glenn made a great poster boy for one part of my credo: I believe in generalists, people who are not limited in scope to the confines of the work they were trained in or are most experienced at, but who have the interest and ability to work beyond the limitations of their résumé.

In the everyday world, you might label this idea as an attractive concept; in the world of Faster, Better, Cheaper, you need to label it as "mission critical."

On Pathfinder, because the core of the team of engineers was multidisciplinary—we hired them that way when we could, and developed them when we had to—we were able to function with a much smaller staff than had been used on similar projects in the past. For the entire management team, in particular, I insisted on generalists and let them know they were expected to think and act that way.

A community of generalists allows faster decision-making, makes the transitions between different phases of the project less inefficient and more fluid, and makes it easier to cross-train workers.

There will always be a need for the in-depth skill and knowledge of specialists. But I'm committed to the idea of giving specialists the opportunity to expand their horizons, and have seen this principle translate into success time and again. A prime example on Pathfinder was Miguel San Martin, a tall Argentine with a easygoing style that turns quite intense in the heat of wrestling with a technical problem. Miguel has one of the best grasps of fundamental physics of anyone I know, can see to the heart of an intricate problem, and can explain complex issues clearly, particularly in his specialty of attitude control. That's why so many people trust his judgment and input.

Before joining Pathfinder, Miguel had been on the Cassini project, where his work involved writing the algorithms—the equations, the mathematical relations that would govern the way the spacecraft would fly; somebody else would then translate his algorithms into computer code, and a third person would test the solution. When Miguel came over to Pathfinder, we said, "We want you to figure it out, we want you to code it and then we want you to test it." Where in the past he had been given a limited assignment and had done just what he was asked for, we were asking for more.

Was he successful at working outside the small box he had been in? Beyond successful: he had flight software running on Pathfinder before the corresponding algorithms were even coded on Cassini—though they had started the project four years earlier. Miguel was excited and quite proud of what he had achieved. He told me several times, in his wonderfully rich Argentine accent, "This is why I became an engineer. Pathfinder is the best job of my career."

Glenn Reeves, another example, had been working on software to run the ground-support equipment for JPL space missions. Slim, blond, quick to smile and just as quick to engage in barbed banter, Glenn brought an unusual ability to the job. While many software engineers don't know much more about hardware than how to turn on their computer, Glenn had worked on the hardware side as well. I accepted him as head of the Pathfinder software team even though he'd never led a flight software development project and would find the job a major challenge. Software is notorious for eating budgets and schedules, but my instincts said that this energetic, sometimes acerbic young man could do the job.

He took the reins, letting me know early on, and often, that *I* was really working for *him*. As he put it, "Software rules, hardware drools"—meant to insult my background as a hardware engineer. Instead of being offended, I fired back a challenge: "Prove it." Glenn and his team did just that.

But one area where Glenn failed miserably was in estimating the scope of the effort, a classic failing and one that generally sinks a software job. Pulling an initial estimate out of Glenn was like pulling teeth, and when he finally gave me one, it was to prove wildly wrong: he estimated the complete package would have 20,000 lines of source code. At launch, the software contained 155,000 lines.

Yet his team wrote all that code—eight times more than he anticipated—without a proportional growth in budget and schedule. How was that possible? The explanation lay in the incredible productivity of Glenn himself, and the productivity he was able to wring from his small team of eight programmers.

The industry standard for a software programmer was then about ten lines of code per person per day. To anyone not in high tech, that

Major elements of the Pathfinder spacecraft, top to bottom: cruise stage; backshell (the long objects are the deceleration rocket motors; the parachute is packed into the canister in the center); the lander with airbags in stowed position; and the heat shield.

Tom Rivellini, airbag designer, with airbags before a test.

Airbag test in the huge vacuum chamber at Plumbrook Station, Ohio. The angled ramp is covered with rocks simulating the Mars surface; the netting keeps the bag from bouncing around the chamber after it hits the ramp.

Members of the cable team who called themselves "the Seven Dwarves." Only six are shown because "Grumpy" was not present for the photograph.

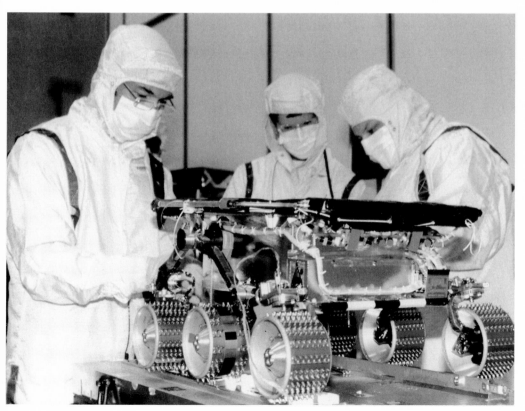

The self-propelled rover vehicle Sojourner featured six-wheel drive and four-wheel steering. Note the steel wheels, specially designed for traction on a variety of surfaces.

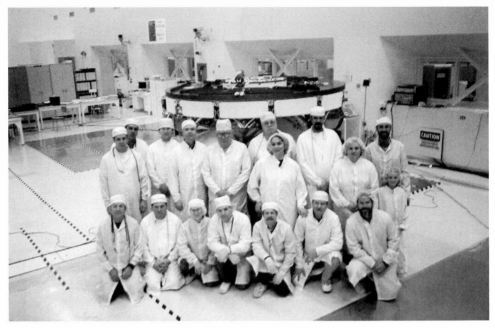

Some of the Pathfinder engineers and technicians gathered for the traditional picture taking on completion of assembly. Front row: Carl McNutt, Don Benson, Linda Robeck, Mike Mangano, Kelly Taylor, Tom Shain, Rob Manning. Back row: Bob DeBusk, Larry Broms, Burt Turney, Brad Gibson, Don Herriot, Chuck Foehlinger, Lorraine Garcia, Jim Pearson, Maralee Murray and Brian Muirhead with daughter Alicia.

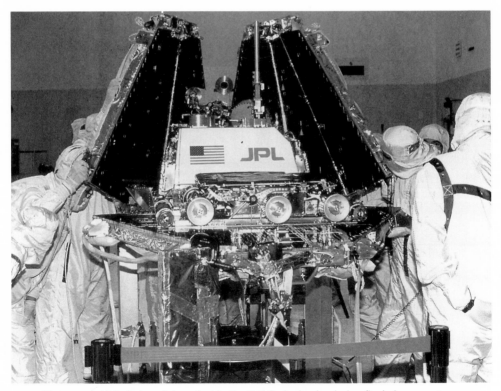

The rover vehicle fastened down inside the Pathfinder lander during final close-up at Cape Canaveral.

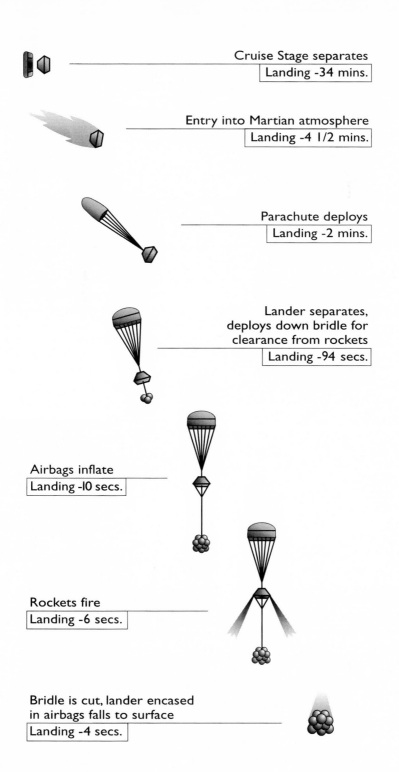

Cruise Stage separates
Landing -34 mins.

Entry into Martian atmosphere
Landing -4 1/2 mins.

Parachute deploys
Landing -2 mins.

Lander separates,
deploys down bridle for
clearance from rockets
Landing -94 secs.

Airbags inflate
Landing -10 secs.

Rockets fire
Landing -6 secs.

Bridle is cut, lander encased
in airbags falls to surface
Landing -4 secs.

The extraordinarily complex sequence of events for Pathfinder's entry, descent and landing.

Dave Gruel watches as Jennifer Harris, flight director for "sol 1," the first day on Mars, rehearses for operations on the surface. Observing them are Richard Cook, Rob Manning, Brian Muirhead and visiting actor LeVar Burton.

The control room just after receiving confirmation that the spacecraft had landed safely. Seated: Chris Salvo, Robert Manning, Guy Beutelschies (partially hidden). Standing: Matt Golombek, Dara Sabahi, Tony Spear, Sam Thurman, Brian Muirhead, Richard Cook (back to camera).

The first photo mosaic shown to the world on July 4, 1997, the evidence of a successful landing.

At a press conference on landing day, Brian Muirhead, right, uses a model to explain the steps of the lander opening its side panels. Listening are, from left, NASA Administrator Dan Goldin, Associate Administrator for Space Science Dr. Wesley Huntress and Pathfinder project scientist Matt Golombek. (Photograph by Bill Ingalls, NASA.)

The first photograph received on Earth showing that the rover had successfully driven off the lander onto the Martian surface.

figure must sound absurd—even my seven-year-old can write ten sentences in a day, why shouldn't a professional programmer be able to write many more lines of code?

Answer: What we're talking about is ten lines of *fully tested, bug-free* code. The challenge lies not in writing the software, but in writing, testing, fixing . . . and repeating that cycle over, and over, and over, until it does what it's supposed to do under every fiendish circumstance the test team can conceive.

Instead of the standard ten lines of good code a day, Glenn's team averaged *twenty-eight*.

What's more, the software went beyond the usual straightforward sequence of step-by-step events, "Carry out the instructions in this line of code, then do the next line." For Pathfinder, the team had to work to a newer paradigm, putting more complexity on board to make the spacecraft more independent of ground control. So, for example, in determining when to issue the command to open the parachute during descent, the program would evaluate the quality of the data it was receiving. If the accelerometer had malfunctioned and was feeding bad data, the software would shift to a simple but less certain backup plan, triggering at a predetermined time.

The secret of the software team's effectiveness grew out of Glenn's attitude. Not the type of person to hand out assignments and let his people just "sling code," Glenn made his assignments in terms of what operation the spacecraft needed to perform, what sensors provided the inputs and what control functions would be available. That left the programmer to think not just in terms of software code but in terms of functionality, of operating the spacecraft.

In any development project of a complex system, most problems show up at the interfaces, the places where two of the subsystems meet or interact. I suppose what best characterizes the nature of a generalist is the ability, and the willingness, to look across the interfaces, to understand the world of the people developing the other subsystems. At the project level, the generalists are the people who glue the whole system together. Glenn rose to the challenge; even more, he got his team members to do that, as well.

As their basic way of functioning, some managers give directions, some give direction. Glenn, like so many of the other Pathfinder leaders, led by showing the way.

IN THE SPIN

All spacecraft are tested for their ability to withstand the mechanical ravages of vibration at launch. Pathfinder would also have to endure an extreme g force as it penetrated the Martian environment and, worse, the high g's of multiple bounces on first reaching the surface of Mars—forces that could last for seconds and be greater than fifty times the force of Earth's gravity.

The challenge of withstanding the forces at launch are tested on a giant vibration table that forms the top surface of something like a huge speaker cone. For the entry forces, we would have to test in a centrifuge. Everyone has seen video clips of astronauts and test pilots, their faces distorted like Silly Putty under the forces in a spin test. But those forces reach a maximum of about 14 g's. Our hardware, fastened to the end of a long arm and spun much faster than an astronaut, would have to withstand 55 g's.

While pieces of space hardware are routinely tested in the chamber, within my knowledge no other *planetary* spacecraft built at JPL had ever been centrifuge-tested before. The first time I visited the centrifuge, a bunker with thick concrete walls, I appreciated what the mechanical team was up against: the walls were deeply scarred in several places, evidence of past test failures. Clearly the centrifuge had the potential for turning into a spacecraft death trap.

This testing presented three major worries for our test leader, Greg Davis, and the mechanical team leader, Mike Mangano. They would have to be absolutely certain the designs for the test hardware were foolproof, guaranteed not to come apart under the high g forces of the centrifuge. And they would have to design and build a 100 percent reliable fixture for attaching our hardware to the centrifuge arm, good enough that they could be dead certain it would not give way.

But the risk was compounded by a decision made much earlier. It's standard on a spacecraft project to build and test three units—an engineering model for working out design concepts; the flight unit; and a spare, as backup in case something disastrous happens with the flight unit. To save money, I had decided we would not assemble spares for any of the electronic components. My reasoning was that if we had problems with a board, we'd use the engineering model as a stand-in while we fixed the flight board. Only in the case of a disaster would we spend the time and money on assembling the spare. So for the centrifuge test there would be no choice: they would be testing our one-and-only flight hardware.

The third worry lay in the test itself. What if the operator set the limits wrong? What if the test controls failed? Not idle worries—I had seen these things happen many times, and they could subject the spacecraft to much higher forces than we'd designed for.

Sure, there's an emergency cutoff, a panic button we call the "chicken switch," but in a centrifuge test there's simply too much momentum. If the machine ran out of control, the damage would be done before that massive arm could be slowed and stopped.

The best workers are those who rise to a challenge. My experience with Mike, who had worked for me in various jobs over ten years, gave me confidence that he would make sure every element of the test was idiot-proof. We both knew this was no time to experiment with new approaches.

Together Mike and I inspected the hardware and fixtures. If anything broke, the responsibility would be on Mike's shoulders, but the nightmare would be everyone's—we were still saddled with that paradox of "Take risks but don't fail." And, of course, avoidable failures, failures caused by dumb mistakes, would permanently scar the reputation of everybody around.

In the control room in early July '95, I sat looking over the shoulder of the centrifuge operator, the "chicken switch" within his easy reach. Noise from the large gasoline motor outside began to change from a throbbing to a higher-pitched whine as the arm increased in speed. Looking through the small porthole, I couldn't believe how fast the arm was spinning. I likely stopped breathing for some moments.

But the mechanical team had done itself proud. The test went fine. There would be days more of centrifuge testing ahead, in different orientations, but Mike and the testers had proven to themselves and the rest of the team that they could handle a very high risk situation and come through flawlessly. Though the project would have plenty of other all-or-nothing challenges still to come, the success of the team in this round gave everyone a notch more confidence that we would persevere.

SPIRIT

Here's a riddle: What's critical to a high-technology space mission and yet is low technology? What task is one of the last to be defined but must be one of the first delivered? If you answered, "the cabling," you're clearly an experienced spacecraft builder.

On a spacecraft project, only when all the electronics designs are finished can the engineers start figuring out details of the wiring that will route the power and electronic signals among all the various components.

Most jobs in the space business have a certain glamour attached to them, the satisfaction that you're creating a widget that's going to fly to Mars. It doesn't hurt any that this also makes great cocktail party conversation, and will look wonderful on a résumé.

(I love answering the question "So what do you do?" Most of the time I use a response I picked up from my friend Hoppy Price: "Oh, I build interplanetary spacecraft." Some people think it's "cool," others want to start a conversation about aliens.)

The cabling job, by contrast, is not exactly glamorous. It's intricate, extremely precise, exacting, demanding work, requiring perseverance and arduous attention to detail, but offering little glory. Every strand of wire has to be very carefully stripped of its insulation, exactingly coated with solder, positioned at the one and only opening it's intended for out of thousands, carefully inserted into this very fine opening, and soldered in place. All these wires then have to be gathered into bunches—cables—and routed to their destination, where the stripping and soldering must be repeated on the other end of each wire. A tiny nick in a wire could weaken it enough to break during the vibration of launch or the g forces of landing. An easily made error like soldering the wire onto the wrong pin could burn up some part of an electronic system.

Despite all the downsides, on Pathfinder the cabling team turned into one of the great stories of the project. The team consisted of six ladies and their quality inspector, who came to call themselves "the

Seven Dwarfs." Each of them adopted the nickname of one dwarf—team leader Linda Ponce called herself Doc, Dopey picked her label because she liked to act that way at times, Happy and Bashful really were, Sleepy found it tough to get started in the mornings, Sneezy was allergic to something in the shop, and the quality person was Grumpy. In most cases the names were laughably appropriate. Especially Grumpy.

The cable drawings weren't finished until spring of 1995; testing was scheduled to begin June 15. The Dwarfs had about three months to make more than 2,000 connections with the fewest possible errors, and then to route the cable bunches, almost as stiff as metal piping, totaling more than 2 miles of wiring.

I dropped in on the cabling shop every day, sometimes twice a day, making sure the team members never forgot how much we were counting on them, and to see if any bottlenecks had appeared that might need my attention.

Could this possibly be worth the time of a project manager with so many high-level issues to attend to?

I believe it's far too easy to focus on the obvious management matters of budget and schedule . . . and overlook the less visible elements until something has reached the crisis stage—requiring you to shift into "fire-fighting" mode.

A project boss needs to identify which elements are both critical and high risk, and give these few items personal attention. For the cabling team, "high risk" meant the impact on the project if they lost enthusiasm and started to grow careless because of overwork, or if they didn't finish on time—especially difficult because of last-minute design changes caused by engineering mistakes that twice required pulling out cables already completed, and reworking them.

Why didn't I just tell their immediate manager, "This is critical, check on the progress every day, keep me updated, come to me if there are any issues you can't handle"? Why, as leader of the entire flight system organization, did I take the time to be so directly involved? Two reasons: Because I knew that my being involved in this way would convey a clear message—to the ladies themselves and to every member of the Pathfinder team—that the cabling work was absolutely mission-critical and had priority over almost anything else going on. And because the cabling work is based on inputs from virtually every part of the flight system organization, and the rover team as well; questions, issues and problems that the cabling group encountered had to be handled by someone who had clout over every part of the organization—clout that no individual element manager has.

Would this kind of leadership involvement at the working level be possible in industry? The answer is, "Yes, but . . ." Yes, but only in a relatively flat organization (we had only a single management level between me and the leader of the cabling team)—which an effective Faster, Better, Cheaper operation demands anyway. So any FBC leader should be able to take this degree of personal, hands-on involvement on those few areas that are make-or-break for the project.

Though the cabling ladies were as highly motivated as any other team on Pathfinder, I dangled additional bait in front of them, telling Linda, "If your team can deliver this harness with three errors or less, I'll buy everyone a bottle of tequila."

She wasn't about to let me off easy: "If it's Cuervo 1800, you're on."

So we had our bet. As her team finished the first build and took their octopus-like harness in to be tested, they were flushed with excitement and anticipation—not so much about the bet, but about having finished an intense challenge under enormous pressure.

Two days later, we had the results: only three errors, all easy to fix. The Seven Dwarfs had won the bet; Tony threw an all-hands party at his home, and I paid with great pleasure.

You can't order that kind of team spirit, you can't command it. But you can show the level of management concern and involvement that convinces people their work is important, valued, recognized.

Months later I noticed a sign over the door of a restaurant in Florida: "In the race for quality, there's never a finish line." It could have served as the motto for Linda and the Dwarfs.

TEAM SPIRIT AT THE TOP

When people talk about team spirit, you invariably find they have their sights focused on the workers. Or at best, the lower-level managers. How about looking for team spirit among the people at the top of an organization, the top of a project? Does no one talk about this because they always assume it's a given?

Or maybe it's because they know it simply doesn't exist in most organizations.

During the thirty-seven months of Pathfinder, my flight system operation faced a financial crisis about twice a year in the first two years: too many unexpecteds, too many never-happens that happened anyway. When it was clear that we were burning reserves too quickly, and since we all well knew there was no point in asking NASA for additional funds, there was only one choice: pass around the tithing plate among the managers of the non-flight system areas—science, mission operations and ground systems.

Tony Spear called these sessions, which he held offsite in a lecture hall on the top floor of the geology building at the nearby Caltech campus. (I always had a suspicion he chose this isolated setting—there were no classrooms or offices nearby—in case emotions ran high and the little group grew overheated and noisy.) Setting the tone for these meetings, Tony would admonish us, "This is not going to be a witch hunt. We're all in this race together and we all need to finish together."

All the managers in turn would stand up and explain their current funding situation and the problems they were facing, while the rest of us listened, trying to figure out what things might be cut or done differently within that program to save money.

At one of these meetings, Al Sacks found a way of expressing the frustration all the other managers felt at the give-money-to-Brian process: in the middle of the session, he stood up, whipped out a gun and fired straight at Tony's chest, launching an uproar. The "gun" was one of those children's toys that fires a stick with a suction cup on the end. Everyone thought this was hysterical; even Tony laughed. Then I picked up the gun and held it to my head, bringing a cheer. The brief interlude certainly broke the tension.

One of the best examples of team spirit at the top came early in the project when I was struggling to pay for an improved lander solar array. We had planned to use silicon cells but the power they could provide on the surface of Mars looked marginal. What I really wanted was high-efficiency cells made of gallium arsenide, but that would take an additional $300,000 I didn't have. Al Sacks looked at his budget, reasoned that more power on Mars would mean less work on Earth for the operations team, and gave me $300,000 out of his budget. Call it enlightened self-interest, but I'd never seen it happen before. And as the story circulated, it raised the spirits of the entire team.

At Tony's cough-up-some-money meetings, though, nobody was volunteering, yet everybody knew the bottom line. Under the project success criteria agreed to with NASA, we would be counted 70 percent successful just by landing on Mars, which meant that the flight system took priority. Pathfinder could scrimp on ground systems, could give up things from the science program . . . but cutting corners on the spacecraft would mean cutting the throats of everybody in the room. The others knew we were not walking out of the meeting until more money had been found to increase reserves. And everyone knew those reserves would eventually be going to me. So these were not pleasant meetings.

Still, Tony made sure that the bloodletting was never too serious. Each time, we all walked out of the room ready to dive back into work.

COMMITMENT BEGINS AT THE TOP

Commitment represents another of the manager's paradoxes. It's essential, yet not something you can create, command or control; it can spell the difference between success and failure, yet only arises from within the individuals of the group.

But while you can't create commitment, you can create the kind of work environment, the kind of atmosphere, in which people are *willing* to commit.

It should be self-evident, though since we sometimes manage to overlook the obvious it's worth noting up front, that the leader of any organization is the role model for commitment, as for virtually all other behaviors. As the leader goes, so—in most cases, about most attitude and behavioral issues—goes the organization.

The leader who wants people to be committed—clearly an essential for any Faster, Better, Cheaper effort—had better be committed herself. But that's not enough. He or she must be *seen* by the people of the organization to be acting in ways that show commitment. That may mean coming in earlier or leaving later (or both) than the posted work hours; it may mean a willingness to roll up the sleeves and pitch in when the deadline nears.

It definitely requires a willingness to listen to the views and suggestions of others. An experienced leader knows she doesn't have all the answers—knows that even an entry-level worker may have recognized a problem before anyone else has seen it, may have had an invaluable flash of insight, may have come up with a remarkable solution.

So the committed leader is a *listener*, someone who recognizes that the next great idea or solution may come from an unexpected source. Most people will only share their ideas when they think they might be listened to. And in any organization, everyone at the working levels knows which bosses are willing to listen and which are not.

The committed leader is also willing to accept criticism and reassess a decision, willing to say, "I was wrong about that, I like your idea, let's go that way instead."

The committed leader lets people see that she is committed to them and their careers—defending them, backing them up when needed. But more than that, the committed leader knows his people well enough to know their career goals, their hopes and dreams, and helps to nurture those goals by creating opportunities to fulfill them.

Acknowledging your people engenders commitment; commitment engenders a willingness to pitch in and do the best possible job, no matter what the hours, not just as an individual but as part of the team.

The Pathfinder team had a level of commitment beyond the ordinary, but even within the team there were people who stood out. People like Tom Shain, who was responsible for setting up the Assembly and Test electrical environment and overseeing all electrical integration operations, one of those rare, most special people who can create something out of nothing (beautifully described by screenwriter Michael Browning in the movie *Six Days, Seven Nights* something like this: a guy "who can go into the jungle with a penknife and a Q-Tip, and build a shopping center"). When we needed a custom-designed box to route power to the spacecraft in testing, and needed it yesterday, instead of asking someone else to do it, Tom sat down, designed it, and then built it himself.

He earned the nickname "the Scrounger" for his uncanny ability to find the hardware and cables we needed from other JPL projects that had leftovers, or from little-known storage areas, or from I'm not sure where. But the ground support and test hardware he provided saved us something probably approaching a million dollars.

Another outstanding commitment example was Lorraine Garcia, one of our quality-control people. In most organizations, quality workers can't help but be seen as adversarial, creating an atmosphere of confrontation—inevitable, since their assignment is to look over people's shoulders and pass judgment on other people's work, "This is acceptable, that's not acceptable."

Lorraine characterized the different approach the Pathfinder project took to quality. Instead of coming in as "inspectors" sent by a different department to find problems, our quality people were integrated within each development team, where they were expected to behave like team members, and use their skill and experience as inspectors to keep us out of trouble.

One issue too often overlooked in this: even though quality inspectors in a project like ours are examining the work of professional engineers, while they themselves don't usually hold engineering degrees, they nonetheless have experience that can be valuable. The problem they're looking at may be one they've seen before on another spacecraft or instrument project. Unsatisfactory solder joints? Improper handling procedures? The quality person may have encountered the situation before and may have a good suggestion. Or may recognize a situation early enough to warn of trouble ahead in time to steer clear of the problems.

I remember in my days as a hardware engineer, the quality people were notorious nay-sayers. Their favorite reaction when something didn't meet their standards was to call a halt to operations, creating a crisis and costing us valuable time. Quality-control people are much more likely to make a constructive, positive contribution when seen as part of the team they're working with.

Lorraine would do whatever was needed. If she found a board that needed to be rewired, she'd go nab a technician qualified to do it. Pleasant, outgoing and friendly, she spread a trail of goodwill wherever she went. Once, when she was working with an engineer who had a way of losing control, she said very simply: "Honey, you're making me nervous." That's all it took; he settled down and behaved.

Commitment is infectious. Both Tom and Lorraine, and so many others like them, energized many around them by their commitment, raising the level for everyone.

THOUGH THIS BE MADNESS, YET THERE IS METHOD IN IT

I held two required leadership meetings each week, back to back, every Wednesday. The first, beginning at 1 o'clock, was for the top managers—the other two members of my leadership troika, Rob Manning and lead system engineer Curt Cleven—plus leaders of the principal teams: mechanical, attitude and information, power, propulsion, telecommunications, and financial. We'd spend about an hour or a little longer covering the items on my "Top Ten" list, which included budget, schedules, and major programmatic issues and changes.

At 2, the systems team would arrive, representing every subsystem as well as other key members of the project staff. This session could last anywhere from one hour to five, and it was a full house: at our peak, as many as thirty people would be crowded into the room.

I look on these technical sessions quite differently than other JPL project managers. They're traditionally known as "design team" meetings; to me, that sends the wrong message. This pack of engineers wasn't there to twiddle the knobs and come up with a design neater or more wonderful than the last one. They were there to design something and *build* it. "Design team" suggests that when their design is finished, they're done, they can go home. Watch out for labels that give people the wrong focus. I called this group the "implementation team."

Another difference: these sessions of mostly engineers are customarily run by someone from the JPL Systems Engineering operation. I saw this as our principal forum, really our *only* forum, for airing every technical problem any subsystem team had run into that might impact the system design, resources (such as mass and power), or programmatic reserves (budget, schedule). Breaking with JPL tradition, I chaired these meetings myself.

I know that most engineers are hard-wired to think in technical terms. I needed more; I needed them to think at a programmatic level as well. And not just the managers but every engineer. On

Faster, Better, Cheaper projects, every person needs to include cost, schedule, quality and risk in his or her thinking. For the Pathfinder group, I expected this would take some training, some leadership by example, and probably some cajoling. Not every engineer or professional is comfortable in this role. It calls on people to stretch; those who rise to the challenge grow in their management skills and the project benefits enormously.

In particular, engineers on the front line, at least at JPL, had rarely been called on to think about budgets; in a Faster, Better, Cheaper effort, they have to. Our engineers at every level had to be worried about the bottom line. And while NASA is a nonprofit organization, the importance of engineers thinking bottom line clearly is even more important in a profit-making business.

Rob Manning chided me that these sessions were "very distinctively Brian," because I was willing to hold the technical brains of the project in a meeting for the entire afternoon while we not only heard the problems but, when needed, dealt with the problems right then and there. If we came up with a solution, great. If not, the item would go onto my Top Ten list, to be brought up later on and worked again, and if necessary again and again, until it was solved.

That took a lot of people by surprise. In the familiar pattern of handling a meeting, someone gives a report about a problem encountered, the group discusses the situation, and if there are no brilliant or easy solutions forthcoming, the manager assigns someone to form a committee or team to tackle the issue. It's then out of sight, "handled," and the group goes on to other concerns. Challenging the whole crowd of managers with critical-path problems tackled in real time was, I think, unprecedented. But it worked.

And many times the ideas for solving problems came from someone who wasn't directly involved. This is a team functioning at its best.

As for the Top Ten list, my experience is that by the end of a meeting, everyone attending has a different version of what was agreed on, what needs to be done, what conclusions were reached. To avoid that, I have one "official" Top Ten, which I prepare myself. We then distribute the list to all managers, and everybody is eating lunch from the same plate.

One caution, however: it's easy to get carried away with the next great idea, the next powerful improvement, until the product is delayed so long it can no longer find a place in the competitive market. The efforts of even the most creative team still have to result in a product that makes it out the door in time to serve its purpose.

Though plenty of people took part when there was an issue on the table, one person in particular acted as my conscience in these meetings. When something new was proposed in a Wednesday meeting, or problems showed up and a solution was offered, I could always count on Guy Beutelschies to provide a counterpoint if one was needed. Perhaps a course of action was being decided and I was ready to say, "Okay, great, go do it," and get on to the next problem. Guy would be heard from. "Hold it," he might say. "Why do we even need to do anything here, this isn't really a problem, we're making this better but it doesn't need to be better." Or maybe, "We don't have to fix that software, we can take care of it operationally."

His governing principle was, "Don't change anything if you don't need to." That's absolutely right on target, especially in a Faster, Better, Cheaper effort. Sometimes I was just missing it. I told Guy repeatedly, "Keep me honest," and he did.

(Guy had joined the project doing basic systems work including block diagrams, requirements, keeping track of resources and the like. Recognizing his sharp talent and his enthusiasm, I would later give him the crucial job of spacecraft system test director.)

I never asked Guy to play the role of my conscience. He was just "doin' what comes naturally," as the song says. It was his nature. All Faster, Better, Cheaper project managers need a Guy Beutelschies.

One notoriously difficult problem that plagues management meetings has been described by management consultant Charlie Prather in his Bottom Line Innovation course. He talks about a conflict that often drags down a problem-solving effort. When the group is trying to identify the problem and brainstorm solutions, the people you want to hear from are the divergent thinkers in the group, who will come at the problem askew and are more likely to suggest the non-obvious solution.

Once you've settled on an approach, that's the time for the convergent thinkers, who, Prather says, tend to be people with a low tolerance for ambiguity and a high comfort for closure. After three minutes of discussion, they want to say, "Hey, let's finish this and move on to the next item." For them, moving down the list of items feels like a successful meeting.

The problems come at a session when people don't know what stage of this process the discussion has reached. The confusion of ideas when some are talking closure while others are still brainstorming can shut down the creative, right-brain thinking too early. And when it should be time for phase two, the same confusion can defeat the efforts to move into implementation. A conversation like this, at cross purposes, can drive people crazy.

The leader of the group needs to understand the distinction and keep people at bay if they're in the wrong phase. Without being obvious about it, the leader needs to convey the messages, "We're gathering ideas now, we need divergent thinking," and then, "Time to bring this to closure, let's take it to implementation, we need some convergent thinking." This avoids the too-common situation in which part of the group is trying to brainstorm, part of the group is trying to come to closure, and everybody else is trying to figure out why they can't understand what's going on.

SCIENTISTS + ENGINEERS = TEAM

In this spirit of teamwork that came to characterize Pathfinder, I found quite remarkable the cooperation between the engineers and the scientists. Particularly remarkable because, for readily understandable reasons, these relationships have frequently been mired in conflict. The science community proposes instruments that are then selected by NASA through a highly formal competitive process. The spacecraft engineering teams have to figure out how to integrate the science into an already crowded capsule.

And of course the scientists, who are if anything even greater masters than engineers at finding better ways to do things, want to make refinements and improvements to their experimental packages through the years that the spacecraft is being designed, built and tested. And since they're all eating from the same trough, problems in the science area take money away from the spacecraft and vice versa. The typical result: a love/hate relationship and an "us versus them" mentality.

A large part of the credit for avoiding that battle on Pathfinder belongs to the man who carried the title of "Project Scientist," JPL resident geologist Matthew Golombek. Small in stature but big in energy and effervescent to the limit, Matt operated on a principle of "Let's make the most of the mission, let's look for how we can use what you're already doing, to produce more scientific return." That's a team attitude, another example of "We're all in this together," providing a strong antidote to the inevitable frictions.

The solution to one especially perplexing challenge was made possible by this unusual atmosphere of cooperation between the science and engineering teams. The question was, how would we tell the high-gain antenna where in the sky to point in order to communicate with planet Earth? A seemingly simple problem, but given our constraints, one that required significant effort.

The Pathfinder team explored a number of different possibilities. We could program the antenna to pan across the sky while the receiving antennas on Earth listened for a signal; this looked complicated, expensive, and probably unreliable since the weak signal from Mars would be hard to detect. We could add a sun sensor to locate the sun, then have the onboard computer use the sun position and the time to calculate where Earth should be. This choice would require additional electronic hardware that we didn't have space for.

The solution came from outside, from our "science team." The camera that would take the photos of the Martian surface was being designed and built by a group working under Peter Smith, at the University of Arizona, Tucson. Peter's camera, a very clever, low-cost stereo imager (nicknamed "IMP"—Imager for Mars Pathfinder) was capable of scanning the entire sky and would look directly at the sun as part of its science mission.

It's one of the unwritten but nearly inviolable rules of the spacecraft business that you "keep your interfaces clean": you don't allow complex interdependencies among the different groups working on a mission. Nonetheless, the Arizona team was asked if its camera would be able to help in the effort to aim the high-gain antenna by providing data on the sun's location. A member of Smith's team, Chris Shinahara, gave the answer: "Sure, we can do that." They developed the additional software needed, tested the hell out of it and, on Mars, the solution worked beautifully. So well, in fact, that the antenna was pointed from Mars far more accurately than we ever expected, pointed with such accuracy that we were able to transmit at a data rate eight times faster than we had anticipated, providing much higher-resolution photographs, and many more of them.

Matt Golombek also led the effort to decide where on the surface of Mars we would attempt to land. A most difficult choice. The scientists wanted a place with a good selection of rocks, preferably a place that looked as if it might have rocks of different kinds. The project people like me wanted a site that would be reasonably safe, fairly flat and—okay, rocks, but not huge boulders, and not so many that our airbags would be unlikely to survive.

The site-selection team Matt had assembled included most of the big names in Mars science; naturally they held some strong opinions. Matt understood the pros and cons, but it took him *three* separate review sessions before he could finally bring the group to a consensus. Even then some panel members held out for a safer site, arguing quite reasonably that the promise of good science wouldn't do anybody any good if the spacecraft was destroyed on landing.

The location that Matt and his site-selection panel chose looked like a fine compromise. Relatively free of craters and mountains that could trap our lander, but in what looked like a floodplain where a huge volume of water, thought to be equivalent to the volume of the Great Lakes, had probably once flowed in just a week, very likely depositing a large variety of rocks—an excellent balance between the risk of landing and the promise of good science.

Once the decision had been made, radar observations and thermal-emission measurements of the site provided convincing evidence that the location was about as rough as the sites where the Vikings had landed in 1976. A great confidence-builder: based on what we then knew from our entry/descent/landing tests, and especially from the airbag tests, I was convinced we could land successfully on terrain like the Viking sites or even more rugged.

It would turn out that Matt Golombek's predictions about the site couldn't have been much better if he had walked the ground himself. When the project was over, Matt would be honored with

NASA's highest scientific award for his work on this mission. He richly deserved it.

A TEAM SPORT

Once upon a time, companies treated their suppliers in a mostly arm's-length relationship. "We need some goods according to these specifications, let us have your bid." Defective items would be shipped back for credit or replacement, and a year or two later, the same bidding dance would be repeated.

We've come a long way. Today many enlightened businesses have established alliances with suppliers based on mutual benefit and mutual respect. It's now standard practice in forward-thinking companies to invite contractors in at a very early stage of product development and say, "Here's what we're trying to do, have you any products, materials or ideas that would help us? Are you working on anything that we would want to know about? Can you develop something that would contribute to our product?"

Sure, it's ticklish unless there's a high level of trust—on both sides. The Pathfinder team went well beyond this enlightened state, to treat our suppliers as full members of the team. Key contractors like the computer developers, ILC Dover on the airbags, Pioneer Aerospace on the parachutes, and Lockheed Martin Astronautics on the aeroshell, weren't just given specifications to follow. We sat down with each of these companies and explained in detail the whole concept of the mission and the part their effort would play. And then we invited, we *expected,* that they would contribute their best ideas. What we found, in many cases, was a willingness to put out an extraordinary effort, far more than we had a right to ask for (though very much what we needed, to get Pathfinder done on time and within the constraints).

A collection of outside organizations, some eighty in all, played a role in developing, building and flying Pathfinder and doing the science on Mars—corporations and universities, as well as the three NASA research centers, Lewis, Langley and Ames, that were absolutely critical to the effort.

If you can engage your vendors so they feel and act just like members of your in-house project team, you have a highly powerful win-win combination. There will always be issues—you have your needs and expectations, the vendor companies still have to show a profit—but your goal should be to make things work like one team.

Not every company will be able to participate at this level of teamwork. The key is having the same level of openness and trust with your vendor's managers as you do with your own. If you can't establish that level of relationship and dedication, then be prepared to manage by the contract and don't expect anything more than what's written down.

The bottom line: It's comfortable, and traditional, to think in terms of the project on the one hand, and of the contractors on the other. But it's more profitable, more successful, to develop project work into *a team sport.*

9. Robustness and Risk

It is incumbent on those who accept great
charges to risk themselves on great occasions.

—Thomas Jefferson

Nobody takes a risk in the expectation it will fail.

—Peter L. Bernstein, in *Against the Gods:
The Remarkable Story of Risk*

COUNTDOWN: 1 YEAR, 2 MONTHS TO LAUNCH

Few human endeavors come burdened with more inherent risk than landing on the surface of another planet. The complexities of hardware and software for a 300-million-mile voyage, the difficulties of the entry and landing, the uncertainties about conditions at the landing site, and the hostile environment make a mission like Mars Pathfinder an extreme technical challenge.

One of the keys to managing risk on Pathfinder was understanding where the risks were very early in the project, and then developing plans to mitigate them. Usually, "mitigate" translated into "test." When we had created a new way of doing something, like the airbags, we tested, tested to its limits and beyond, which taught us where its limits were.

So we took risks by accepting new ideas but then made sure they would be successful. When you have a standard way of doing business and somebody says "Take more risk," there's a good chance you'll try to do that by cutting corners on the same practices that have worked in the past. You'll probably fail.

NASA Administrator Dan Goldin delivered the message to me personally about failure not being an option for Pathfinder. In the fall of 1995, at lunch in the JPL cafeteria, someone mentioned that Mr. Goldin was on site to see firsthand how the Cassini mission was coming along. And there he was, a few tables away.

I went over, reintroduced myself, and said, "How would you like to see JPL's premier Faster, Better, Cheaper mission?"

"I would, indeed," he answered. "But don't tell the Cassini guys you invited me, tell them I asked you." (A bit of Washington-style intrigue, but understandable: the people of the Cassini team, with a big expensive mission they were recasting in leaner, meaner form, were eager to impress the big boss, and were not too happy when they learned about the distraction of his taking time to visit Pathfinder.)

We toured the High Bay assembly area, where our spacecraft's components were all on hand but still in pieces. He met the team members and chatted with them, and was quite complimentary. Describing his vision for doing many inexpensive space projects, he drew a vivid picture of "darkening the skies with planetary spacecraft."

And he shared with me his concern. Yes, Faster, Better, Cheaper meant taking risks. But as NASA's first deep space FBC mission, Pathfinder must not fail, could not fail. This was the paradox that defined the project, directly from the top man himself, the self-contradictory demand to "Take risks but don't fail."

One novel way we followed that edict involved our approach to testing. Often when a project is on a tight budget, people say, "Well, we can drop some of the tests." We took exactly the opposite approach: "We're on a tight budget, we're going to have to take risks, we better test the hell out of it." And the same reasoning when we were running out of reserves.

Tests of our all-important radar altimeter were due to start in mid-November 1995, at the China Lake Naval Air Warfare Center, in the Mojave desert northeast of Los Angeles. We knew that if the altimeter didn't work, the chances of firing the rockets and releasing the airbags at the right instant would range from quite small to nil. That made the altimeter one of the high-risk items, hardware we had to be sure of. Honeywell, the company that was building the unit, had already spent a lot of time testing it, and so had Sam Thurman, the engineer who was personally honchoing this one with the help of radar expert Bryan Honeycutt.

If all the hardware elements of the entry/descent/landing system were extremely difficult to test, the altimeter fit that description in spades. Tests in the lab wouldn't tell us much; we had recognized we'd have to take the hardware out to the big open spaces, and drop it from a helicopter. But even then, there are many exceptions. The atmosphere is so much more dense than on Mars, the temperature is so much warmer than the awesome chill of the real thing, the terrain that the radar signal will be bouncing from is so different.

Little wonder that Sam kept showing up in my office to say things like, "A new glitch has shown up that we can't explain. We need to do more testing." And he'd hand me a sheet of paper detailing the new tests he was proposing, and how much money he was asking for to run them. Money that would have to come out of reserves. But Sam was usually able to convince me, and usually got the money he asked for.

In testing, the altimeter often worked well. Yet occasionally it would be fooled, we didn't know by what, and would produce potentially disastrously wrong readings. Rob joked with macabre humor about the spacecraft arriving at Mars and undergoing something he called "lithobraking"—*litho* being from the Greek for "rock," and *braking* being wordplay for its homonym, *breaking*. In other words, breaking against the rocks.

One test had produced just such a failure. Blessedly it was not a live test but only a computer simulation. Still, it had been a most sobering experience.

The essence of any Faster, Better, Cheaper project rests on accepting risks but acknowledging from the first that you must then develop ways to "retire" each of them—by design, by testing, by whatever other means—until each has been reduced to the point where it's no longer a risk item, or at least the probability is so low that you don't need to worry about it any longer.

Other high-risk items included the rest of the unique entry/descent/landing system—especially the airbags, of course; the software approach; the high-technology telecommunications subsystem; and the complex mechanical assembly. Some were easier to retire. We would still be trying to lower the level of others when the spacecraft was already atop the Delta launch vehicle at the Cape.

By the time Sam Thurman took the altimeter into the desert in November 1995, I was fairly confident he would find it was giving us accurate data. The test procedure called for dropping the device from a helicopter, tracking it as it fell, and then later, back in the lab, comparing the altitude moment by moment as recorded by the tracking instruments against the height reported by the altimeter itself.

Sam was using three instruments simultaneously to gather the tracking data—a laser device and two optical telescopes. For this final series of tests, the altimeter was set swinging underneath its parachute, approximating the way our calculations showed it would likely be swinging during its actual descent to Mars.

In the space business, there are not many inexpensive items. With rental of the tracking devices, an operator for each device, and the helicopter and pilot, each drop could easily cost $10,000. And once you're out in the desert, you don't do one drop and go home; each test series usually involved five or six.

The altimeter itself cost about $15,000; we spent about $500,000 testing it, still a bargain compared to the millions if we had tried to build one from scratch. And well worth it—when Sam reported the results of the November tests, I was left feeling satisfied that the altimeter would come through for us. There are no absolutes, of course, no guarantees. But this had become one more item I felt we could strike from the risk list.

RISK IN THE BUSINESS SETTING

Most managers, as Peter Drucker has pointed out, don't really want their people to be risk-takers and won't allow people to consider projects that involve a lot of risk. This fits very neatly with the "druthers" of most workers. People by nature prefer avoiding risk, sensible enough since risky actions carry the innate danger of failure. We have a sense that great people are remembered for their successes, and the rest of mankind for their failures. So we recall Babe Ruth for his 714 home runs, not his 1,300 strikeouts, and Lincoln for his presidency, not the long string of elections he lost earlier in life.

Leaders of Faster, Better, Cheaper projects will find that most of their people don't take to risk naturally, but must be coaxed, induced, tempted, wheedled or cajoled along this often uncomfortable path. And of course they must believe they will not be punished for taking a risk which fails, that the reward goes to those who overcome their hesitancy and dive into the waters of uncertainty, that disdain is reserved for those who stay on the shore, self-protective, keeping themselves safe but potentially endangering the project. In any risk-taking endeavor, all team members must know without doubt that their manager will stand behind them when they willingly accept a risk.

Yet the leader has to make sure everyone knows the obligations that go along with playing in the risk arena. Probably the first obligation is not holding back information, keeping one's manager advised of any significant change in status, most of all with anything that changes the character of a high-risk item.

It's not my style to yell at people; I get upset occasionally—who doesn't?—but I try to keep my anger in check. One incident, though, tested my patience because it put the project schedule at so much risk. In High Bay One, the assembly crew was ready to begin installing the ISA, our "million-dollar beer cooler" that would keep our electronics at the proper temperature on the surface of Mars. The schedule allowed just enough time to install it before a critical test due to begin shortly. But the ISA hadn't been delivered yet.

The young man developing the ISA, Eric Slimko, had been doing an incredible job. A very junior engineer, he had undertaken the project after one of the most qualified companies in the country turned it down as too complicated, and he had solved the technical problems, coming up with a design that was buildable, met the performance needs, and made sense in terms of cost. An achievement that even a seasoned engineer would have been proud of.

Except that now, at a critical moment for his subsystem, he hadn't bothered to let anyone know he would not be ready to deliver his unit to assembly on time. Everything had come to a halt.

I lost it. I yelled. And in front of others, which I know perfectly well is something a good manager never, never does.

He got a short but heated lecture about taking responsibility, about the role of a professional engineer, about the risk he had placed the project in. I doubt he will ever forget it, but, knowing Eric, I'm confident it's the lesson that stuck, not the pain of the experience.

It's the responsibility of everyone on a Faster, Better, Cheaper project to meet the obligations of schedule, budget, quality, and the other make-or-break categories; meet them, or speak up the moment you become aware you might not. To avoid putting the entire effort at risk, the project leader needs to make that obligation clear to everyone at the outset, and remind people of it regularly. Somewhere here, *I* had fallen down, too.

OUT COMES THE NOOSE

For reasons that are a little too obvious to explain to anyone not familiar with the terms, electronic connectors are referred to by gender, male and female.

Don Hunter, the team leader for electronic packaging, had achieved brilliant, amazing things, inventing new ways to condense the electronics into a very small volume. Still, as the cliché says, nobody's perfect. When the cabling was delivered to the High Bay assembly area, looking like a nightmarish plate of oversized spaghetti, the assembly crew found a cable that ended in the wrong kind of connector.

And then a second. And another. In all, a total of five.

The plans were correct; Don had drawn them himself. But when it came to doing the work, in five places he had failed to follow his own plan.

This was the kind of foul-up we could not afford to be making. I went through the roof (this was a period of especially intense pressure for the project, and for me), but had calmed down a little by the time I had gathered people together for a meeting.

Throughout Pathfinder I had dangling from a hook high on a wall in my office (and still have) a hangman's noose made of heavy rope, just like the real thing. It had become a standing joke of the team to ask whether I kept it to use myself, or to use on any team member who screwed up.

When everyone was assembled I took down the noose and slammed it on the table. "Who's first!" I challenged.

To his credit, Don raised his hand. "Me," he said, as everyone dissolved in laughter, breaking their tension. And mine.

Earlier I had established a policy that if somebody screwed up the interface, that person was responsible for fixing it, which put Don on the spot. But it would have taken longer and been more expensive than the alternative: the cabling ladies had already done several corrections to clean up errors made by engineering. Now we were looking to them once again. Linda Ponce spoke up even before being asked; she and another of the Dwarfs, Maralee Murray, would handle the effort themselves, though it meant they would have to do their unsoldering and resoldering in the High Bay, precariously working right next to the spacecraft.

This was another good wake-up call—a small screw-up that made me see the need for redoubling our efforts to avoid bigger ones. The team got a new challenge from me: "I want a complete check, end-to-end, to make sure the hardware is right."

The search turned up a few more mistakes, found before they got onto the critical path and slowed our momentum.

I don't spend a lot of time berating people or being unhappy with them. The most effective course, I've found, is to make a commotion, let it be known that you're highly dissatisfied . . . and then go back to the job.

He who remembers a wrong too long will never set it right.

MAKE THE PEOPLE RESPONSIBLE, NOT THE POLICY

In any organization tied to rigid "proven ways of doing business," taking risks can lead to an *increased* probability of failure. Given a setting of that kind, probably the only hope for a Faster, Better, Cheaper effort lies in negotiating to have the standard rules lifted, allowing project people to look for clever ways of mitigating the risks by *doing things differently.*

On Pathfinder, we had been able to have ourselves exempted from most of the demands and "thou shalt nots" in JPL's rule book for deep space missions. For example, we didn't have to do intricate, time-consuming analyses like the "failure modes and effects analysis" on every element of the spacecraft.

This approach worked very well, putting the responsibility for success directly in the hands of the front-line engineers, who felt personally responsible for making their systems reliable. They understood that blindly applying the operating practices spelled out in some rule book would not meet the requirements. The personal sense of responsibility for handling risk meant their job wasn't done until the spacecraft had arrived safely on Mars.

Make the people, not the policy, responsible for the system.

TEST, TEST, TEST

Deciding to build Pathfinder with few backup systems made us rigorous in our commitment to what Tony Spear colorfully termed "test, test, test."

Risk was also reduced in the early stages of the project by building hardware and software "test beds," beginning much earlier than on other projects. We had integrated into the flight system test bed about 80 percent of all spacecraft electrical subsystems, including the scientific hardware, before spacecraft assembly and testing even began. (Besides being a focus of our efforts, the test bed was especially popular with visitors. To add realism, we had covered the ground with sand, brought in some appropriate rocks, and hung a large backdrop photo of the Mars landscape. In what we called our "sandbox," visitors could see the lander looking as if it had recently descended to the surface, and the rover trundling about in response to the team's commands.)

One outgrowth of our philosophy on testing turned out to be an important factor in reducing the risk level of Pathfinder: we had started the assembly phase very early—eighteen months prior to launch.

Beyond starting early, we actually *added* tests as we went—the original plans called for five airbag drops and we did a total of eighteen, twelve parachute drops and we did forty-nine. The early testing helped us make sure that when the bigger, more complex tests came later on, they were more likely to go smoothly.

The mechanical chief engineer for the lander, Bill Layman, has his own description of this process: "You're always looking for ways to get the job done that minimize the risks in as many areas as you can. Make decisions where you can be confident the judgment is sound without having to involve six months or six engineering teams to evaluate the approach.

"But then," he says, "there are always a few places where you don't have time or money to come up with some other way of getting the job done. You just swallow hard and accept the risk."

As we built up the lander in the High Bay assembly area, we conducted six major system tests with progressively more complete hardware and software in the loop. These tests were conducted in the various spacecraft operating modes—prelaunch, launch, cruise, landing and on the surface. The results proved extremely valuable in directing specific changes to the software modules that would control the phases of flight, particularly entry/descent/landing.

Starting so early allowed time to resolve issues about making the pieces fit together—what works on paper doesn't always work when you have the physical pieces in hand. We were moving so fast that the engineers weren't always able to verify every detail of the interfaces and we got bit too often. But as in decision-making, it was more important to keep the momentum going than to have every last detail worked within what we engineers inelegantly call "a gnat's eyebrow."

Starting early also let us subject most of the electronic parts to over 2,600 hours of operation, substantially reducing the risk of an electronic part failing in flight or on the surface.

A key figure in the testing was a recent mechanical engineering graduate from Rensselaer Polytechnic Institute. One of the babies of the team, Dave Gruel was hired about the time Pathfinder started, originally to work in the test bed doing mechanical chores—setting up the facility, handling the installations, and so on. In Pathfinder style, when we were shorthanded for somebody to debug hardware, he offered to pitch in, we gladly accepted and he proved to be an ace, eventually becoming the manager of the test bed.

I wrote earlier about encouraging people to become generalists; by its very nature, the test environment leads people in that direction because there's always such a variety of things needing to be done. Another personnel shortage appeared when we lost our fault protection engineer, who's charged with looking at possible failures, figuring out how to recognize them, what the consequences would be, and how the spacecraft should react. Again Dave Gruel stepped up to the plate.

A big guy with a butch crew cut and an outgoing, gregarious style, Dave is one of those people who keep a workplace lively. So in addition to everything else he was doing, we asked Dave to create tests to determine whether the ground crew at their control panels would respond appropriately to problems—devising challenges to throw at them the same way airline pilots are tested with emergencies while sitting in a flight simulator on the ground.

He proved to possess a Machiavellian genius for dreaming up devious "what's wrong now" scenarios for the engineers who would be flying the spacecraft, and for the other team who would later be handling the lander and rover after we reached Mars. Frustrating but extremely valuable, these tests earned him the nickname "Gremlin," a term popularized in World War II for an imaginary creature that creates problems in otherwise reliable hardware. Dave "the Gremlin" Gruel dreamed up cruel, near pathological tests that sometimes left the controllers and engineers steaming, while teaching them how to deal with the uncertainties of operating a spacecraft.

He was building a level of robustness in them and a level of confidence in me that they would be able to handle whatever lay ahead.

FROM RISKY TO ROBUST

Robust—a term I've discussed earlier in these pages—became one of our most important vocabulary words on the Mars Pathfinder mission. The precise meanings have to do with being powerfully built, being sturdy, and having endurance, and I use the term to mean something that's almost the converse of *risk*. Risky and robust are two ends of a spectrum.

Robust products and systems grow from the combination of sturdy concepts and relentless testing. Robustness also means building in margin by crafting solutions that are highly tolerant to the uncertainties, yielding a product or system that's likely to work in whatever circumstances it might encounter.

With the parachute, the airbags, the decision to use deceleration rockets, the telecommunications system—in fact, throughout the Pathfinder spacecraft, we were willing to accept risk initially because we were confident that careful design and meticulous testing could "kill" the risk and yield a robust system.

The key to getting flawless or nearly flawless performance out of machines is robustness, and the key to robustness is people. The secret lies in the hands of the people who design and build the machines, people applying their hearts and minds to being sure the basic concepts are inherently robust, and every detail is worked to something approaching perfection.

The challenge is in getting the right people and getting them to work together. A Faster, Better, Cheaper project requires talent, of course, but it also demands strong personal dedication and a high level of integrity from every member of the team. One engineer who has doubts about his design and doesn't surface them and ask for help could lead to a product that falls severely short. A software programmer who is just a little sloppy about his code, who leaves something untested on the theory that it couldn't possibly cause a problem, can put at risk the product or mission, even the reputation of the company.

Good enough but not robust isn't good enough.

Everyone in your organization must know that, understand it, believe it at a deep, fundamental level. Robust products don't "just happen." They come about only as the result of the combined efforts of dedicated people who understand the goal and are committed to it, and leaders and managers who show the way by their own example.

Make *robust* part of your vocabulary and culture . . . and then make it part of the vocabulary and culture of every designer, engineer, and programmer in your organization—everyone, indeed, who has responsibility on products or projects.

ROBUSTNESS REQUIRES INNOVATION

Space telecommunications systems historically have had a higher rate of failure than other components, not so hard to understand when you consider how complex they are. The radio that Leslie Livesay's team developed for Pathfinder, for example, would have to locate and lock onto an extremely weak signal coming from Earth, virtually hidden in the hiss of electronic noise arriving out of the blackness from every direction. The outgoing signal of only 12 watts—in a lightbulb, anything less than about 50 watts is too dim to read by—would only be detectable on Earth if Pathfinder's antenna could beam the signal in the right direction with incredible accuracy.

In the telecommunications system, almost every component was new and would be flying for the first time. We could not shake the sense of uncertainty from failures on other missions in the past. We wanted more margin, we wanted to make our communications more reliable, more robust, if we could find the way.

Weighing in heavily against any notions of adding a backup radio were the same strictures of mass, volume, schedule and budget that afflicted every other aspect of the mission. We devised an innovative way around the dilemma, a compromise of using an additional "half a radio"—a lightweight transmitter with a single-minded function: if all other communications failed, the backup would be able to come to life after the spacecraft landed to let us know that Pathfinder had safely reached the surface of Mars.

We had given the assignment to develop this unit to engineer Sam Valas. Now, a year later, he had the unit completed and ready for installation onto the spacecraft, a feat that should go down in the history books of space: it usually takes two years, three, even longer, to develop a radio that meets the rigid requirements of reliability, sturdiness, ability to withstand extremes of temperature and all the other yardsticks for gaining admission to a deep space craft. Sam had turned in a spectacular performance, and added significantly to the robustness of the overall telecommunications system for the mission.

ROVER ARRIVES

As the end of 1995 approached, the rover team finished work on its vehicle and delivered it to us for installing into the lander. This little thing, smaller than a child's wagon—so small that visitors often asked, "Is that full-sized or a scale model?"—became my responsibility.

The rover now had a name: Sojourner Truth, after the escaped slave who gained fame and admiration as an abolitionist and worker for the rights of women. Rover manager Donna Shirley, after launching a national campaign to pick the name (it was won by twelve-year-old Connecticut schoolgirl Valerie Ambroise—her essay ended with the words "Sojourner will travel around Mars bringing back the truth"), found herself in hot water with the NASA Science Office, which by policy had the responsibility for picking names. But the complaint came too late to stop the contest. "Sojourner Truth" it would be.

Meanwhile the backup for Sojourner, named Marie Curie, would continue testing under simulated Mars conditions, preparing like any good understudy to step in should something happen to the star.

ROBUSTNESS WRAPPED IN A BLANKET

You wouldn't expect to find a blanket maker at a place like the Jet Propulsion Lab, but it's a craft of great importance, requiring a unique set of special skills.

These are, of course, blankets for helping keep the interior of a spacecraft at a temperature that is "comfortable" for the intricate components. The deep chill of deep space approaches absolute zero, creating a curious predicament for the designers of a spacecraft. Buried inside are those electronic components, generating heat in tiny amounts, but enough that ridding the spacecraft of it presents an engineering challenge. On the outside of the Pathfinder, the face that sees the sun stays warm, while the temperature of the others sinks toward zero. So we put space-age blankets in place, enveloping all the contents of the interior in a cocoon-like wrapping.

JPL is renowned in the industry for doing clever things in the design of these one-of-a-kind blankets, fashioned individually for each spacecraft, each requiring more painstaking hand work than a gown for a Paris haute couture fashion show . . . and even more expensive. And like designing the gown, creating the blanket is an art, not a science.

At the time of Pathfinder, our blanket maker was JPL's resident expert, a young man who was the only remaining person on staff with the required knowledge, skill and experience. Unfortunately he became mired in a battle with the institution over an issue as mundane as rules about travel expenses. I went to bat, arguing for the rules to be relaxed in his case. Such a small point, but neither side would yield. Before we could find some amicable middle ground, he announced he was fed up . . . and quit.

Asking around, I heard rumors of another young man on staff, Andy Rose, who was also said to have done some blanket work. But when I sought him out, he was candid about his experience: "I can make you a blanket, if somebody else designs it," he said. "I don't know how to design them."

That wouldn't be enough: much of the skill is in the design, which must translate a set of requirements from the "temperature control engineer" into a system that provides just the right amount of protection to maintain a specific range of temperatures under a wide range of conditions—power on, power off, in sunlight, out of sunlight, and so on.

JPL blankets are built up out of extremely thin sheets of Mylar plastic, interspersed with a material that looks like wedding lace but laid on in such a narrow thickness that the Mylar sheets—aluminized on both sides—look as if they're almost touching each other, something like sheets of paper in a notebook, typically about twenty of them, the exact number suited to meet the specifications from the temperature control engineer.

Again like a fashion designer, the blanket maker, at the spacecraft assembly in the High Bay, marks patterns on sheets of brown paper. Back in his shop, technicians cut the material to fit the patterns and sew the pieces. The blanket maker tries it on the "model"—the spacecraft—and makes adjustments until he has the proper fit. One of the challenges that makes the job into an art is the problem of fashioning seams and corners so tight that they allow no heat to leak, which could destroy the effectiveness of his work.

Clearly this is not a process one learns out of a book, or masters in a few weeks of trial and error. With no one at JPL able to do the designs, I could think of only one possible way of getting our many blankets made, and that was a long shot. JPL's longtime resident guru blanket maker, a true master of the craft, had recently retired. Hugh von Delden, an eccentric, much loved and admired at JPL, and someone I considered a good friend, had been working for me in his last position, and I had given the main address at his goodbye party, something of a roast.

It would save my butt if Hugh would agree to come back for this one final project. But he had told me on leaving, "I'm not going to do this like so many other people, say I'm retiring and then come back part-time. I'm done. I'm never coming back." He clearly meant it.

Reaching him by phone, I started to explain our dilemma. News travels fast—he had already heard.

He said, "You're going to pay through the nose for this."

"I'm willing," I answered. So we agreed and, to the delight of many JPL people, Hugh came back. It was wonderfully reassuring to have him among us, just as committed to Pathfinder as the rest of the team. With Hugh at his side, Andy agreed to take charge of the project and the two of them got the job done (Andy in the process learning to be a great blanket designer as well as builder).

But there would be some major land mines along the way that would make it much tougher than anyone anticipated. We would be testing Andy's and Hugh's dedication all the way to launch.

GOODBYE, 1995

In November I made a decision that I would come to look on as risk of another sort. JPL's director for Space and Earth Science, Dr. Charles Elachi, called me to his office and said he had a request to make based on my track record of doing tough missions under tight constraints. Would I be willing to accept the job as project manager of another mission—not instead of Pathfinder but *at the same time.* Given the challenges already on my plate, I wondered why he thought I'd even consider it.

I was being offered the chance to lead a mission that would eventually be known as Space Technology 4/Champollion. The goal: land on the surface of a comet and analyze what it's made of.

The mission, which would be in partnership with CNES, the French space agency, had been given the name "Champollion," after the Frenchman who broke the code of the Rosetta stone, making it possible to decipher the ancient Egyptian hieroglyphics.

The job would mean developing a machine to do an absolute

first-of-a-kind mission, demanding a host of new technology, daunting the designers with a great many unknowns, challenging with a great many risks. It made no sense to accept such an overwhelming challenge in addition to Pathfinder.

And of course I couldn't turn down an opportunity like this. Somehow I would find the way to do both projects simultaneously.

There was hardly time to catch my breath on Champollion before the holiday season was upon us. But no holidays for Pathfinder. The spacecraft wasn't even assembled yet, a lot of unknowns still lay ahead, and we couldn't afford to relax. I announced that we would take two days off at Christmas, and one day for New Year's, but would otherwise work right through the holidays.

They called me the grinch. But they showed up, the whole team, right through the holidays.

10. Innovation

The person who walks in another's
tracks leaves no footprints.
—Anonymous

A scientist discovers that which exists,
an engineer creates that which never was.
—Theodore von Kármán,
founder of the Jet Propulsion Laboratory

COUNTDOWN: 11 MONTHS TO LAUNCH

We were party to the near-magical process by which constraints and limitations turn into catalysts for change, the driving mechanism for innovation. What had at first appeared to the Pathfinder team to be merely tough constraints proved instead to be powerful motivation for putting aside the familiar tools, techniques, approaches and business methods, and becoming highly effective at finding new solutions.

Limitations induce innovations. Innovations can guide you to breakthroughs.

Sure, life would have been much simpler with more money, a longer schedule and less need for technological wizardry. The point is that confronted by roadblocks, the team repeatedly found ways to surmount them.

Early in 1996, we faced just the kind of situation that demanded what might be called a "scheduled invention."

With the launch window opening on December 2, we had entered the new year hoping that all major surprises were behind us. That dream shattered at the beginning of February during what should have been a routine series of tests of the deceleration rockets at China Lake, in the California desert.

The arrangement we had settled on used three solid-propellant rockets, each producing 1,800 pounds of thrust. The rockets came with admirable credentials: the propellant had long ago been proven and accepted as "flight qualified," and the basic design had been used successfully for years as the separation motors for the Titan series of launch vehicles.

In February, the final helicopter drop test was going smoothly, everything seemed to be working as expected. The rocket engines seemed to fire properly but then things went haywire, the parachute failed and the hardware augured into the ground.

All was not lost. The computer had miraculously survived, and the data stored in its memory served us much like the black boxes recovered after an airline crash. Those data showed an unlikely and highly disturbing event. A chart of thrust plotted against time revealed that the thrust had tailed off just a little too quickly—the rocket boost hadn't lasted long enough. Only a slight difference but to rocket experts like Les Compton and Leon Strand, it was significant.

Another chart showing pressure inside the rocket during the burn revealed a pressure oscillation as the likely cause—the burn had become unstable. This scared the hell out of us—it could be a mission-killer.

The style of rapid decision-making that the Pathfinder team had developed as a fundamental way of doing business, combined with the hands-on, micro-knowledge management, allowed us to deal with tough problems without wasted energy. Nobody had to say what the process would be; when faced with a problem that demanded a quick, innovative solution, the process was always the same: Get to the bottom of the story, get the options on the table, make a decision, and go with it.

The company building our rockets, Thiokol Corporation, among the best in the country, had produced hundreds of similar units that worked as designed. What had gone wrong? Was there a chance one or more of the three rockets on our flight unit could suffer the same quirk and ruin the mission? Not being able to pin down the cause of the problem was frightening.

This was the stuff of Ph.D. dissertations, but time was running out on us. Unable to study the problem at length, we would have to select the most reasonable scenario for the mishap, decide on a fix, have new rockets made up, and take them out to the desert for retesting as quickly as possible.

How long would all this take? At that point I just didn't know. To make the launch window, we would have to start moving the spacecraft to Cape Canaveral by no later than the first week of September, and the date was coming on us too fast.

CORPORATE-LEVEL INNOVATION

Peter Drucker maintains that few of the successful entrepreneurs he's worked with over the years have the type of personality traits people think of as necessary for an entrepreneur. Yet he says he's known "many people—salespeople, surgeons, journalists, scholars, even musicians—who did have [those traits] without being the least bit 'entrepreneurial.'"

These people shared in common not some unique personality characteristics but "a commitment to the systematic practice of innovation"; their best ideas sprang from a conscious, purposeful search for those few situations where innovation is possible.

While Drucker was focusing on the kinds of major innovations that launch an entire product or even launch a new product category, it's intriguing to note the "areas of opportunity" for innovation he has observed. The most straightforward opportunities grow out of unexpected occurrences, like the one that faced IBM in the early thirties. The company had developed the first primitive machines for accounting, with an eye on the huge banking market. But the timing was lousy—in the midst of the Depression, banks weren't exactly in position to spring for newfangled machinery. The company could have died for lack of sales.

Folks from the New York Public Library showed up on the scene at the opportune moment: they wanted to buy one of the new machines. IBM recognized the opening—banks didn't have money to spend, but, thanks to the New Deal, libraries did. Quickly refocusing its marketing effort, the company sold more than a hundred machines to libraries, staving off ruin.

IBM showed its marketing innovation again fifteen years later. Computers had become an established product for solving complex science problems. When business began to see the possibilities of adapting the computer to handle a completely different kind of challenge, doing repetitive, routine chores like payroll and inventory, market leader Univac showed no interest. One can imagine Univac executives looking on such applications as below the dignity of their highly vaunted "thinking machines." IBM stepped into the breach, redesigning a machine along Univac lines. Within five years it owned the corporate computing marketplace.

(As a contrary example, Drucker cites the experience of the German scientist who created novocaine, the first non-addictive anesthetic. With it, a surgeon would be able to numb just the part of the body being worked on. Surgeons of the day, it turned out, preferred a general anesthetic to a local, while dentists enthusiastically adopted the stuff. That didn't please the scientist, who reacted as if the use by dentists demeaned his product. He spent the rest of his life lecturing at dental schools, trying to forbid the future dentists from giving their patients novocaine because this was not the use he had intended.)

Other categories of innovation cited by Drucker involve exploiting incongruities, like the shipping companies, suffering from years of declining profits, realizing how to adapt so their ships could handle the container loads that had already been in use for years in the trucking and railroad industries; and "process needs," which in the early 1900s led AT&T, after seeing data predicting that in less than a decade it would need every female in the United States to be working as a switchboard operator, to develop the automatic switching device for connecting calls without an operator. (For more on Drucker's views, see his 1998 book *On the Profession of Management*.)

You may have already pieced together the two elements I would add to the Drucker equation. The first comes from recognizing people who have the ability to innovate, even if they haven't shown much evidence in their previous jobs. The second depends on creating the right kind of environment, where people are not only given the opportunity to innovate, but actively encouraged to do so.

INNOVATIVELY CHASING YOUR TAIL

Spacecraft chief engineer Rob Manning, who has a colorful way of expressing himself, is vivid in his explanation of how innovation has sometimes become a double-edged sword to space missions:

> The more money that's involved, the less risk people want to take. The less risk people want to take, the more they put into their designs, to make sure their subsystem is super-reliable. The more things they put in, the more expensive the project gets. The more expensive it gets, the more instruments the scientists want to add, because the cost is getting so high that they're afraid there won't be another opportunity later on—they figure this is the last train out of town. So little by little, the spacecraft becomes gilded. And you have these bad dreams about a spacecraft so bulky and so heavy, it won't be able to get off the ground—never mind the overblown cost.
>
> That boils down to the higher the cost, the more you want to protect your investment, so the more money you put into lowering your risk. It becomes a vicious cycle.
>
> They always said, "Here are all the requirements, how much is it going to cost?" And then when they got the answer, they'd say, "Uh, oh, we can't afford that."

Instead, Manning insists, management should say, "Here's how much money I have, and here's what we'd like to accomplish, what can you do for that?" The free variable now becomes the scope of the task, not the amount of money, and the role of innovation becomes finding clever ways to realize the most "bang for the buck."

NURTURING INNOVATION

On any project, it's easy to achieve a robust solution in your design by playing it safe, by sticking with already-proven components and concepts. Or by the alternate tactic of "gold-plating" everything, the eternal temptation among technical people to create a system that will stand as a monument to engineering science, a tendency referred to in techie-speak as "queer for the gear"—making your object the most wonderful ever built but losing sight of the original goal.

These highly appealing and all too common approaches clearly fly in the face of "faster" and "cheaper," and even run counter to the "better." Safe designs avoid risk but don't likely lead to advanced products that can roll over the competition and capture the marketplace. Design teams need to know, not just that it's okay to be innovative, but that it's essential. Project leaders must let the designers know that innovation is expected of them, demanded of them.

The catch is this: People who innovate make mistakes.

But that's okay. It's okay to make mistakes, *smart* mistakes . . . as long as they're made while there's still time to fix them without encountering the level of expense that throws the whole project into trouble. (An old business adage says that if it costs $100 to correct a mistake in the design phase, it will cost $1,000 to correct if not caught until the mockup phase, and $10,000 if in manufacturing.)

A major ingredient in the brew for nurturing innovation, I believe, comes from throwing people into a hotbed of activity where there is a *mix* of talents. When buyers of electronic hardware work only with other buyers of electronic hardware, and fault-analysis specialists spend their days mostly with other fault-analysis specialists, and C software programmers sit in a room surrounded by other C programmers, then there's little stimulus to look for the light at the end of the tunnel.

On Pathfinder we began, whenever possible, by choosing multi-discipline people, who bring to their workplace a broader perspective right from the outset. And then we made sure that the teams lived in close proximity, working together, talking together, every day. We added enough generalists sprinkled into that brew to provide catalysts who could help the specialists understand one another's vocabulary, perspectives and needs. This is a major advantage of creating a single work environment for the entire project team—the "collocation" theme drummed on in an earlier chapter.

These conditions throw together people of very different mindsets, different views of the world, and the payoffs can be enormous. Creation is indeed a lonely act, yet it rarely thrives in a vacuum.

Pathfinder programmer David Smythe had been struggling with the tough problem of writing software that would trigger an event at exactly the right moment. It looked as if he would have to spend hours, perhaps days, writing code for this single step.

Right across the hall from him, separated by only a six-foot open-landscape wall, sat hardware engineer Chris Devine, who was working on the hardware that David's software would be controlling. Dave stepped over and said, "Chris, can you give me a trigger in your hardware that I could time my software from?"

"No problem," was the reply. Incredibly, it took only fifteen minutes to fashion the hardware solution, which was not only a saving of the programmer's design and subsequent test time but also provided a more reliable, more robust solution.

In fact, the whole idea of putting hardware people and software people together was for JPL an innovation that not everyone applauded. It meant we were taking people away from their individual silos, the fiefdoms that usually maintained control over their services, and moving those people physically into our organization. For the first time, engineers in the attitude control group, devising the systems that govern how the spacecraft flies, and the command and data group, developing how we command and manage the spacecraft, were working shoulder to shoulder.

The point is that opportunities for innovation don't just lie in brainstorms by engineers, scientists and inventors; managers can be innovative in the way they design the structure of their organization, the processes, and even in areas as seemingly mundane as the seating arrangements, the architectures of the way people interface.

WEARING THE BIG HAT

In early 1996 we received some very bad news: there might be a serious problem with the computer.

The project had already been kicked around in one of those corporate buy/sell ballgames: Loral had purchased the division making our machine from the original contractor, IBM, but then had later turned around and sold the operation to Lockheed Martin Federal Systems.

Now Lockheed Martin was advising us that a company which had purchased the same computer had encountered a problem with the memory chips. Lockheed had already investigated and discovered a difficulty that might have affected our unit as well: when the memory chips had been installed on the computer board, the soldering had been done at too high a temperature. The excess heat could have damaged the memories of our unit.

For people who build spacecraft, *maybe* isn't an acceptable word. The memories would have to be replaced.

But that led to still another problem. It turned out that the memory modules had been adhesive-mounted so tightly that the shop had to machine them off. In the process, the operator had cut into the printed circuit board; even if no electronic traces had been cut, the board had been weakened.

It was much too late for Lockheed Martin to build a new one for us in time. Fortunately another JPL project, Sea Winds, had liked our choice of the RAD-6000 and had selected the same computer. Since the Sea Winds' bird was still three years from launch, project manager Jim Graf agreed to let us have one of his flight units. The replacement unit from the manufacturer would arrive in plenty of time to meet the Sea Wind's need.

This is an example of what I call "big hat" thinking—the idea that the success of an organization depends on the success of every project. Jim was under no obligation to help me, but in today's environment, projects within an enterprise need to come to each other's rescue when they can. A project manager whose attitude is "me first, to hell with everyone else," weakens the entire organization.

Tom Gavin of the Cassini project was the archetype of "big hat" thinking, perhaps even was the person who coined the term. He made available to Pathfinder a large array of high-quality electronics that we built into our designs at very low cost.

Not that another JPL project manager wouldn't have provided the computer as the Sea Winds manager did, but with Jim the agreement was struck in minutes in a single telephone call—today's equivalent of sealing a deal with a handshake.

PICKING PEOPLE WHO CAN INNOVATE

How do you choose people who will be able to innovate? I've never found a foolproof way of doing that, so I approach the problem differently, guided by a view that is a paraphrase of a famous Thomas Edison maxim; my version says, "Innovation is 1 percent inspiration and 99 percent perspiration." So I look mostly for people with energy, and then sprinkle in a few highly creative types to provide the innovative spark.

It takes an enormous amount of energy to make a good idea work. Invention may indeed be the offspring of necessity, but in my observation invention leads only to the *kernel* of a new idea. The inventor still needs to transform it into reality. So what I look for is people who will stick with a challenge, people who have the initiative to take a good idea and pursue it tenaciously until they've made it work.

And I try to avoid people who will wander down dead-end alleys where they'll become stuck because they're trying to go it alone instead of asking for help when they need it. I want people who will eat, sleep and breathe the problem until they've licked it and have an item that works, does the job, and has been tested and proven. To me, that's where the true nature of innovation lies.

The determination to stick with a challenge could be seen wherever you looked among the Mars Pathfinder teams. Perhaps the most vivid example came in the face of a problem that had us panicked.

Magnifying the situation, this one occurred at what seemed like the worst possible time. I don't blame people for wanting to further their careers, but we found ourselves pinned to the wall when within the span of a few weeks three of our software engineers announced that they were leaving, a combination of family pressures to escape the Los Angeles area, and the temptation of higher paying jobs in industry.

It's a familiar story for people with high-tech skills in California. Programmers in particular are in very short supply, and many get phone calls from headhunters at least once a week, dangling offers that are hard to resist. If the offer is from a startup or young company and the target employee has a compelling enough background, the offer will probably include a quite sizable chunk of stock, frequently enough to translate into a million dollars, or several, if the company succeeds and goes public.

So our incredibly small staff of eight software engineers shrank almost overnight to only five. This was one of those situations in which the head of the team, Glenn Reeves, insisted he didn't want to hire new people because it would take too much time to train them. Apprehensive about the software not being finished on time, I kept leaning on Glenn to accept some help, and he kept insisting he and his four remaining engineers could do the job if I would just leave him alone.

And then the situation became desperate. The test team, working with parts of the software that were already done, found that something was going wrong. On occasion, the computer was "resetting," which is similar to what happens when your desktop computer locks up and you have to restart the machine.

We had intentionally designed the software to behave in a very nonstandard way if it encountered a glitch. Typical software systems include the ability to analyze a freeze or lockup, determine what part of the software is causing the problem (in the desktop analogy, this is like asking "Is it the word processor that's frozen? Is it the browser?"), and restarting just that part of the software.

We had taken an entirely different view, summed up in our joke that "Resets are our friend." In part, the approach was forced on us: we didn't have the time, money or people to write all that analysis software. More important, the analysis can take minutes to run; if we encountered a software hang-up during the four and a half minutes between entering the Martian atmosphere and the landing, the spacecraft could crash to the surface while the computer was still trying to locate the problem.

So we had decided, If the software has a glitch, don't wait, restart. That would have the computer back on line in less than twenty seconds, fast enough that it might still have time to resume control of the descent and landing.

During tests of the spacecraft in the High Bay, the computer was restarting just as we had intended. But what was causing the restarts? We had to know, and quickly.

The problem was happening infrequently, with no discernible pattern. Intermittent problems are the worst: because there's no repeatable circumstance that causes them, you have to wait till one happens and then try to figure out what was going on.

At this crucial period, that "stick-to-it-iveness," that commitment which characterizes the necessary companion of innovation, came into play: two of the programmers who had left the project,

Dave Cummings and Carl Schneider, were so dedicated that they flew down from Silicon Valley in northern California on weekends to continue work on the software. Dave in particular was probably the only person with the knowledge and experience of the operating system to go about solving that vexing reset problem.

Dave wrote "traps" to insert into the software; when a problem showed up, the traps would capture and record what the computer was doing at the moment of the problem. The resets had first appeared in April; by July, Dave and team leader Glenn Reeves had isolated the problem.

When an engineer, after a painful struggle, finds the source of a problem like this, there's usually a big yowl of joy—"I found it!!!"

This usually produces excitement all around, quickly followed by skeptical demands of "Are you *sure*?!" Not until the problem has been fixed and the new solution thoroughly tested can we really declare victory and breathe a sigh of relief.

But Dave had indeed correctly found the cause of the problem. After the challenge of the hunt, the fix was easy—handled by adding a few standard lines of code.

Without the commitment of people like Dave Cummings, Pathfinder could not have been successful. Not just the knowledge and experience but the dedication to stick with a challenge to the very end made the mission possible.

This would not be our last software crisis, and the headaches in this area would continue almost until touchdown. By late 1995 the programmers had completed 95 percent of the flight code, and we thought we were in software heaven. No project had ever been so far along with its code a year before launch. Completing the last 5 percent, though, would turn out to take every minute of the remaining year.

And even then, with such complex software, it's never possible to test every aspect. We would test and test, and still not be entirely sure. This would remain to the very end one of the big question marks hanging over us.

ROCKETS: BACK IN THE GROOVE

The enigma of the erratic rocket burn had produced furrowed brows and worried looks. After much analysis and discussion with the experts, we were left with two competing theories. One, the more likely, was mechanical, figuring that the mounting of the rocket motors had set up a vibration in the mockup spacecraft. The other pointed a finger at the formulation of the propellant. The standard formulation used 16 percent aluminum, but we had reduced that to 2 percent so there would be less chance of throwing off the scientific measurements of the Martian soil. (If the rover's instruments sent back data showing a significant amount of aluminum in the rock and soil samples, nobody would be quite sure this wasn't simply our own rocket powder debris contaminating the top layer of the material.)

In case the cause was due to theory number two, after obtaining the reluctant blessing of Matt Golombek and the science team, I decided to go back to the original 16 percent aluminum, and we placed the order for the flight set of rockets with this formulation. Meanwhile Les Compton ran some tests with another set of rockets already made up, with the 2 percent aluminum, to see if the problem would recur. This time he loaded the assembly with instrumentation and tethered the rockets to a test stand, to capture a more detailed picture of what was going on. But the rockets fired and burned perfectly. Was that good news?—on one hand, we were glad the problem hadn't appeared again; on the other, we weren't any closer to knowing what was really happening.

As soon as rockets loaded with the new 16 percent aluminum formulation were ready, Les Compton and his team went back out to the desert for one more round of testing. But even though I had called for these tests myself, they made me quite nervous: this time the rockets would be mounted to the engineering-model backshell, our only spare. Any serious test mishap, even a clumsy handling, could mean we would go to the Cape with no fallback.

Les called as soon as the tests were finished. The firing had gone without problem. When he returned, the other members of my top management troika—Rob Manning and Curt Cleven—sat down with Les and me to figure out what all this meant. Conclusion: we were fairly confident the underlying problem had been due to the way the rockets had been mounted on the test structure. If so, we were home free: the flight structure was much better damped, with very little transmission of energy from one rocket to another. Another critical problem that I decided could be checked off as "killed."

THE MANY FACES OF INNOVATION

Everyone in business who has ever worked for an organization large enough to have a purchasing department knows the frustration of having a high-priority need that purchasing isn't set up to handle on a high-priority basis. Certainly at JPL, where the typical major project runs over several years, another week or three for sending out the next request for proposals or purchase order isn't a make-or-break issue.

In the world of Faster, Better, Cheaper, those leisurely work habits can strangle. Yet it's not realistic to think that with some kind of dog-and-pony show, you can convince the head of procurement that he has to revamp his organization and procedures to meet the needs of your one project.

We took a different approach, by establishing, right at the beginning of the project and with the support of the Procurement Division, what we called a "hardware acquisition team." Its assignment: provide end-to-end tracking and problem-solving on subcontracts and other procurements. The team was led by a senior manager from procurement, Randy Taylor, along with Ed Kellum, an experienced hardware engineer.

Randy was designated to handle the full range of Pathfinder business matters, and was freed of all other duties. An experienced hand, a lawyer by training (but we didn't hold that against him), he knew the ins and outs of contracting and procurement, and also knew better than most the organization and people of the Lab's procurement organization. He became part of our staff but at the same time remained part of the procurement organization.

Randy knew which buyers to go to when something needed to be done in a hurry, and then he knew how to help them get the work finished and out. Those skills enabled him to keep things moving for us in a way we could never have achieved by leaning on the organization from outside.

The job for Randy and Ed went beyond just contracting; they were responsible for making sure everything we were buying from contractors and universities would arrive on schedule, when we needed it. Just as a band leader directs the actions of the players, so they orchestrated the deliveries of the vendors.

And not only the vendors. Many times a company couldn't move ahead because it was waiting for some data, instructions or decision from someone on Pathfinder. Whenever that happened, Randy would be just as hard-hitting with the engineer, the manager, or even with me—whatever was needed to keep things moving. The man was absolutely tenacious—just what we needed.

Once when a vendor was falling behind, Randy paid a visit to the company. He met with the president and shoved our red/yellow/green "Fever Chart" under his nose, pointing to the line that showed his job as a red-flagged item.

"Who sees this?" the president asked.

"It goes to NASA headquarters every month," Randy told him.

The next morning, the president was out on his shop floor personally to make sure they got back on schedule. Score another for Randy Taylor.

The other key player of this duo, Ed Kellum, took on the task of keeping tabs on the schedule of every request for proposal, contract, and design review for every job being done outside the Lab. He set up and maintained a master schedule of all procurement steps on some fifty major contracts. This is detailed, methodical work, but highly important to success. Fortunately, Ed thrived on it, bringing a bulldog attitude that saw all of his status questions answered promptly. He kept us constantly up-to-date on delivery issues before they turned into problems.

These managers were accessible to the entire team for status and resolution on procurement issues. Other members of the hardware acquisition team consisted of JPL contract technical managers, procurement negotiators and project element managers responsible for delivering hardware. We held regularly scheduled monthly meetings, supplemented by weekly follow-up meetings when necessary, where each procurement status was reviewed.

I also had the good instincts to pick Craig Sholes as my financial manager. A tall, soft-spoken guy whose three-piece suits didn't quite match my wardrobe of jeans and T-shirt, he heard from me at the outset that on this project it was more important to produce the numbers fast, even if it meant they were only approximate. He proved able to cover much more of the total business management job than anyone I'd ever worked with. In direct contact with the engineers and managers, he was generally a step ahead of me in identifying problems that could impact the budget and our dwindling reserves. Craig took a huge load off my shoulders, allowing me to focus more of my attention on the engineering challenges.

My experience with Craig and Randy has since led me to push for opportunities to develop broad-based businesspeople capable of multiplying the effectiveness of the management team they support.

The moral of all this: Don't look just to your engineers and designers for innovation—it needs to be a common quality throughout the project organization. Innovation can have many faces; it will come as a surprise to many that innovation can even come in three-piece suits.

WE HAVE A SPACECRAFT

On the first Sunday in March '96, with both my daughters in tow, I stopped by JPL to check on the activities in High Bay One. Jenna, the younger, chose to stay in the control room, but Alicia came in with me. As we suited up to enter the clean-room environment, I chose the smallest gown available for her. The selection of course doesn't include any children's sizes; we tried turning up the hem but it wouldn't stay. She walked in with me dragging a train behind her like a diminutive Snow White.

Mike Mangano, who was spearheading the arduous effort of assembling the flight spacecraft, had early on been certain his team would not be able to finish this complex task on time. Together he and I had reworked the schedule on several occasions, juggling deliveries and replanning operations. Each time he was still left full of doubts. But his doubts didn't stop him and his team from giving 150 percent to get the job done.

This day marked a major achievement: what Alicia and I found was a team that had just finished the first full-up assembly of Mars Pathfinder.

Here was a milestone to be cherished. We called the JPL Photo Lab, which sent down a photographer who captured the moment with the team that had completed the assembly, their smiling flight system manager, chief engineer Rob Manning, and of course, Alicia.

Monday morning the team began installing the spacecraft into a special container for a short voyage. Once packed, it was driven out of the High Bay and up the hilly JPL campus, at about 3 miles an hour, toward the environmental test chamber. Many of the team and a lot of other JPL workers gathered to watch as we accompanied the slow-moving vehicle taking our Pathfinder on its first short journey.

Earlier we had done vibration and environmental tests on subsystems and groups of subsystems. Now we would be doing similar tests, and some much more intricate ones, on the whole spacecraft.

Once it was installed in the environmental chamber, the first item on the agenda was an acoustic test: we aim a gigantic horn at the spacecraft, and let loose with a blast of noise at around 146 decibels—enough to turn a human being into mush. This approximates the level of sound pressure that Pathfinder would experience during launch. We anticipated no problems, and found none.

One of the tests in this final series at JPL was especially pleasing to me because it was, I thought, so highly innovative. The challenge turned on the fact that our spacecraft was a "spinner"—to keep it stabilized, we had designed it to spin about its main axis like a gyroscope. We were now ready for the tests to check on how good a job we had done with the thermal design and blankets, ensuring that the spacecraft wouldn't grow too hot or too cold. We would need to subject it in the environmental test chamber to the conditions of deep space.

But a spacecraft that's a spinner continually changes the side being exposed to the sun. How would we twirl the craft in the test chamber?

One approach would be to build a rig that could spin it, just as it would spin in flight. Pathfinder presented a complicated, intricate exterior; the challenge would be to design a rig that could securely attach to such a complex device and still leave it free to spin.

The thermal test engineers came up with a novel solution, one that had never been used before at JPL, the kind of solution that makes everybody else wonder, "Why didn't I think of that?" Instead of rotating the spacecraft under an intense light simulating the sun, they designed a large gridwork of infrared lamps. Controlled by computer, the lamps would heat the spacecraft uniformly from all sides, similar to what the craft would feel from spinning, its surfaces in succession being exposed equally to the heating of the sun—like a Weber charcoal grill, but with the coals all around the inside (which sounds like a great concept for a zero-gravity barbecue). This setup worked extremely well, and although it cost about $500,000 to develop, did the job and turned out to be a bargain.

Again we had found people able to innovate when presented with a challenge and given the license and resources.

A BURNED-OUT SWITCH

It's not news to an observant manager, and a point I've made more than once in these pages, that the attitude of the person at the top of any organization, work unit or team colors the attitude of every member. One characteristic of leadership that's essential in a Faster, Better, Cheaper environment is to maintain an air of confidence; this needs to be sincere (phony is soon detected), but I've seen many teams perform heroically when things looked darkest because the leader was able to project confidence. Necessary even though not sufficient by itself, this air of confidence about the outcome can be enough to screw people up to the superhuman performance that the greatest of the mission's challenges will demand.

I was put to the test of maintaining equanimity and a sense of "we can meet this challenge" when we discovered in April that one piece of the spacecraft hardware had burned out. The item, called a waveguide transfer switch, on command changes which of the two radio antennas is in use. A small item but a critical one: locking up in the wrong position at the wrong time, it would prevent us from sending orders to the spacecraft or receiving data from it.

One annoying characteristic of this switch: if its power is left on for more than about two minutes, its rotor windings go up in smoke. To prevent damage, the software programmers had added some lines of code that would allow power to be applied for only a short duration.

During testing of a Mars surface sequence, the software commanded the switch to change antennas. Then, before the action could be completed, the computer encountered a problem and reset. That's common in testing and not unexpected. But before the computer could finish its restart sequence and again take control of the switch, a mistake in the settings of another piece of hardware, a timer, caused the computer to go into its hibernate mode . . . with power to the switch never turned off.

It happens so often in developing high-tech products that you've built in all the appropriate protections, and then *two* errors happen simultaneously. You could create a corollary to Murphy's Law that says, "If software can cause hardware to fail, it will." Our switch difficulties only happened because the sleep mode started in the middle of the computer reset.

We set about figuring out when in the schedule it would be possible to pull the lander hardware apart and replace the switch, unhappily located deep inside the lander.

At the same time we put the engineers to work designing another layer of protection, a hardware circuit to cut off the power after a specific period if the software protection didn't work. We discovered a way of gaining a major head start on this: the engineers on the Cassini project, with their bigger budget and more time, had counted on these two levels of fault protection from the first, and had already designed the hardware part. We had only to take their design and modify it to the needs of Pathfinder.

Fine. Except that all these changes were being added at the last minute. We might not have the chance of testing them thoroughly. The software, and even more likely the hardware, might be bringing new problems we could not anticipate.

Would the new hardware truly be "bulletproof"?

"Yes," send Pathfinder designer Rocco Scaramastra. "It's well tested, it's safe to fly."

"Can we be certain that a software problem won't create a situation like this again?"

"No," said the Gremlin, Dave Gruel, our tester par excellence. "We can't guarantee that some other problem like this couldn't occur."

Given Dave's answer, it was a no-brainer to decide on putting in the new electronics. For me, this was a lesson in innovation. Software can't be made completely foolproof, and I'll never again rely on software for protecting hardware against damage.

But the clock was running against us. With no time for building a new switch, "big hat" assistance once again came into play as it had with the computer: the Deep Space 1 flight system manager gave us one of hers. It would have to be installed after the spacecraft reached Cape Canaveral.

Meanwhile this last phase of environmental testing at JPL wasn't over yet. And another crisis lay just ahead.

11. Communications: Data to Information to Knowledge

I like to listen. I have learned a great deal from listening carefully. Most people never listen.

—Ernest Hemingway

COUNTDOWN: 6 MONTHS TO LAUNCH

Even for people who live by technology, sometimes technology turns around and bites its masters on the backside.

We generated a much smaller volume of paper on Pathfinder than is typical: rather than using the time to generate a lot of documents, memos, written requests and written reports; instead—again thanks to collocation—much of our communication was verbal.

That was made easier by a personnel pattern novel in the space business. Most major spacecraft projects have at least three sets of workers, in different time periods—first the folks who design and build, then a different bunch for the testing, and finally the operators, who control the craft en route and operate it at destination. On Pathfinder, though, we followed a practice that we described as "builders become testers, testers become operators." Many people, finishing one job, would take on a new role they had never handled before.

The project benefited, too, because the people themselves became our archives—another very important and very effective aspect of growing generalists. We didn't have to make a fetish of documenting every step and every decision—if you needed a piece of information, even though our project librarian Susan Roberts did a yeoman job, much of the time you didn't go poring through the archives, you simply asked the team member handling that particular area.

This approach brings one compelling benefit: "human archives" store more than words, drawings and data; they store knowledge. The response may not bring the answer to the question you asked, but a more valuable, more insightful response based on an understanding of the problem you're seeking to solve.

PRISON IN OUR FUTURE?

When two of our engineers early in the project tried to apply technology to a communications challenge, they stirred up a hornet's nest. Groups around the country were working on separate parts of our flight software, like the University of Arizona team developing the critical code that would locate the position of the sun. How could we best keep all the players up to the moment on all the code being written in all these places, so anyone who needed a piece of information about someone else's software would be able to find it immediately?

One of the guys said, "Let's just use the Internet and make this available to all the people who need it." At this point, in 1994, the Net was still in its relative infancy, still being used almost exclusively by the military, universities, researchers, and national labs, and looked like an ideal solution for making our software available. We weren't using any classified military items, nothing in the code was proprietary, and putting everybody's software up on-line would give immediate access to the most current version, twenty-four hours a day.

So they posted much of the Pathfinder software on the Internet, and things worked out just as they had figured. Until the NASA Inspector General's Office found out about it.

The problem, we learned, grew out of the Ronald Reagan/"Star Wars"/cold-war era. In that climate any spacecraft was considered to hold the potential for being used as a weapon (a view no less true today). The Pathfinder team had unknowingly violated ITAR, the

International Traffic in Arms Regulations. We were technically law-breakers, and the crime was treated as quite serious. It sounded like a John Cleese movie plot, but nobody was laughing.

One thing a high-pressure project doesn't need is a major distraction. The Inspector General ordered an investigation, called for detailed backgrounds on our two engineers and everybody else in any way connected with the misdeed—including me—and demanded a huge stack of documents. Project work slowed as we dug out the paperwork and ran the copying machines overtime.

They also wanted a complete list of Internet hits showing who had visited the site and what they downloaded. A major Japanese telecommunications company, we discovered, had taken every line of software.

Not that it could have done the company much good. That, I think, was what saved our necks: the software on line was not usable operational code—to run it would require a compiler no one else had, and an operating system that didn't yet exist. The equations embedded in the software—for things like ordering the spacecraft to rotate—were all in the public domain, things routinely taught in college classrooms.

The NASA IG gathered the data, but—talk about a federal case—the actual decision on our fate was in the hands of the State Department, responsible for the initial ruling. After keeping us in suspense for several months, they decided no serious infraction had occurred. (The NASA Inspector General, though, didn't close the case until 1996.)

It would turn out much later that our unhappily gained knowledge of Internet security issues would become a valuable lesson as Web use exploded through the ensuing years.

The effort had taken a lot of the team's time, and a lot of my time, over a mistake we could hardly have been expected to know about. But at least no one had to stand trial facing a prison term. We got back to work, relieved and, if not any wiser, at least a little more cautious.

MESSAGE FROM OHIO

While the spacecraft was undergoing its testing at JPL, the entry/descent/landing subsystems were completing their qualification testing. Because each of the elements—parachute, deceleration rockets, airbag, and radar altimeter—had to be tested in a different kind of situation, this work was being done separately, in parallel. When finished, the flight hardware would all be delivered directly to the Cape.

Ann Mauritz's parachute qualification program went off without any problems. In fact, people from the vendor, Pioneer Aerospace, were so confident of their design that they subjected one of the qualification units to a "dynamic overpressure" test—loading the parachute to greater than three times its flight limit load. The chute survived undamaged.

For the airbags, we had devised a series of final tests that would be the most complete of all, including, for the first time, chilling the whole assembly down to minus 40 degrees Centigrade before inflating the bags. Always on guard for some nuance of physics that might have been overlooked, we wanted the most realistic conditions we could get. (And I remembered the lesson of the Egg-Drop Challenge.)

As Tom Rivellini prepared for these final tests at NASA's Plumbrook facility in Ohio, I again gathered the "entry/descent/landing brain trust"—Bill Layman, Rob Manning, Sam Thurman, and Dara Sabahi—into my office to make the final decision about how fast we should drop the device, with Tom on the phone from Plumbrook, just hours away from test start. The test, of course, *had* to be successful—if a final qualification test comes up a failure, there's no hiding it. Suddenly, everything is thrown into question. All the powers-that-be who are looking over your shoulder begin to wonder what *else* might be wrong.

The latest simulations told us that the absolute highest likely velocity of the lander as it reached the surface, if everything had worked as planned, would be about 28 meters per second—62 miles per hour. Yet the calculations also told us there was less than one chance in a hundred of the speed actually reaching this worst-case maximum.

The dilemma was plain: If we told Tom to drop it at that speed and it failed, we'd have shot ourselves in the foot. But if we used a lesser speed, say, 24 meters per second, would we really be confident about the results? Would we be able to convincingly justify our decision if challenged?

After we had chewed it over, I went around the table taking an informal vote. We settled on 25, which bounded 95 percent of the thousands of simulation cases. Tom left the conference call to go tell his guys the number.

The next morning, when my alarm went off at 5 as usual, I was immediately struck by the realization that no call from Tom had wakened me. What could it mean—bad news or good? I called Plumbrook but Tom and his team weren't there.

He reached me later in the day to report that the whole team had knocked off at 3 A.M.—as soon as the test was over, before waiting for the chamber to be returned to normal pressure, so they could all grab some much needed sleep and come in fresh to fully assess the results. He now had the answer: the test had been flawless. For the first time ever, the airbag had survived without a single tear.

Finally, the biggest uncertainty that had been hanging over us from the very beginning was put to rest.

HEATING UP

Practically everyone on the face of the Earth considers that he or she has a great sense of humor, a characteristic so universal it's almost a joke. And in the same way, some proportion of the human population that I suspect closely approaches 100 percent considers themselves excellent communicators.

This number of course includes every engineer and manager. While members of my august profession are not always models of clarity in trying to express ideas to those outside their own field, among ourselves—blessed by access not only to the everyday language of ordinary people but to the advanced vocabularies of the specialist, plus the language of mathematics, and the visual depiction of mechanical drawing and circuit diagrams, to name only a few—their communications skills are impeccable.

With all these tools at our command, no wonder our communications are so flawless and totally free from misunderstanding.

Your own communications skills being what they are, you will have detected the underlying note of sarcasm running through the above. No matter how much management attention we apply or how hard we work at it, communication is always an issue, an almost endless source of problems. Though the collocation of so much of the Pathfinder team made communications one of the most successful aspects of the project, so that we were blessed with few communications gaffes, still, when we miscued, it could be a whopper.

As tests in the environmental chamber continued, I received an alarming phone call from Dr. Yi-Chien Wu (known to everyone as Y.C.), the lead of the temperature control team. "Brian, we've been running the hot case"—simulating the early part of the flight, with the sun beating down on the slowly rotating spacecraft. "And it's not looking good."

"What's happening?"

"The cruise solar array is running hot. Thirty degrees hotter than it should."

"Oh, shit, what's going on?"

"We don't know yet."

"Y.C., is there something wrong with the instrumentation?"

"We already checked that, Brian. I didn't want to get you upset over nothing. We just spent most of the day going all over everything. Whatever's happening, it's not the instrumentation."

When we got to the bottom of it, we did indeed have a serious problem on our hands. The reality was just as the test had indicated. With the spacecraft operating exactly as our engineers had designed it, the solar arrays would be 30 degrees Centigrade (54 degrees Fahrenheit) too hot, which meant they would produce lower voltage than designed, which in turn meant that late in the mission, they might not be putting out enough "oomph" to recharge the battery.

Even if Pathfinder managed to land safely in that condition, it might lack the energy to open its petals. But the petals had to open so the lander solar arrays could be exposed to the sun—the only way of providing power for the operations on the surface. Petals that couldn't open would mean there would be no data collection, no rover, no pictures.

At an emergency meeting I called on Saturday morning for the entire team, the testers reported that the situation was even worse than it had at first seemed. The lines carrying hydrazine propellant to the "thruster clusters"—the two groups of four small rocket motors that we fire to spin, rotate and orient the spacecraft, and to give thrust for mid-course corrections—were in danger of freezing up. Thermostats designed to control the fuel-line heaters were located in places where they were experiencing the same overheating as the solar arrays and therefore were not turning on as they should. If the lines froze and broke, we would lose all ability to steer and guide the spacecraft. End of mission.

But these problems were not due to the failure of some part, a bad solder connection or some other typical breakdown. Everything was working *as designed*. I was not so much angry as panicked about how we would climb out of this deep pit. And wondering how on earth it could have happened.

The trail led back to a pair of our engineers, and I had been witness to their conversations more than once at the weekly technical meetings. In front of everyone, the solar array specialist had asked the thermal specialist, "Give me the most likely temperature that the solar panels will be at when we arrive at Mars." The thermal engineer had understood the request to mean what we call the "cold case," when the solar array is being warmed by the sun but the rest of the spacecraft is feeling the chill of deep space, which is the coldest the spacecraft would experience during the flight. Each time he gave the same number he had been using all along, minus 10 degrees Fahrenheit. He had been over and over the calculations, and he was sure.

Nothing wrong with his calculations. To the thermal engineer, the request was for the *coldest* temperature to be encountered, and he built a simple, straightforward mathematical model for calculating the answer. But it didn't account for all the blockage on the back side of the solar array—the propulsion system, electronics, the blanketing, and the meteoroid protection. All this hardware blocked the exposure of the solar array, leaving it little surface area for radiating its heat off to space. So the solar arrays were running hot, and the fuel lines were in danger of freezing.

A prime example for my earlier remarks about specialists and generalists. This highly capable engineer was thinking like a thermal specialist, not like a systems person. He was so involved with solving the particular problem that he wasn't looking "over the wall," wasn't stretching himself to consider the problem that the person on the other side of the interface was really trying to solve.

I remembered an incident on the Galileo project, when I was working on the interface between the spacecraft and the Centaur launch vehicle with another engineer, and a question came up about the coordinate system—the reference frame for designating the location and orientation of things that comes into play when engineers are figuring out how a part built in one lab will line up during assembly with a part built in another. Digging into the documentation, he discovered that the Galileo and the Centaur attitude-control coordinate systems were 180 degrees different—one system upside down from the other. If the problem had not been caught, after launch, when time came to release the spacecraft, it would have been sent spinning in the wrong direction, and there would have been no way to recover it—a catastrophic and most embarrassing failure.

That experience had been an incredible wake-up call for me. I know now how important it is to check rigorously all those things that people *assume.* It's the high-tech stuff that consumes everybody's attention but the little things that can cause your downfall. The attitude infiltrated the whole of the Pathfinder team; I'd smile when I heard one engineer telling another, "It won't be the computer, the actuators or the pyro devices that get us, it'll be something butt simple." We worked hard at making sure we didn't overlook the simple things.

And yet, no matter how careful you think you're being . . . Here we were with just that kind of major issue growing out of a small problem in communications, interpreting words differently. As usual, it would have been really easy to uncover if we had only looked at the problem more closely.

Often when there's a breakdown like this, managers start posting a lot of rules to make sure it doesn't happen again. That's a perfectly natural inclination . . . and entirely wrongheaded. Pretty soon the organization has been loaded down with so many rules (the origin of which frequently become lost in antiquity) that innovation is stifled and people start losing the initiative to try anything different. Meanwhile nothing has been accomplished in addressing the root cause, the quality of communications.

But for us, what counted now was fixing the problem. If we could.

My senior management team decided with me that we would suspend the environmental testing and attempt a fix, with the spacecraft still in the test chamber. Nothing too clever about that decision—we would be sending the spacecraft on its journey to the Cape in less than two months; there simply wasn't time to pack it up, move it back into the High Bay, rework it, and return it to testing.

The only fix we could see that could be done quickly enough involved stripping off the blankets and reworking them to adjust for the temperature patterns as they actually existed instead of the ones we had anticipated. At the same time we set Mike Shirbacheh and his battery team looking for alternative techniques to charge the battery. If neither of these approaches produced an effective answer, and they might well not, then we were in deep trouble.

The indomitable Hugh von Delden came back in to help us through the crisis, again teamed up with Andy Rose, and the two of them put in a string of long days and long nights. In half a week, they had reworked the blankets and installed them back on the spacecraft, and we could resume testing.

We started, of course, by redoing the "cold" temperature tests. The results were mildly encouraging: conditions had improved some, but not much. The temperature of the solar array had dropped by several degrees. Enough? We couldn't be certain. Meanwhile the battery guys were still looking at their options.

The propellant-line story was even less certain. Our lead system engineer for propulsion, a tenacious engineer named Morgan Parker, was unsatisfied with the ambiguous results. He wasn't going to let this one go, and insisted on a very detailed thermal analysis. The analysis revealed that the propulsion lines were still showing some dangerously cold segments.

Our maneuvering room now growing more and more limited, we were forced into a radical step. Once again Hugh and Andy removed the blankets covering the propellant lines, and painstakingly reworked them, and put them back in place one last time.

But there would be no further testing. We were out of time and had to move on. We had reviewed the data from the thermal analysis over and over, which concluded that this last fix should be enough to solve the problem, and I felt confident the analysis was conservative enough, and accurate enough. Now our only proof would have to come from the real thing, the performance of Pathfinder in flight.

The entire reworking of the blankets had, incredibly, been accomplished in a single week. For his heroic efforts, I would later nominate Andy Rose for the JPL Excellence Award.

COOLING DOWN

With the shipping date now just six weeks away, in July the lander and Sojourner were scheduled to begin a series of tests under conditions simulating as closely as we could the situation they would encounter sitting on the surface of Mars.

We had to run a gamut of complaints, cautions and criticisms for this one. The test chamber was designed for simulating the conditions of cold in the vacuum of space. We needed to test for cold not in a vacuum but in the thin yet significant atmosphere of Mars, and planned, at great expense, to run liquid nitrogen through piping inside the inner walls. But even this thin atmosphere would convey the deep chill to the outer steel walls, which had not been designed to withstand this condition.

Our structural engineers had thoroughly examined the chamber, run their calculations, and said, "The chamber walls are sound and will withstand the test without problems."

But some old JPL hands said, "NO!—too risky. It could damage the outer walls." Their caution was understandable: a damaged chamber would require time-consuming and extremely expensive repairs; other projects after ours, scheduled for time in the chamber, would be left with no place to test.

We agreed to do a preliminary test run with the chamber walls fully instrumented on both the inside and outer surfaces. The tests confirmed our earlier analysis—the chamber did fine. And so did the lander and rover when they underwent the actual testing a week later.

END OF THE LINE AT JPL

At the end of all other testing, there was one final step in the schedule. With each subsystem, component or element, you start with a requirement in mind—what this item needs to do, what function it needs to perform. "Antenna: beam communications to Earth."

"Waveguide transfer switch: switch radio signals between the two antennas." "Altimeter: measure the height above the surface during descent." That requirement is then written down as a set of technical specifications of how the device must perform to carry out its contribution to the mission.

What happens if you lose sight of the original goal and design an element that meets the technical requirements you've written down, measures up on every test against those requirements ... but in some way fails to perform the task it was meant to achieve? How do you protect against that possibility?

So we would round off this phase of the project with what we called an "end-to-end functional test," designed to ensure that all parts of the spacecraft would work properly to produce the performance we had intended.

Guy Beutelschies, who had written down most of the requirements and was now in charge of testing, had insisted that each team write a formal procedures document for these tests, and for later operations during the mission. These documents are a communications tool, recording the knowledge of how things should work. Preparing the documents is a pain, few engineers write them willingly, but Guy and the other leaders of the test team knew they could save our skins. Guy personally wrote many himself, and reviewed and signed off on every one of the others.

For five days, with the lander, cruise stage, and backshell all separated but hooked together by a maze of cabling (provided by our scrounger, Tom Shain), we ran the spacecraft through all its modes—prelaunch, launch, cruise, preparation for entry, entry/descent/landing, and operations on the surface. This was a full-up dress rehearsal for the entire mission.

As a final step in this final testing at JPL, the team ran a short "plugs out" test, in which all support systems are disconnected. Just in case the performance of some function was being affected by a peripheral item or piece of test equipment, we would operate our bird the way it would operate in space. That follows an adage familiar to spacecraft engineers: "Test what you fly and fly what you test."

Though the end-to-end test results looked good, we weren't free of concerns. That new waveguide switch would have to be installed at the Cape, as well as some hardware elements like the flight batteries. And the software still wasn't in its final state. Looking at the items still not checked off, I decided I wanted to repeat the end-to-end functional testing at the Cape. We moved the ship date forward by one week to allow time for repeating this test.

With the final JPL testing now completed, the Lab's Press Office issued its first press release citing the goal of exploring a planet with a first-ever self-propelled, free-ranging robot. Certainly we didn't yet have much to brag about. Yes, we had built an innovative, advanced spacecraft on remarkably little money and a tight schedule, but none of that would count for much unless it would fly, reach Mars and land in one piece.

The team members were starting to show the wear and tear on their mostly young faces—some looking noticeably not as young as when we had begun together. But we were still about a year from the real challenge, landing on Mars.

REVIEWS AS A COMMUNICATIONS TOOL

In addition to the formal reviews before a board of seasoned space mission professionals and top spacecraft project managers, we had through the course of the project held many more "peer reviews." As described earlier in these pages, the formal board reviews are sometimes elaborate dog-and-pony shows, sessions that give project management a kick in the butt about things the board believes the team hasn't paid enough attention to. But their greatest value lies in the weeks of laborious preparation that force the team to closure on still-unresolved issues. The benefits of preparation generally outweigh any new insights from the review.

The peer reviews, on the other hand, are much less of a distraction. Shirtsleeve, no-holds-barred sessions involving a smaller number of people—peers, not high-level executives—and focused on a particular aspect or narrow range of topics, each took only a few days of preparation by the people who would be presenting. I believed strongly in the communications and learning value of these sessions for making sure we weren't overlooking things and were keeping within limits on schedule, volume, mass and money, and for ensuring all the key people understood what decisions were being made. We held over a hundred of these "user friendly" peer reviews during the three years of developing Pathfinder, an extraordinary number.

Another user-friendly communications tool was the "Problem/ Failure Report" for tracking problem resolution—a familiar tool that was rendered less formal and less intimidating when Dave Gruel took the initiative of creating an electronic version. It proved much more effective than on earlier projects, not just for keeping track of problem issues but in helping us focus on the important ones and documenting our actions in closing them.

To give a ranking to problems, we used a familiar two-number shorthand coding system, rating each item on whether it was mission critical (1 = negligible mission impact; 3 = mission catastrophic), and whether we knew the cause of the problem and how to fix it (1 = known cause and known fix; 4 = unknown cause, unverified fix).

An entry on the Problem/Failure Report may be a straightforward issue that's easy to correct, or a complex problem that we would be working on for a while, or, sometimes, an issue that showed up once, never came back, but could be catastrophic. Many were related to testing the software. We generated and addressed more than eight hundred of these electronic reports.

An item rated as 2, 3 or worse achieved an unwelcome status we referred to as the "red-flag domain," indicating that it was mission critical, and we didn't know the cause or didn't know for certain the problem had been fixed. The project manager had to sign off personally on these items, which are so crucial to the project that it would be a failure of responsibility for the top person not to be aware of them.

The team had done an extraordinary job of resolving nearly every problem that had occurred during development, and well in advance had closed all remaining red-flag items.

We were ready to travel across the country.

TO THE CAPE

Wednesday, August 7, 1996. On this red-letter day (not to be confused with a red-flag something), we began the half-week process of loading three trucks—a pair of wide-load air-ride vans and a lowboy—that would carry the fruits of our labor to Florida.

Tom Shain had cooked up an unlikely contraption for housing the cruise stage and aeroshell, a sealed cylindrical container kept purged with nitrogen so the heavy, humid air of the southern U.S. summer wouldn't cause moisture to condense inside the units. For further protection, he had the cylinder wrapped in an insulating blanket. And on top of all that, he had provided an air conditioner that could circulate cold air inside the blanket if the caravan got stuck somewhere with the hot sun beating down on it. That promised to be effective but was certainly weird-looking; what would a government-UFO-cover-up theorist have made of seeing this? What would the *National Enquirer* have done as a photo caption!

What, indeed. Surely it seems paranoid, but we actually worried about some weirdo with a rifle taking potshots at our caravan, which would be a bit too obvious to escape notice—the pair of oversized vehicles trundling down the freeways, with a third vehicle bringing up the rear, its yellow roof lights flashing to warn motorists of the wide trucks ahead. The vehicles intentionally carry no markings—no NASA label, no JPL label, no American flag.

We wondered, If our spacecraft took a bullet, would we be able to repair it? Looking back, it sounds a bit overwrought, but we actually discussed it.

On Friday, several dozen or so people showed up around midnight to see Tom and his caravan set off, an experience that I think must be a bit like seeing an only child off to college, leaving home for the first time. The late hour of departure is traditional, allowing the trucks to escape L.A. while the traffic is light, and cross most of the California desert before sunup. I brought a bottle of champagne, intending to "launch" the caravan by cracking it against the bumper of the lead truck; caution ruled—liquor isn't allowed on the grounds of JPL and, concerned over the possibility of bringing a security force onslaught down on our heads that could delay departure, I demurred.

Besides, I wasn't entirely in the mood for abandoned celebration. This was a milestone, sure, but I would be staying behind. There was still so much to do at JPL—helping get the team ready for controlling the spacecraft in flight and on Mars, staying on top of the drive to finish the software and complete its testing. My schedule included short trips to the Cape on occasion, but I was leaving the responsibility for readying the spacecraft in the able hands of Curt Cleven, Mike Mangano, and Guy Beutelschies. Staying behind was the right decision, still, knowing I would not be present for much of the final preparation was not easy.

To lose as little time as possible in transit, two teams of drivers would keep the trucks moving twenty-four hours a day, the off-duty drivers sleeping in their trucks' fancy cabs. The small van provided work space and accommodations for Shain, quality inspector Lorraine Garcia, and some technicians. Monitoring equipment continually measured temperature and vibration of the components, and were rigged to set off alarms in case of a problem.

Around lunchtime on Tuesday, August 13, sixty-two hours after leaving JPL (and another record), the caravan pulled up to the main gate of the John F. Kennedy Space Flight Center, Cape Canaveral, Florida. It was given an escort to lead it to SAEF 2, the Spacecraft Assembly and Encapsulation (truly!) Facility building, specially designed for housing systems that carried explosive materials like our rockets and propulsion system—coincidentally, the same facility that the Viking mission to Mars had been prepared in some twenty years earlier.

PROBLEMS AT THE CAPE

Before the team members at the Cape could begin reassembling the spacecraft, they faced a string of tasks that still had to be performed. The lander had to be torn down to its electronic chassis so they could replace two fuses that had blown and replace that damaged waveguide switch. Also spacecraft typically are launched with a fresh, brand-new battery; Pathfinder's new battery, delivered directly to the Cape by the manufacturer, BST, Inc., would have to be installed.

At JPL, for personnel safety, we had been working with a rover that did not yet have the heating elements of its heater units installed: radioactive plutonium. The rover team had tried to avoid using radioactive material, appalled that the Cassini project had supposedly spent $25 million just preparing *documentation* for its plutonium—a sum equal to the entire budget for the rover. But Bill Layman became convinced there was no other alternative, and coaxed agreements from NASA that limited the amount of documentation required.

Even though the stuff is not weapons-grade, and the rover needed only tiny amounts, each piece about the size of a baby's fingernail, the delivery looked like a scene from an overwrought Hollywood action movie. On the appointed day, a large black eighteen-wheeler reinforced with heavy armor plating rolled up to our facility at the Cape, escorted by a caravan of unmarked vehicles. Almost before they pulled to a stop, a squadron of guards armed with machine guns leaped out and formed a cordon. For our assembly team, the scene provided an amusing diversion.

When the team members at the Cape had finished installing the new waveguide switch and the flight batteries, and making the other changes, they began the repeat of the final verification test I had called for.

I knew the team understood that with Pathfinder, JPL's most complicated spacecraft ever, we were always just one weak screw, one bad transistor, one faulty wire away from failure.

But this time, thankfully, no new problems appeared. We were proceeding smoothly toward launch.

PETAL PANIC

The procedure called a "walkdown" involves going over every major section of the spacecraft—cruise stage, aeroshell, lander using a figurative magnifying glass, examining every item, asking tons of questions of the team, looking over tons of backup documentation. It's an airplane pilot's kick-the-tires walk-around inspection multiplied by a million, a great check-and-balance for team members who have been seeing the spacecraft every day and so may miss something familiar but wrong.

On these critical inspections, it helps to have the fresh perspective of someone from outside the project, so we had arranged that the walkdowns would be conducted jointly by our Bill Layman along with Frank Locatell, former JPLer and now consulting for us. I flew in for these inspections, to be on hand in case of any emergencies.

After the walkdown of the lander open, the team started closing it up. And threw us all into panic mode: one of the three side-petals wouldn't close. It was misaligned—not by much, but enough to represent a serious problem. Yet it had been opened and closed repeatedly at JPL—how could it suddenly not work?

And then it began to dawn on all of us about the same time. At JPL, a crane had swung the petal into place; now when we tried to close it with the actuator motor designed to do the job, the weight of the airbag mounted on the outside of the petal was making the base plate deform.

Each of the petals was machined from high-strength aluminum about 3 inches thick and weighing about 45 pounds—so sturdy no one ever anticipated that the added weight of the airbag fashioned out of "soft goods" could bend that stiff aluminum plate.

We had a full-fledged crisis on our hands.

A leader always carries the responsibility of modeling the right intellectual and emotional behavior. Your people learn as much from how you handle the downside as they do from how you handle the upside. That's so easy to forget at crunch time, and managers seem to fall into one of two categories: those who lose control, unleashing their fury or frustration on anybody conveniently in range, and those who quash their feelings under the misconceived notion that any show of emotion will be taken as a sign of weakness.

I'm a firm subscriber in the middle ground: let people see your concern and disappointment . . . and then let them see how you overcome it, moving out of an emotional place where you're ruled by feelings, up to a level where you're dealing with the facts.

An electronic camera had been set up in the assembly area, taking a still image every thirty seconds that were immediately posted on the Web. I moved the camera to give a close-up view so our team members back at JPL could see directly the nature and magnitude of the problem. A powerful example of the role that the Internet would come to play in our lives, a real-time tool in resolving problems and for sharing information with the world. (Also in classic style of the project, we were entirely aboveboard about the difficulties we were in: not just our teammates at JPL but anyone interested, anywhere in the world, could follow our activities over our Web site.)

What happened next became the subject of a letter I would write two months later to the director of JPL:

Miracles Still Happen

The following contains a reminder of just how special a place JPL is and some specific concerns about its future.

The place is Kennedy Space Center. The date is October 1, 1996, 2 months before the launch of Mars Pathfinder. During the activities to close the lander petals for the last time, the launch team noticed that the petals were not as well aligned with each other as had been seen in other closures and that the cups and cones were not seated properly. Under the pressure of a tight launch schedule the easy thing for the ATLO Mechanical Operations Engineer, Mike Mangano, to do would be to just push them closed and go on. But Mike didn't like what he saw and asked the team that had conducted a detailed walk through that morning to look at the situation with him. Two of JPL's best mechanical engineers, Bill Layman and Frank Locatell (with supporting roles by Carl Buck and yours truly), looked at the problem, made measurements and discussed theories and options until 7 pm. At this point we were looking at a day for day slip, eating into our remaining 7 days of contingency. We weren't sure of the cause but we knew what our options were, but reworking a fully assembled spacecraft, with live pyros, in a Kennedy Space Center clean room, looked very scary.

At 9:00 the next morning, JPL time, we held a teleconference with the lander structure Cognizant Engineer, Jim Baughman, and structures team leader Jim Staats. They heard our assessment of the situation and were asked to evaluate it themselves, start working on a set of fixes devised primarily by Frank, and converge on a design solution by 4 pm JPL time, when we'd be calling back.

Meanwhile we continued our evaluation, developing a more detailed understand of the problem and refining the design solutions. It appeared that the base petal was more flexible than anyone had thought and that it was sagging under the weight of the petals in Earth gravity. Experience told us that this new-discovered flexibility of the petals could represent a problem for the separation of the release nuts on Mars [necessary in order to free the petal for unfolding and providing an exit for the rover]. The odds were that it would be OK but it was not a risk we should take if it could be fixed quickly.

By the time of the 4:00 pm phone call, Jim Baughman was already moving on one option and had removed alignment cups and cones from the development test model at JPL and had the JPL machine shop on line to start re-machining. The design solution was agreed to (increase the diameter of the cups and cones by counterboring them open by about 4 mm) and final dimensions would be agreed to at 9:00 am PDT the following day.

So far we had lost only one day but the new hardware, tooling and procedures were needed at KSC [the Kennedy Space Center] as fast as possible. By some miracle, Jim and the machine shop finished the design, remachined the parts and Jim was on a red eye flight that evening, Oct. 3rd. By the end of the next day, Friday Oct. 4th, the flight lander modifications were complete and the petals ready for closure. What at first had looked like a major mission and launch schedule risk, was now a much more robust design and it had been done in less than 60 hours, across 3000 miles.

The Mars Pathfinder Project recognizes the following for heroic effort above and beyond the call of duty: Bill Layman, Frank Locatell, Carl Buck, Jim Baughman, Jim Staats, 170 machine shop, Mike Mangano, Linda Robeck and the flight mechanical techs from Bldg 18.

There was more to this letter, which I will save for the final chapter.

CRISIS OF THE WRONG NUT

With what we hoped was the last of the problems behind us, the team started on the final close-out items, including spin balancing (just like at the tire store, before new tires are installed on your car), and putting the whole spacecraft back together one last time. For this close-out operation, the team worked ten to twelve hours a day, finishing off by bolting the cruise stage and aeroshell together.

I remained at the Cape for this, so was on hand for what might be called "the crisis of the wrong nut."

Frank Locatell was going over the paperwork for the release nuts, intricate pieces of machinery that are part of the assembly holding the backshell to the lander. Following the entry into the Martian atmosphere, small charges fire, driving stiff pistons, allowing each of the nuts to fall away in three parts and so freeing the bolts that were screwed into them. With all the six bolts letting go, the lander, no longer attached to the backshell, deploys down its bridle.

It says something about the level of detail examined in the walk-downs that Frank discovered a very minor but possibly serious error involving the release nuts: the documentation provided by the vendor showed that one of the nuts on the spacecraft had a serial number not from the flight hardware lot but from the set of engineering models.

How much difference could it make? Engineering model hard-ware generally doesn't have to meet the same standards, doesn't have to be inspected as thoroughly. There was no way we would fly second-class release nuts; if just one let go too early, or didn't let go at all, Pathfinder would end as a pile of space debris in a large hole on Mars. After all our work, not a pretty thought.

We weighed the risk of reopening the entire aeroshell assembly, which was significant. But after a lot of conversation back and forth, the manufacturer's people were able to confirm (in writing) that they had done exactly the same testing for the engineering model units as for the flight units. A great sigh of relief all around, another poten-tial disaster avoided.

We could go back to other concerns.

Returning to JPL, I checked in with the software guys—we still didn't have final software. Meanwhile the mission test team was drilling the software, finding and fixing problems, checking on the "what ifs"—what if *this* happens, what if *that* happens. Sometimes it looked as if the software would never be finished, and even though this is a standard condition faced by virtually every mission, that doesn't make it any more comfortable. As you run out of time, you begin making concessions—"Okay, we can complete the testing of the software for the off-nominal Mars surface operations after launch. Focus on testing and retesting everything for launch and cruise, and anything to do with hardware."

I told Tony, with a smile, "We can always load the final version of software on the launch pad." He blanched, and then decided I was joking. But I was softening him up, planting the idea just in case we really had to.

JPL's mission control building had been designed without a single window, I suspect so that project people, ignorant of the world outside, would go on working unaware that the sun was setting, rising, and setting again. At this final phase of testing they were at it around the clock, largely without complaint.

Mission manager Richard Cook was running the mission control team members through rehearsals of their procedures but worried over whether we were being thorough enough in testing the events and contingencies for the moment when they would "catch the ball": after the crew at the Cape had successfully launched the spacecraft, they would no longer have any way of controlling it. About sixty minutes later, as Pathfinder left Earth orbit forever, the team at JPL would have to play catch and take over the mission.

Never involved in this phase myself, I quietly went around to ask some of the experienced hands, "Does this team look as ready as in past missions?" The answers were reassuring: "These guys are ready." But telecommunications system engineer Gordon Wood, a veteran of many missions, added a little sardonically, "As ready as anyone ever gets."

Still, we worried over a perplexing question: If just before launch our controllers at JPL couldn't communicate with the Cape, should we launch anyway? The answer we settled on was an If, Then: If this happened early in the launch window, when we still had many days of margin—No, we'd wait.

But if it happened late in the window—Yes, we would launch; we had designed the system so there wouldn't be any commands we would need to send to the spacecraft right after launch, and we would risk being able to come on line in time. Better that than risk missing the window and having to wait more than two years for the next opportunity or, worse and perhaps more likely, having NASA cancel the project outright.

TO THE LAUNCH PAD, AT LAST

Most of our crew of about forty people at the Cape were now finished with their work. They could relax after a fashion, but remained on standby in case some ugly circumstance should require opening Pathfinder once again.

Spacecraft are loaded onto their launch vehicle in the middle of the night. There is no air conditioning for the bird during the lift up the gantry; in daytime, the heat of the sun might damage the sensitive electronics, especially difficult in our case because the electronics of the rover were already being warmed by their radioisotope heaters. We agonized over what might happen should there be a problem with the crane, leaving the spacecraft dangling in the Florida morning sun; should we provide an air conditioner, just in case? But it was unlikely, and in any event, no appropriate unit was available—we would have had to patch something together. The cost outweighed the risk. We would take our chances.

On the night of November 21, once again a whole fleet of vehicles pulled up to the front door of our assembly building. Security is always heavy when a spacecraft moves there, but in addition we had live rockets and 200 pounds of explosive propellant.

With our spacecraft protected in a temporary shroud and loaded onto the open transporter vehicle, the caravan crept along at not much faster than a walking pace, moving from the Kennedy Space Center to the other side of the base, Cape Canaveral Air Station, and to launch pad 17B. There a giant crane picked up the spacecraft, raised it some hundred feet, and gently placed it atop the Delta II. Bolting it in place took only a matter of minutes. Technicians then began making the connections to start the flow of power and electronic signals between spacecraft and its launch vehicle, and from there to the blockhouse, control room and JPL.

Pathfinder was now in the hands of the well-experienced Delta II launch team.

12. Plan, Then Improvise

> There is nothing so useless as doing efficiently
> that which should not be done at all.
>
> —Peter Drucker

COUNTDOWN: 3 WEEKS TO LAUNCH

With Pathfinder safely installed at the top of the Delta launch vehicle, the two control teams, one at the Cape, the other at JPL, settled into a routine of practicing countdowns. "T minus four, switch to internal power," and the rest.

We had about fifteen people in our small room at JPL, where from the moment of launch, mission manager Richard Cook would become responsible for the health and safety of the spacecraft; not incidentally, he was also one of our best hands-on flight directors. Other consoles were manned by the ACE, or flight controller, who was in charge of communications over the deep space network; and controllers in charge of propulsion, power, attitude control, systems, software, rover and telecommunications.

The Cape had boomed with raw excitement in the days of the early astronauts, when the good old U.S. of A. was in a space race with the "Commies" and John Kennedy had promised us a man on the moon by the end of the sixties. Warm days, white hot nights of beer and laughter and beer.

Maybe, along with the palmetto bugs and the no-see-ums, some of the excitement of those days still lingers in the air. Maybe. But the excitement that made the blood pound for the members of the Pathfinder team wasn't left over from thirty years earlier. It was the real here and now of this magical time, this special moment, when you've done it, you've really built the machine you set out to build, and it's there, out there under the night spotlights, sitting there waiting for the launch signal to be sent, and it's really going to happen, this thing you've been working on for too many hours a week, for too many weeks and months, it's really going to happen. To Mars!

And there's always this little voice somewhere in the back of your head, this little voice that won't be stilled and can't be ignored, that says, "Something could still go wrong." There are so many, many things that have to go right for this to work. You look around you and know everyone else is hearing the same internal voice whispering the same infernal message but everyone is intent, concentrating, occasionally smiling, not letting on, not saying anything about it out loud for fear of jinxing the mission.

The twenty-six-day launch window would open at 11:09 P.M. California time on Sunday, December 1, 1996. We would have until the day after Christmas to send our bird on its way.

As so often happens at the Cape, we became the victims of Florida weather. The JPL team was scheduled to assemble at 5 P.M. but well before that time, the high-altitude winds increased, and then got worse. When it finally became clear that the situation wasn't going to improve, the launch director at the Cape canceled for the day. We would try again tomorrow. One day down, twenty-five to go.

The next day, December 2, the weather was cooperating. At 5 P.M. as scheduled, the JPL team members took their stations in the mission control room, joining the lengthy countdown already in progress for hours.

So that family, friends and interested JPL employees could share in the event, I had arranged to open the doors of JPL's von Kármán auditorium, where we had large TV displays set up. And since as flight system manager I had no official duties for the launch, I had taken on the job of host for the event.

As launch time approached I sat in the auditorium watching the mission control room activity on the monitor, thinking, "If something goes wrong now and we have to replace a lander part, could we do it and still be back on the pad within the launch window?" Take the spacecraft down and back to our assembly building, gingerly open it up, pull out the defective unit and install a new one, carefully button everything back up, paradoxically working as fast as we could but also as carefully, knowing the grave risk of mistakes and oversights when you're hurrying. But yes, if a problem happened early enough in the launch window and we still had the energy and determination for one last, great, incredibly heroic effort, yes, we could probably do it.

A few years earlier, Mars Observer, awaiting launch in the sultry humidity of hurricane season, suffered damage when an untested air-conditioning unit was turned on, blowing dust and gunk all over the spacecraft. The team had taken it down, cleaned it off, reinstalled it, and gone on to a clean launch. If the need came, we wouldn't likely have it as easy: because of Pathfinder's "Russian doll" design, we'd only be able to repair the spacecraft by taking it all apart.

I should not be thinking these thoughts.

The hands of the clock had not been moving but now showed 10 P.M. And finally, 11. Three minutes to launch. Everything going smoothly, not a hitch, except for my own state of nerves.

Sixty seconds to go, fifty, forty, thirty, and then something is wrong, voices and confusion, the clock is still running but no launch, now the countdown has been halted, does anybody know what the hell is going on?

The air cleared with explanations a few minutes later. Two separate ground computers monitor telemetry from the Delta rocket. The two must agree with each other precisely. They didn't agree. The launch had been scrubbed. Another day lost.

The Delta II is the Old Faithful of launch vehicles, a grandfather in the business, extremely reliable, a graduate of more than two hundred successful launches. (Happily we could have no way of knowing that the next Delta II launch following ours would blow up a few hundred feet off the ground!)

We had agreed early on, as a cost-saving measure, to use only one of the two launch opportunities per day, which gave us only a single instant in every twenty-four hours when the Earth's rotation would point the Delta II in the right direction in space for the launch. You're ready to go at that instant, or you've missed for the day.

For Tuesday the launch window (maybe "launch *slit*" would be a more appropriate term) was at 10:58 P.M. The team was settling in, more relaxed, pretty much over the opening night jitters. I was again hosting families and friends in the JPL auditorium. We had live TV feeds and audio from the pad and our local control room running to our display monitors, and even though it was past 10:30 at night, the big auditorium was full of people eager to share the excitement of the launch. I came up with a way of letting these enthusiasts play a small part in the action and rehearsed them for the moment.

At about T minus twenty minutes, the launch director at the Cape polls all his people, and then the flight director at JPL does the same. We all heard Richard Cook over the audio as he went down the list, receiving a Go from each person in turn. When his voice came over the speakers, "Flight system manager," I cued the audience and they shouted in one voice, "GO FOR LAUNCH!!!"

On the monitors we could see the control team at their consoles, stunned reaction followed by laughter as this unexpected response thundered through their headsets.

The third time was the charm. The countdown went without a hitch or delay. And then all the flames and roar we've seen so many times, but this time, for us, meaning so much more. Off she went, a spectacular sight in the Florida night sky. I felt, we all felt, a true sense of accomplishment, and, corny as it sounds, my eyes still well up with tears when I see a replay of that video.

We watched it through the lens of the remarkable tracking camera, continuing to show us an image of the Delta as the first set of six solid rockets fell away and the second set of three ignited. And then she was gone from sight.

LEARNING TO IMPROVISE

The Pathfinder management team had made it through those three years by striving toward a set of goals, backed by a general plan for achieving those goals that was clear to everyone—while at the same time appreciating that slavishly trying to follow that plan could sink us.

Everybody understands the need for a plan, one of the basic notions drummed into the head of every student of business, the sciences, architecture, engineering, almost every field, in fact, except perhaps the arts. Even my daughters in grammar school have homework planners.

But in the world of Faster, Better, Cheaper, improvising should be seen as an inseparable part of planning, the other half of a complete process. Yet improvising scares some people silly and is overlooked by too many others. Certainly it's easy to become married to the idea that "We've got a plan, we need to stick to it." And there's an unarguable logic to that position, right?—if you're not going to follow the plan, then you've wasted all the time spent creating it.

On Pathfinder, we had a plan but *knew* from the start that the plan was not going to be perfect, that when we "met the enemy," we would need to be highly flexible.

I'm surprised at the number of people who don't have the willingness to improvise, who just want to stick to the plan. Some managers do find life less complicated that way—so much energy has gone into the planning that they want to sit back and say, "Just go do it." And then stay glued to the chair and monitor. They want to know, "How are you doing with respect to the plan?" Even on Pathfinder, we had a senior manager early in the project who actually said, "I planned this, I don't want to change the plan." It didn't seem to matter to him that the plan no longer fit the circumstances. He did not stay with us long.

People too much in love with their plan behave like a robot programmed to attempt moving forward no matter what obstacle it encounters. Such robots rarely reach their goal.

This goes back to the Fourth Level of Change: if you've recognized you're in a situation where a static plan is not going to work (and I think I've never seen a situation where a static plan remained workable), then it follows you must also have recognized that you and your team will need the ability to improvise.

In the fast-paced, rapidly changing world in which we now live and do business, the ability to improvise has risen to near the top of the priority list of managerial skills. If you can't adapt nimbly yourself, then you won't be able to lead a nimble team. Feet firmly planted in concrete = Plan most likely doomed to fail.

A leader needs to recognize and reward people who correct and improvise as they become more knowledgeable, encounter problems and identify opportunities. And a leader must be unafraid to *lead* through the changes. Here leaders play perhaps their most important role—not in making the plan, which is, by comparison, the easy part, but by accepting that they must be prepared to deviate when circumstances change, to identify the new direction and lead decisively in that new direction. This is high velocity leadership at its best.

For three years it had been a wonderful experience to watch the people of the Pathfinder team rising to the myriad challenges. In the atmosphere we created, where everyone knew that improvising wasn't just accepted but expected, we began to see that ability displayed everywhere we looked. But some were certainly world-class champions of the art, people like Tom Rivellini with the airbags; Mike Mangano, Guy Beutelschies and Dave Gruel with testing; Rob Manning with entry, descent and landing; and Richard Cook with Mars surface operations.

And yet . . . Little did we know that the toughest challenges in that department still lay ahead.

AROUND EARTH AND INTO THE SUNLIGHT

Fifty-three minutes after launch, high over the South Pacific, the second and then third stages of the Delta vehicle burn, propelling our cargo out of Earth's orbit and on its way to Mars.

Now completely free of the launch vehicle, Pathfinder's antenna is clear of obstructions and the craft starts sending out a signal, trying to communicate with its makers. Within seconds of when we expected it, the first signal comes through. The small control room at JPL erupts in applause.

At the telecommunications console, Gordon Wood and Laif Harke report the radio signal fading in and out at the rate of about sixteen times a minute, confirming the correct spin rate of 16 rpm as the antenna turns toward and then away from Earth. Everyone is poring over computer screens that have just sprung to life. Everything is looking great. Our baby is in space and healthy.

The first black news hits while the team is still grinning and babbling over how well everything is going. With the spacecraft now out of sun shadow, the voice of Miguel San Martin comes over the headsets and loudspeakers artificially calm, as if he is forcing himself not to show what he's feeling: "The sun sensor isn't reporting."

An immediate chill settles over the JPL control room. Everyone understands what this means. Pathfinder has been designed to fly with a radio antenna pointing toward Earth and the solar arrays oriented to catch the sunlight. Not immediately but soon enough, the spacecraft will need to determine the sun's position so it can orient itself properly. Without a working sun sensor, it has no way of doing this. The mission isn't in any imminent danger, but this is a serious worry. The bubble has just burst on our illusion of a trouble-free beginning.

We start bouncing possible causes and solutions. But it is now 5 A.M. and mission manager Richard Cook makes his decision: "The spacecraft is healthy, it can fly happily for the time being without the sun sensor. We'll tackle this tomorrow."

One by one the people at the consoles stand up and stretch and turn things over to the second-shift team. We've been zapped with the charge of a lifetime, the surge of seeing the hardware we had designed and built and tested, handled and nurtured and fussed over and fumed at, given its fiery sendoff. And, with a single, surely temporary glitch, it *worked*, just as advertised, just as we had imagined it, dreamed it.

Maybe it's human nature, or an engineer's humility, but you can't help but feel surprised when such a complicated machine actually works. We had reached the launch pad on budget and on schedule, and with only a small headache, the machine was flying as designed.

We were heroes, at least in one another's eyes.

CONTINGENCIES

After launch, for many of the team the job was over, for them the mission accomplished, the impossible achieved. The operations team was now in charge, the people who would monitor and control the spacecraft during its seven months of flight and operate it when, we hoped, it would safely land on Mars. I would continue the day-to-day management of the mission while simultaneously running my spacecraft-to-a-comet project, Champollion.

If "Plan, then improvise" had been a main theme of Pathfinder during development, it would have to be that raised to the nth power during flight and preparations for landing. The nucleus of people staying on faced the first test with the misbehaving sun sensor, especially perplexing because the device is simplicity itself— just a solar cell, a piece of silicon, looking out through a narrow slit. So simple that we had never dreamed it would present a problem.

For so many of the other devices we had thought about every possible way they might fail, had planned corrective actions, and tested and trained until the team could do many of them blindfolded. Not enough power from the solar array?—check: we had a plan. Something squirrelly about the star tracker?—they're notorious problem children, and we were ready. And so on throughout the spacecraft. But for the sun sensor—sure, we had five of them, but this early in the mission, only two pointed in the direction of Earth, and we had provided no other "what ifs."

The team was able to verify that one sensor was indeed reading nothing, but the other was working well, just not putting out a very strong signal—only one-fifth the strength it should have been. Miguel San Martin then figured out strategy to fool the software into using the low-voltage reading anyway. (For the technically minded, a low-voltage reading from the sun sensor is considered invalid data, and the reading is suppressed; Miguel devised a way to ignore the "bad data" flag, allowing the onboard computer to use the voltage readings and calculate the spacecraft attitude.)

It seemed that some kind of contamination must be blocking the sensors. Worried the condition might grow worse, I took the lead on this one myself and finally decided it was most likely residue from one of the pyrotechnics of the Delta launch vehicle. (Much later, the Delta people at Boeing, after studying the possible causes and doing some tests, would confirm that the vehicle had one pyrotechnic device right next to the sun sensors that could release material during the firing and leave a residue. We couldn't prove this was the cause beyond reasonable doubt, but, to their credit, the Boeing people changed the design so later missions would not face this problem.)

In our first major effort at improvising on a spacecraft already beyond the moon, the software team wrote some new code, a software "patch," that would direct the system to use the low-signal data from the one working sun sensor, and ignore the other. They ran the software on the test bed over and over, to make certain it was rock-solid and without error.

There's a not insignificant risk here. Nobody likes to change software on a spacecraft in flight. One oversight, one uh-oh, and the attempt to fix a single small problem could create other, giant ones. We had tested this patching process well on the ground but there is always the unexpected, the unanticipated, the never-before. Fortunately we had provided adequate computer memory for storing new software without erasing the old, so we could try the new and still shift back to the previous version if things started going haywire.

It took only three days from launch to characterize the problem, devise a solution, write the new code and verify it. Sending the new software to the spacecraft—"uploading" it—involves a number of steps but is basically a straightforward process. At least on paper.

For transmission through the vast distances of space, this was a comparatively huge file—350,000 bytes. And the spacecraft wasn't able to receive it.

We tried breaking the file into smaller pieces, hoping this would solve the problem. We tried repeatedly, smaller and smaller. Still no success.

We finally tried sending at a painfully slow data rate, about eight bits per second. That made the difference.

Richard Cook would later call this effort "the day from hell." What should have been a simple procedure in the end took twenty long, sweaty, frustrating hours.

But once uploaded, the new software worked fine. Pathfinder was reading the sun signals and interpreting them using just the one nearly blind sensor.

One crisis down. How many more to go?

BURN

Four times on the way to Mars we had planned to give Pathfinder a nudge to refine its course, the same way a sailor makes adjustments as wind and tide set him off the track he meant to sail, or an airline pilot adjusts to follow a great circle path.

The first of these "trajectory correction maneuvers" was originally planned to take place in mid-December, two weeks after launch, but the sun sensor problem had led us to push it downstream another week. Morgan Parker, part of the group that had designed the propulsion system, would be seeing his team's hardware light up for the first time. Finding him a bit nervous and high-strung didn't surprise anybody—there are so many things that can go wrong. Naturally enough, his case of nerves transmitted to everybody else. You could cut the tension with a knife.

We had worked out a slew cf contingencies—If the engines didn't fire in unison and with equal thrust, we'd immediately shut down. If the spacecraft started to "nutate"—wobble like a spinning top—its computer would swing into action with a program of steps to dampen the wobble that the attitude control team, under Miguel, had laboriously worked out and tested to perfection.

The spacecraft was commanded to turn and orient itself in the attitude the navigators had called for. The thrusters fired and worked perfectly so that the spacecraft turned and settled in the right attitude. Once we'd verified that everything looked good, Richard Cook ordered the commands to be sent that would start the big burn.

From the telecom station came the welcome report, "The Doppler shift looks right." The burn was textbook-perfect.

The only unhappy person in the room was Miguel San Martin. He had been looking forward to seeing some nutation, so he could watch the damping program prove its worth. But the propulsion system had been so carefully aligned and balanced, there had been no need.

WHEN ENERGY FLAGS

It would be months before we had to do another burn. With the performance of all the subsystems confirmed and all the high-risk operations behind us, the control room team shifted into a kind of cruise mode, the way an airline pilot, on reaching the assigned flight altitude, sets the autopilot and relaxes, more observer than active operator. The team would take assigned shifts for eight hours at a stretch, three or four times a week, at whatever time of the day or night the pass occurred.

But now the energy level dropped. The team could envision months of routine conditions, no panic projects to absorb every waking moment, nothing much happening. A yawn.

Now a kind of malaise set in, a torpor. People were self-satisfied, proud of what they had achieved, and walking around as if half asleep. The transition from manic to "normal" was more than they could handle.

Richard Cook, Rob Manning and I worried about how to pump the gang up and fire them into motion again. There was still plenty to do. Plans hadn't yet been solidified and tested for the critical first few days of operations on Mars. We knew trying to squeeze too many things into the first day could be fatal—too much chance for making an unrecoverable mistake if the hardware, not to mention the test team, was overloaded. The rover team had always pressed to drive the rover off the lander and onto the surface on the first day. To do that required a set of pictures and a full assessment of whether conditions were safe for deploying the rover. All of that planning had to be done, sequences built and thoroughly tested.

And we still weren't comfortable about the entry/descent/landing software. David Gruel had done as much testing as anybody thought we'd need, and then some, for normal conditions, when everything was working as designed. But for the many "off-nominal" situations, he and his people faced months more work based on the latest results from "the mother of all simulations."

Both of these efforts—testing the operational plans for the first few days, and verifying the entry/descent/landing software for off-nominal conditions—needed access to the Pathfinder test bed. We had not appreciated how much test time would be needed this late in the project. Dave Gruel was grousing, "We can't do all this," and I was beginning to see we would need extra shifts to get all the testing done. Back to extra-long work hours for people who just wanted to coast for a while.

At times like this, the informal, occasionally prankish atmosphere we'd created (not so much by design but because it matched personalities of so many of the team) came to the fore. Jennifer Harris helped keep people from turning cranky with little stunts like bringing in something that looked like an ostrich egg and hiding it in people's offices; anyone who found it got to hide it in someone else's space. After a few days people started to worry about what would happen if it broke, but that didn't stop them from playing with it in the control room. (I could just imagine the smell and mess of a rotten, softball-sized egg broken over the flight director's keyboard.)

Dave Gruel, too, had his own way of nabbing laughs: sticking some inappropriate object into the Mars-terrain test bed, which the team would discover over the cameras in the middle of the next test. One time it was a philodendron plant, another time, a skeleton. Small distractions that helped relieve the pressure of the still-too-long days.

THE CHALLENGE TO IMPROVISE

In March, as Pathfinder neared its halfway point to Mars, we began a weeklong simulation to drill the control team on the operations from the beginning of entry into the Martian atmosphere through the first days on the surface—called Operational Readiness Test Five, or ORT5. It turned into a sour comedy of errors that at least had the benefit of giving everyone a wallop on the side of the head, another wake-up call that worked.

Dave Gruel had done his Gremlin best in setting up unusual conditions and unexpected situations to challenge the team's ability at figuring out what was going on and improvising a quick fix. But the problems began long before reaching Dave's first booby trap. To make the drill as realistic as possible, the test began at midnight and would run on real time, minute for minute as if we were controlling the actual spacecraft from the beginning of its approach. Things had hardly begun before we discovered that the timing clock we were relying on had not been set correctly, so nothing was going to happen at the correct moment. Testing was halted and everybody had to wait while the software clocked through its whole sequence back to the start.

The mission manager had planned events to begin with the final course correction to put Pathfinder on track for the selected target site, then through the entry/descent/landing sequence. Anything that could get bollixed up, did. By the time our simulated spacecraft had landed on the Martian surface, we were well behind the real-time schedule—not by minutes, by *hours.*

They say that airline pilots in a flight simulator being tested on in-flight emergencies work up a sweat and pulse rate just as if they were coping with the real thing. I have no trouble believing it. The operations of getting the first images from the camera, and readying Sojourner for the drive off the lander, had us all tense and edgy.

Before starting the process, the rover team members first had to satisfy themselves the lander had come to rest in a safe condition, so that the two ramps for the rover could be safely deployed. This wasn't difficult—the view from the stereo camera on the mockup lander in our sandy, imitation-Mars test bed showed a 3D view of the ramp that seemed at quite a steep angle but within acceptable limits. The rover guys were ready to command the vehicle to drive off. Richard Cook and I tried to suggest they move cautiously, think the situation through, make sure they were making the right decision. The words of caution were ignored—they had analyzed the situation, damn it, and were ready to proceed.

They were certain but entirely wrong. Cruel Dave Gruel had created a monster headache of a challenge—building a mound of sand in front of the lander, and creating a pit behind it. The rover team recognized the real danger of driving off the front ramp, leaving the rover to negotiate down a quite steep sandy hill on which it would have little traction. That meant they *had* to use the rear ramp. Because of the pit Dave had created, this ramp was sitting at an extreme angle, but at least the rover's unique metal wheels were designed to give good traction on the ramp.

We would later discover that the software program created to determine the steepness of the ramps had an error in it, and was giving the rover people incorrect data, making them think the angle was within safe parameters—shallow enough an incline for the rover to use.

Running a couple of available calibration checks had shown that something wasn't right. Yet the attitude of some of the rover people, so cocky, so certain of their judgment, kept them from stepping back and questioning their decision.

Later, when they saw the test bed setup and realized they had been prepared to drive the rover toward disaster, I didn't have to say a word. The experience had waked us all up.

The time while we fought our way through to sanity on this one only increased how far we were behind our supposedly real-time clock. By the end of the second day, with things continuing to go cockeyed, Richard Cook became desperate for a way to pump in some energy. Using what he would later claim was "a Brian Muirhead method," he attempted to get people riled up. "We need to clear the slate, set the clock back and start all over again," he announced. In fact, I thought he had a point—the whole business was just too frustrating, littered with too many dumb mistakes, one piled on top of the next.

But as Richard had calculated, the team members rose to the bait. "We're making mistakes but we're learning a lot," they said. "Let's keep going." He played reluctant for a bit, then let himself be talked into it, and the test continued.

When the exercise was over I didn't have to tell anybody my conclusion—they had figured it out easily enough for themselves: "We're not ready to land." Gruesome, unnerving. The beast called *fear* had plopped down in our midst.

It was enough to goose the energy level back up. The adrenaline that had carried us through all those months up to launch was flowing again.

Over the following months we repeated Operational Readiness Tests several times, with increasingly better results. It began to look as if we might pull our act together in time, after all.

The original ORT5 session had taught us, among the myriad other lessons, that we had entirely missed the boat by not having a set of procedures written out to guide us from one step to another in the complex timeline. Particularly unhappy about this oversight was Jennifer Harris, the young woman who would be the flight director for the first day on Mars. (A Martian day, called a "sol," lasts twenty-four hours and thirty-seven minutes; Jennifer would serve as flight director on "sol 1.") Richard and Jennifer took the lead in writing the procedures that we should have been working on months ago.

Mission manager Richard Cook had selected Jennifer for the crucial job of flight director, plucking her from a position doing operations planning and software development and testing. Crucial because the flight director is responsible for the health and safety of the spacecraft during her shift—dealing with contingencies, making or approving all decisions, handling all problems or emergencies. Jennifer must have seemed an unconventional choice for the job. Neither macho nor propeller-head techno-nerd, she is quiet and low key, highly competent without being obvious about it.

(Going against the stereotype of a single-minded engineer, Jennifer periodically takes off on missionary expeditions . . . to the Ukraine. Twice during the project when she left on these adventures, my biggest concern was that she might fall victim to some freak accident in the rapidly deteriorating conditions of the former Soviet Union, and never come back.)

The Pathfinder team had become highly skilled in reacting quickly to problems. We had to figure that the first days of operations on Mars would put that ability to its most severe test, especially for Jennifer. The spacecraft might land in a crater. Or the terrain might be rougher than we planned. Or the performance of key subsystems might be degraded. Conscious we could be surprised, we did our best to expect the unexpected.

The test would be how quickly we could assess the situation, determine where we were with respect to our plan, and improvise our way back to our goals. I was growing increasingly confident, as we continued testing, that we'd be ready for almost anything.

By then, when reporters would be writing the story and cameras would be pointing at us, it would be our finest hour or our worst humiliation.

"DO_EDL"

Early in May as I sat at a meeting, my pager buzzed. A call from mission control; I phoned back and the call was taken by Rob Manning. "You've got to come here quick."

"What's happening?"

"No time to explain, just get over here fast."

Something has happened, something so bad he won't tell me on the phone. I set off at a dead run across the lab to the mission control building.

"What's wrong?" I blurt breathlessly as I bolt through the door.

A smile from Rob. "You have to send a command to the spacecraft."

I knew immediately what he was talking about, and broke out laughing, accompanied by grins from everyone in the room. A year earlier I had casually mentioned to Rob what a kick it would be for me to send the command giving the spacecraft the ability to take control and, at the appropriate time, go into the entry/descent/landing ("EDL") sequence on its own. Rob hadn't forgotten, and the time had come.

The control room team had already sent an electronic file containing the command to the deep space network station at Goldstone, where it had been loaded onto their computer, ready for the order to transmit it to the spacecraft.

Now, at the communications console, the monitor in front of me showed a list of the files in the directory of the Goldstone computer. With everyone crowded around to watch (and to make sure I didn't do the wrong thing!), I clicked to select the file called "Do_EDL," then moved the cursor to the on-screen button labeled "Transmit," and clicked.

Minutes later the spacecraft responded that it had received the command, and had switched into EDL mode. She was on her own. From that point on, we were just monitoring—though still able to retake control right up to entry if something happened that the spacecraft couldn't handle.

All I had done was click a mouse button twice. Such a small effort, but I would never forget it.

13. Celebrate Success

The most incomprehensible thing about the
universe is that it is comprehensible.

—Albert Einstein

What if you spent years building a magnificent bridge connecting New York City to the Long Island resort communities of
the Hamptons, and when you finished, hardly anybody knew it
existed?

"Ridiculous," you say. "Everyone would know." Well, yes, a project of that magnitude would hardly go unnoticed. Yet this same
attitude of "Everyone will know" seems to infect many team leaders, project managers, product managers, and department heads—
many of every job title who haven't yet understood that
communicating the results, benefits, profits from your achievement,
should be one of the checkoff-list items in every effort or project.

It's not a matter of seeking personal glory or promotion or financial reward (nothing wrong with those, but we're looking here at
something much nobler and of ultimately greater benefit). Your next
project when this one is finished, your access to funds and other
resources, your reputation for handling difficult challenges, grow
not from achievements but from people *knowing* about the achievements. You owe it to yourself and your team to make sure your
accomplishments are not overlooked.

What's more, you owe it to your boss, who needs regular input
from you about your progress, intermediate successes, overcoming of

obstacles and reaching of milestones, so that he or she can gain support up the ladder, the kind of support that, again, may translate into the bigger budgets and the more challenging, higher-profile projects.

There's a payoff from making the success well known internally and among peers, as well: building prestige and reputation of the group. This translates into morale, pride and satisfaction among the team members when others in the organization have heard of the successes, perhaps even been awed by them. And it tends to bring the best workers from other groups knocking at the door, wanting to become part of this successful group that is building a reputation for overcoming barriers and getting the job done. What management consultant Arynne Simon calls the "A" Players are people who want to be part of a winning team.

Yet there's obviously a significant risk to high visibility. If your project is not the success you'd hoped for or promised, if—everyone's nightmare—it becomes an out-and-out failure, you will have no place to hide.

The experience of Pathfinder taught me that you must educate your peers and management early about the inherent risks, and prepare them for the possibility of failure. If your project also (hurray and alas!) has high visibility in the public domain, you need to educate the media as best you can on what could go wrong. Openness and honesty are clearly the best policy. People can smell it when you're not being truthful and that can breed a public relations disaster.

But when you succeed, let people know it. Let no significant achievement go unheralded. Celebrate success.

CONGRATULATIONS

It was the merest coincidence, yet somehow fitting, that all those mortar explosions of our spacecraft, all those fiery displays and pyrotechnics, the parachute and rockets and all the other events of the landing described earlier in these pages, should happen as Americans were celebrating the most important day in our national calendar. We could not have conjured it better if we had been able to select the landing time by design.

On that July 4, once we knew that Pathfinder had safely landed on Mars, I took advantage of a silent period when the spacecraft was not transmitting, saving its batteries, waiting for the sun to rise, to slip briefly away. I hadn't been outside our windowless control room since well before dawn and stepped out to be greeted by a beautiful sunny Southern California afternoon. As I walked across the Lab, a place that should have been deserted over the Independence Day holiday, people appeared from every direction. Some called "Congratulations!" or "Great job!" Others, most of them strangers, came up to shake my hand and pat me on the back. As I walked on, accepting the outrush of greetings, my steps grew a bit springier, my head and shoulders a bit straighter.

With a little help (okay, more than just a little) from CNN, television news, and teams of reporters and photographers, we were celebrating success. Sure, your own project for building a new factory, planning a new sales effort, launching a new pharmaceutical, or installing a new customer-support program may not bring a swarm of national media people. But the principles are the same: let people know of your achievements. And not just at the end of the project, but throughout the journey.

ROVER PROBLEMS

Shortly before 7:30 P.M. on landing day, I sat down next to Jake Matijevic, the rover manager. A friendly, affable guy, more college professor than hard-nosed manager, he had done an excellent job leading the rover development after taking over from Donna Shirley. But now his usual smile was missing; my adrenaline level took another leap. Jake said, almost calmly, "We haven't heard from Sojourner since 3:20 this afternoon."

My first thoughts went right to the worse-case scenario: the rover's dead. Could we have come so far only to stumble on the one-yard line? But just as quickly my knowledge and experience and positive outlook all kicked in. "We've had problems before with the rover communications and we've worked them all out. Jake, let's not panic," I told him. "Not yet . . . "

The rover team, trying to make sense of the problem, had managed to pin it down to a communications glitch but couldn't tell whether the garbles were on the lander side or the rover side. The rover and lander talk to each other through those commercial radio modems (the ones about which we had joked that Motorola warned they would not honor the warranties on if we sent them to Mars). How ironic if a $150 box, so small it would fit into a shirt pocket, took down Sojourner, star of the mission!

But why would a system that had been working earlier in the afternoon suddenly go haywire? We tried the only remedy available—cycling the units on and off. This "fix" had worked during testing.

Not this time.

If we couldn't communicate, the scientific contributions of the rover would be virtually nil, a prospect none of us wanted to dwell on. While the vehicle did carry a backup program that would start automatically within days, it wasn't likely to provide the results we had hoped for, if it worked at all. It was going to be a long, sleepless night for the rover team.

I went home exhausted, still with a cloud hanging over me. Over all of Pathfinder.

MORE ROVER PROBLEMS

The next day I was seated next to Art Thompson at the rover control console at 3:30 when the rotation of Mars put us in communication once again. A magazine writer on hand in the control room later wrote that in my excitement I *shouted* the news, "We have rover data!"

The gods were with us. During the night, the lander computer had unexpectedly reset, clearing the problem that had so plagued us the day before. The rover and lander were talking to each other again.

A palpable sense of relief flashed through the control room. Matt Wallace, power engineer for the rover and lander, described the moment at a press conference later that day by saying, "It felt like we'd been invited back to the party."

Next, the sequence of commands for deploying the ramps designed for the rover to drive off the lander, much the way new cars arriving at an auto dealership are driven down a ramp from the delivery truck. These ramps were another ingenious innovation, dreamed up by an adroitly clever and highly competent member of the rover mechanical team, Lee Sword.

 (VideoNotes: www.HiVelocity.com, "Rover ramps unfolding.")

Imagine a strip of metal like a slat from a metallic Venetian blind, the kind with a curl in each slat; now imagine rolling up this slat like a narrow strip of carpet, and fastening down the roll. When you free it, the strip will spring back out to its original long shape. A pair of such strips, with some nylon webbing stretched between them, and you have a rover ramp.

Our design provided two separate ramps, one at the front of the rover, one at the rear, giving us a choice in case a rock or hill stood in the way, or some other problem made one unusable, as in Dave Gruel's test months earlier. At least one of the two, we fervently hoped, would end in a suitable position.

At the same time the ramp deployed, we commanded the rover to perform its first trick: a bit too tall to fit in the spacecraft, the vehicle's suspension had been partially collapsed for the voyage. The driving motion of the back wheels against the fixed front wheels causes the rover to stand up and lock into its normal position for operating. Yet again we figuratively held our breaths—in the testing, the maneuver had not always worked.

This time it went without a hitch.

 (VideoNotes: www.HiVelocity.com, "Rover configuring to drive.")

AIRBAG IN THE WAY

When we received the photos showing the deployed ramps, the front one appeared to be unfolded but, perhaps a little too stiff for the Mars gravity, extended straight out like a diving board instead of touching the ground. The rear ramp was deployed but partly covered by one airbag that had not fully retracted.

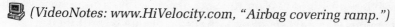 *(VideoNotes: www.HiVelocity.com, "Airbag covering ramp.")*

We thought there was significant risk that the rover wheels, with their sharp cleats designed to provide good traction both in deep, loosely packed dust and on a hard or rocky surface, could grab the fibers of the airbag, which might wrap around the wheel, lock it up and cause the rover to topple off the ramp. It wasn't designed to withstand a fall. Even if it survived a short drop, landing on its side or back would be end of story, that's all she wrote. Nobody around to set it upright again.

Some of the rover team and I went to our sandbox test bed and replicated what we were seeing on Mars, driving the flight spare rover, Marie Curie, up and down a lander ramp with a section of airbag draped over it. No snags, no wrapping. Previous reports to the contrary, everything worked fine. Howard Eisen, the lead rover mechanical engineer, finally looked at me and asked, "Can I go build the sequence to deploy Sojourner now?"

"What are you waiting for?!" I demanded, giving him a push on the shoulder as he turned to hurry out of the room.

We sent the command for the rover to start driving off backward, down the ramp that was partly airbag-covered.

Minutes later the "wheel counter" numbers began to change on the monitor displays, indicating that the wheels were turning—Sojourner had started its trip down the three-foot ramp to the surface. But just as a company launches a new product and has to wait patiently to find out if it will sell through, so we had to practice patience as well.

The scientists had already picked out the rock they wanted to visit first, one that appeared less layered with Martian dust than the others, but covered with curious features that looked like barnacles. The idea that we might find fossils flashed through our heads, a naive thought, yet in the excitement of exploring something for the first time, the imagination is given license to run free. Still, we would have to keep our wildest musings to ourselves: unfettered speculations that reached the ears of the media could damage our scientific credibility.

Partway down the ramp, the telemetry signal bringing data from the wheel-rotation counter dropped out. Again that sinking feeling. Maybe the signal quit because the rover flipped off the ramp and was lying upside down on the soil like a helpless June bug. We'd know when the next set of pictures came through. Until then . . .

As if Pathfinder were playing a fiendish game with us, the first picture of the rover moving was followed by various pictures of rocks and the lander, then another rover picture, then more rocks. We'd see a picture that showed the rover's wheels on the ramp, then nothing but rocks. (Of course, we had set up the picture-taking priorities ourselves, so had no other man or machine to blame for the frustrating wait.)

Finally, at 10:59, only minutes before we lost the communications link, there it was: Sojourner, sitting squarely on the surface of

Mars, 6 inches from the foot of the ramp, patiently waiting for instructions. Mankind's first mobile exploring machine, our 25-pound geologist, was ready to go do science on Mars. Rob Manning summed it up for all of us: "Life is complete."

🖳 *(VideoNotes: www.HiVelocity.com, "Rover on Mars, awaiting instructions.")*

SHARING THE NEWS

It was time to share the news at yet another press conference, the fourth and last of the day.

For this 11:30 P.M. function, breaking with all precedent, I invited the entire team. High-fiving one another and hooting like a bunch of cowboys at a rodeo, the vibrant Pathfinder bunch streamed into an auditorium still crowded despite the hour.

We stood to the side and cheered as Jake Matijevic presented the image of the rover on Mars. The press, normally so reserved and blasé, cheered right along with my exuberant teammates.

The reporters sensed that this group was different from what they were used to. We openly showed the emotions we were feeling, even on camera and at the press conferences. We didn't follow the familiar pattern of conservative clothes (I had decided we would not wear ties at the press conferences, since polo shirts and jeans were more our true style). Our genuine excitement and frankness—just the Pathfinder team members being themselves—seemed to be the right touch for connecting with people.

One of the reporters told me later, "I've covered big sporting events, the Indy 500, the Super Bowl, but the electricity of the Pathfinder team as they streamed through the auditorium was beyond anything I'd felt before."

It was Sunday morning at 2 A.M. when I got home. Leslie and I opened the Dom Perignon we had put on ice, and talked until 5.

OVATION AND A BRIEF DETOUR

I woke late, regretting that I had agreed some weeks earlier to give a talk at Planetfest, a gathering organized by the Planetary Society to celebrate space exploration. What could I have been thinking of? Still, Pathfinder would be asleep on Mars for several more hours, and to be a no-show for an announced speech was unthinkable.

My copy of the Planetfest schedule showed me speaking at noon, not 12:30 as I had remembered. And it was almost that time. Fortunately the site of the meeting, the Pasadena Convention Center, wasn't far away. When I reached the building, society president Lou Friedman was standing in the corridor, waiting. Hoping, I guess, that I wasn't going to let them down.

We walked into the large room and I was met by a spontaneous cheer. The next moment they were all on their feet, applauding. A standing ovation! Not something a mechanical engineer receives very often in his life. Reaching the microphone, I said breathlessly, "I guess this must be the right place."

This sea of faces, hundreds of people on their feet, clapping. And beaming at me. And I had entertained a fleeting thought of not coming! It was an experience not to be missed for all the world.

Since there had been no time to prepare, instead of a speech, the audience heard an off-the-cuff, personal and highly charged recounting about the last forty-eight hours and the emotional roller coaster we'd been riding for three and a half years. They laughed, and clapped, and seemed to cherish the stories, though later I would be unable to recall any of what I had said. After the speech it seemed as if everyone wanted to shake my hand. I was even asked for autographs. Autographs! I thought, "This is rock star stuff, not engineering!"

Afterward, starting back to JPL, I realized the sun wouldn't rise on Mars for another two hours. My car lease had run out a week ago but I hadn't been sure what to do, uncertain whether I'd still have a job if Pathfinder failed. I had made myself a little promise: If we landed safely, I would treat myself to the car I'd been wanting.

My watch showed two hours to make it happen. I drove to the Lexus dealership, pointed to the car I'd set my sights on, and made a good deal. The loan manager was excited to find out I was a Pathfinder person. "My wife and I were glued to the set all day," he told me. Who wouldn't respond to that kind of enthusiasm? I took the Pathfinder pin out of my lapel and gave it to him, and drove away in my new car in time to arrive back at mission control before the spacecraft called.

GOING FOR A DRIVE

As you might expect from scientists and engineers who had been raised on video games and Saturday morning cartoons, and in some ways never grew up, the boulders and larger rocks that looked to be of special interest were soon given names—Scooby Doo and Barnacle Bill, Shark, Half Dome and Wedge, Ender and Prince Charming. And landmarks, too—Little Crater, Rimshot Crater, Mermaid Dune, Far Knob and *Really* Far Knob.

Rover driver Brian Cooper, who ranks as an unofficial master of the video game domain, had learned to practice patience, slowing down from the blur of hand and finger motion of an expert game player to the sleepy pace of controlling Sojourner. Once he sent a command for the rover to move—say, "Turn the wheels fifteen rotations"—the message would hurtle through space for eleven minutes before reaching Mars, and then, once the command had been carried out, another eleven for the report of the action to come back and appear on his monitor. Nothing happened very fast with the rover— the little vehicle had been designed to trundle at a snail-like, excruciatingly slow 2 feet per minute.

📟 *(VideoNotes: www.HiVelocity.com, "Rover maneuvering on Mars.")*

The rover also had a kind of bug-like intelligence built in as self-protection. Relying on a primitive but ingenious combination of lasers, sensors and software, Sojourner knew when it was in danger and, usually, how to maneuver back to a state of safety. Shining two laser beams along the ground ahead, and then detecting whether the beams were straight, angled up, or dropped out of sight, the rover could decide on its own whether the ground ahead was flat enough to continue, blocked by a rock it needed to steer itself around, or falling off in some kind of crevasse or precipice it needed to avoid altogether.

Driving the rover to a desired location, Brian would back up the vehicle until snuggled to a face of the target rock, pressing against it a scientific instrument called an alpha proton X-ray spectrometer, which would then measure the elemental composition of the rock material.

 *(VideoNotes: www.HiVelocity.com, "Rover examining a rock.")*

The lander carried its own suite of instruments—weather station, dust magnets, and a color stereo camera that sent back dramatically vivid three-dimensional photos with the impact of virtual reality. Together, lander and rover were busy gathering data for the scientists and everyone else with any curiosity about the red planet.

MAKING ACKNOWLEDGMENT HAPPEN

In the career of the fortunate few, thanks to talent or happenstance or just being at the right place at the right time, there will come a project or effort that turns out to be so successful, so notable, that it effectively promotes itself. People clamor to heap praise, share in the credit, bask in the glory. That was Pathfinder—a level of success we never imagined.

The mission was honored by being chosen International Project of the Year by the Project Management Institute. Individual members won prestigious NASA Leadership awards and "Lauriettes," the Oscars of the space business, given by *Aviation Week and Space Technology* magazine. Project scientist Matt Golombek was honored with the prestigious NASA Exceptional Scientific Achievement medal. And a year later, some of us flew back to Washington where, at a black-tie affair, we were presented with an award that carried high honor and meant a great deal to the twenty of us in attendance: the Current Achievement Award, given by the Smithsonian Institution's National Air and Space Museum. This honor put us in company with past recipients including the project teams of Voyager, Magellan and the Boeing 777.

Never anticipating I would one day find myself and other members of the team popular on the speaking circuit, I'm still surprised to receive attractive offers of speaking engagements and to see such excitement from audiences as we retell the tale.

At the risk of further offending modesty, but for the sake of the record, I will also mention the feature story in the March 2, 1998, issue of *Design News* magazine naming me as its "Engineer of the

Year," with a grinning picture of me on the cover, superimposed over a shot of the rover on the Martian surface. (My daughters were unimpressed, which helped me maintain perspective.)

The renowned scientist Eleanor Helin, discoverer of many asteroids and comets, would later name a celestial body after me: Asteroid Muirhead. I was told she picked this particular one to pin my name to because it was moving uncommonly fast and was somewhat eccentric—appropriate enough, since I see these as two characteristics that serve me well as a manager. An amusing honor that tickles my sense of humor. And Tony Spear, Matt Golombek and Donna Shirley were also honored in this way.

SHARING THE PRAISE

Earlier in these pages there appeared part of a letter I wrote to the management of JPL about a particularly remarkable achievement of the Pathfinder team—a letter that was another aspect of my "celebrate success" efforts (but that also addressed areas I believe may threaten the Lab's future unless changes are made). In one section this letter acknowledges the uniqueness of JPL people:

> This kind of miracle is not unusual at JPL. Anyone who has worked on a flight project has seen them. Mars Pathfinder has had more than its fair share (the electrical, RF, mechanical, and integration/test teams have all worked major miracles over the last two years) but there is a common thread to these happy endings and it boils down to the following things: experienced generalist and specialist engineers trained through hands-on work, skilled technicians willing and able to work any hours to get the job done, the facilities and tools required to do the job and a total personal commitment to the success of our missions.
>
> We have this caliber of talent because of a development cycle that starts with the kinds of missions and challenges that attract talented, motivated engineers and technicians, who are over time trained as discipline specialists and generalists, who in turn develop, integrate, test and launch even more exciting, challenging missions, a process that equates to performing miracles on demand.

As far as I have experienced, JPL is unique in the world. It is still a place where a project or task manager can find everything from a single specialist with the required background, to the hardware-experienced generalist, the system engineer.

This breadth and depth did not come by accident. It is the direct result of giving people hands-on responsibility, allowing individuals to own end-to-end responsibility for a product.

"When the project ends, reward the uninvolved," says a caustic, mocking business adage. While the above section of my in-house letter to management heaped praise on the special qualities of JPL's people, the principles of celebrating success also call on you to "reward the involved," lavishing praise on individual contributors to your project in more public ways.

We shared the glory—by looking for opportunities to give as many people as possible the chance to be seen and heard at press conferences. By keeping alert, throughout the project, for ways to let team members know they were being widely recognized and acknowledged for their efforts and achievements. By nominating for a variety of NASA and JPL awards some sixty-five team members, the largest number of people ever (though twice that many deserved recognition).

But what if Pathfinder hadn't done so well? Tony Spear, Pathfinder project manager, had told me much earlier that if the mission was successful, he'd let the team take the credit, if a failure, he'd take the responsibility on his own shoulders. A noble sentiment but not realistic. For those of us who had been on the front lines in defining and implementing Pathfinder, there would have been no escaping the consequence of a failure. The entire team, but especially Richard Cook, Rob Manning, Curt Cleven, John Wellman, Al Sacks, Jake Matijevic and I, would share responsibility. Together we'd succeed or together we'd fall.

Success is much easier to handle.

DON'T HOLD BACK

Most people set up goals and benchmarks against which to measure their level of success. While Pathfinder was still en route to Mars, I had a benchmark in mind for measuring public interest in the mission: the front page of the *New York Times*. We would have a shot at it, I figured, if we were able to capture even a single good color image. The landing itself might be seen by press and public as "just another planetary mission." But a good photo . . .

We got that photo, and thousands more. We made the front page of the *New York Times* . . . as well as the front page of what seemed like every daily newspaper on the planet. *Time* and *Newsweek* both heralded the accomplishment with cover stories.

But we greatly underestimated the extent of public excitement. We had planned on handling a huge number of Internet hits. Who could have expected 46 million in one day, an Internet record?

Within hours after Pathfinder had successfully arrived, I had the honor of representing the project team, along with JPL Director Edward Stone and NASA Administrator Daniel Goldin, as the three of us took a phone call from Vice President Al Gore. "This is a new way of doing business, and its validity is being borne out by your dramatic success today," the vice president said. "The whole country is proud of what you've accomplished." President Clinton issued a statement that declared, "Our return to Mars today marks the beginning of a new era in the nation's space-exploration program."

Some time later, California Senator Dianne Feinstein, on a special visit to JPL just to see Pathfinder, told me that the NASA budget had come up for a vote in Congress the week before. "It sailed right through," she said with a smile—clearly convinced that our achievement had helped to pave the way.

The reputation and future opportunities for your team, your organization, your company depend not just on the success of the efforts you undertake, but on letting those efforts be known. It's good for your team and it's good for business.

Holding back doesn't pay. Praise your project, praise your team, let people know what's been achieved.

14. Putting Faster, Better, Cheaper to Work

> You only live once, but if you
> work it right, once is enough.
> —Comedian Joe E. Lewis

When asked by interviewers in the past about machines versus humans in the exploration of space, a debate that has been raging since the beginning of the space program, I had always responded by saying that to truly understand a planet like Mars, we'd need to send human scientists. To learn whether life ever existed on Mars and how it might have evolved would require that humans land there and explore. Even a single geologist using just her eyes and a few basic tools could decipher the geologic history of a place from examining a few rocks and their context. Only by direct experience would humans be able to use their insight to begin piecing together the secrets of something as complex as another planet.

But Pathfinder, a project that had been intended mostly as a demonstration of technological capabilities to point the way toward future missions, had gathered a phenomenal amount of scientific data. That, and the process I witnessed of scientists reaching new understanding from studying those data, led me to question my previous beliefs.

Then, when people from NASA's Ames Research Center set up at JPL a system providing high-definition stereo TV of our Mars images, we saw a virtual-reality environment so realistic that we could practically fly inside a rock. The technology is becoming so sophisticated that virtual exploration may one day truly be just as effective as the real thing.

The lander and rover sent back to Earth a trainload of information—2.6 billion bits of data, more than *16,000* images, and weather reports of temperature, wind and dust conditions. We are so proud that Pathfinder managed to achieve all this and a great deal more.

From these data, scientists have come to new understandings about the red planet. Some of its mostly volcanic rocks appear to have an unusually high silica or quartz content. The red Martian dust is highly magnetic. The planet has high clouds of water ice highly like Earth's that wax and wane daily. Surface temperatures at the landing site varied from 15 degrees Fahrenheit during the day to minus 150 degrees Fahrenheit at night, with changes of as much as 30 degrees in half a minute. Winds were described as "light and variable" (sounding like a Los Angeles weather report), but with frequent whirlwinds—"dust devils." The scientists were able to determine that Mars has a central metallic core like Earth's, and to provide convincing evidence, though not yet definitive, that it had once indeed been a water-rich planet, probably more Earth-like than we had previously understood.

THE HISTORY MYSTERY

When a project is completed in an organization, what becomes of the accumulated knowledge and experience gained along the way? Ninety chances out of a hundred the wisdom is carefully stored . . . in the heads of the project team. For as long as memory lasts. And when key employees leave, too often their share of the company archives walks out the door in their memory banks. Cautious firms protect their hardware by posting guards and spot-checking bags, but how does a company protect against this kind of intellectual and experiential drain?

On Pathfinder, when we wanted to design the heat shield and the parachute, people ran around asking, "What did Viking do on this? What did Viking use?"—trying to find the records or someone who remembered. We made a determined effort not to let that problem face the projects that would come after ours. I cajoled all the managers and subsystem leads to write up "Lessons Learned" reports, which we then shared at two half-day briefings with one another and anyone else interested. Their reports plus notes of the review session fill a large volume, a copy of which is permanently filed in the JPL Archives, along with videotapes of the two sessions.

Jennifer Harris took the responsibility for compiling an end-of-mission report—a hard struggle, since most of the people she needed inputs from were busy at their new jobs on other projects. But she got it done. It's available for all future missions, and also posted on the Web.

We've made it possible for details and lessons of Pathfinder to be remembered long after memories fade and people move on; this book is part of that record.

As a realist I know this to be only a half-baked legacy, a small stepping stone in the right direction. Information on a shelf is information that won't get looked at very often. On my new project, we're storing all data on line; virtually every piece of information is recorded electronically, where it's accessible to all project people at any time of the day or night.

Most of this digital project library can be accessed over the Web; though it remains behind a so-called firewall (I don't want to land in another of those "giving away national security secrets" hassles), the contractors working on the project with us can find up-to-the-minute information about virtually any aspect of the project whenever they need it. Outside providers in other countries, thanks to the borderless nature of the Web, have just as immediate access (albeit with restrictions) as the people working down the hall from me.

For their own version of Lessons Learned at the end of a project, some companies are already going a step beyond, doing what might be called "video history" segments—oral history taken to the next plateau—of key project people. One plan I admire organizes these interviews into very short clips, as short as a minute, focused on a single subject. Someone who wants to know, "What did past projects do about risk?" (or explosive bolts, or computer memory, or . . .) simply types in the key words, selects from a list that appears of every project person who addressed that topic, and screens the clips right on the computer terminal.

Why do hard-copy reports seem to get read so little these days? Maybe we're spoiled by all the information easily available over the

Web or otherwise accessible without leaving our computers, maybe we're growing lazy, maybe we've all become so busy that if something can't be in hand in a nanosecond, we don't have time to pursue it.

Whatever the reasons, the invaluable information from previous company projects needs to be captured, stored, and made instantly available. This will be an essential ingredient for all next-generation Faster, Better, Cheaper efforts.

Still, the most effective way to transmit lessons learned is person-to-person. People with experience talking to others, people sharing their knowledge and experience as they work shoulder to shoulder with others. People applying what they learned in doing a Faster, Better, Cheaper project and adapting it to new circumstances on new jobs.

I love hearing people say, "Well, on Pathfinder we did it *this* way."

THE FASTER, BETTER, CHEAPER LESSONS OF MARS PATHFINDER

Aside from the lessons learned about building a spacecraft, I gathered my own personal set of lessons about running a Faster, Better, Cheaper project. The two most important, the answer I give when someone asks, "How did you do that?" and doesn't want a forty-five-minute lecture, are these: the Team, and Hands-on Leadership. But there are a number of other take-aways that are in the second rank, and very nearly as important.

Rob Manning described in *Design News* magazine what he called "the synergism, the electric, very positive tension" of the Pathfinder team, which he thinks made possible our ability in "charting new courses, crossing new kinds of ground within an otherwise very conservative and very traditional institute." And he articulated the criterion that is my measure of a well-run Faster, Better, Cheaper operation: one that can set its own ground rules within the traditionalist structure of the larger organization.

Some have asked what made the Pathfinder team so special. I attribute it to selecting people who, even before being hired, showed an enthusiasm for the project or the challenges, a burning desire to be part of what we were trying to do. We also went for people with a higher than normal energy level (who else would be willing, or even able, to endure the work weeks of sixty hours and more, necessary to meet schedules and keep up!).

One point about the team members that surprised even me: they *liked* working in a slightly understaffed condition, a few people short of enough. Somehow it conveyed the message that every single person was critical to the success of the whole mission, which helped all of us rise to challenges. As a result, practically all the members of the team performed beyond their previous experience; I suspect even beyond what they imagined they were capable of.

The notion of demanding hands-on leadership has emerged out of my own experiences and observations. Whatever else I do, I will look for managers whose natural inclination is to work hands-on. None of those sit-in-the-office-and-draw-up-schedules managers for me. All people work harder, with greater dedication and greater verve, when their management is seen, involved and part of the action, not behind a closed door or tied up at meetings; people want to know the manager is right in there with them. And that goes for the boss's boss, and the boss's boss's boss, too—they need to be visible, they need to be in there, showing they know what's going on, calling individuals by name, asking questions, asking for suggestions . . . and then actually *listening* to the answers before taking action.

At the same time, once you've set up the conditions for the team, and the right people are working the right jobs, then *get out of the way.* Touch base, monitor progress, show support and be there to help, all part of being hands-on, but grant people all appropriate authority—apply the grease, then step aside and let them do the very best they can do. Stay close enough to the action that you're there when needed, but give them the space to maximize their personal performance.

When hiring, I ask previous bosses whether a candidate has this "hands-on" quality. Then in interviews I sound out the person to see how he or she describes attitudes, work day, and leadership strengths and weaknesses. I talk about the hands-on attitude I expect, and watch the reaction. If there's a sparkle in the eye when they describe their own experiences, I'm looking at someone who may have the right quality.

Other leadership qualities, nearly as important, that I believe allowed us to succeed against the expectations of many: the insistence on working with trust, honesty and openness at every level . . . the willingness to reverse a bad decision as soon as it was recognized.

Another practice we valued was making people stretch by putting them in jobs they were not "qualified" for by experience but that I felt, and they felt, they could handle. Nearly everyone on Pathfinder, including me, was tackling a job with demands and responsibilities way beyond anything we'd done before.

Two others that belong on this list were important implementation features for Pathfinder: collocating, bringing as many of the team as possible to work in a single building or set of adjacent offices, and the determination to spend only the first half of the available time on development, which allowed devoting the entire second half to testing. These early resolves proved to be the kind of architectural decisions you look back on after it's all over, and say, "That was a damned good call."

All these principles clearly belong to the high velocity leadership style required for working at the Fourth Level of Change.

THE FIFTH LEVEL OF CHANGE

Many people, once they have grasped the idea behind the Four Levels of Change, ask, "What's the *Fifth* Level going to be?"

With most organizations not yet operating at the Fourth Level, it's early to be making predictions about the steps beyond. But management consultants Price Pritchett and Stephanie Snyder, reading early signals by watching the forward-looking ideas of some pace-setting companies, make the point that the Fourth Level is definitely not going to be the last.

Three patterns appear to be emerging: leading this list is a shift to technology-based organizations. The computer networking firm Cisco, looking like one of the best examples of a "tomorrow" company, is structured around "organizational networks" instead of hierarchies. Something approaching 2 million pages of information are available electronically to every employee. Individuals become much more empowered to make decisions because they have access to information once available only to managers.

Second, the growing need for employees to be able to "multi-task" between the technology side and the business side—engineers learning to understand, plan and present the business equation for their projects, and businesspeople reaching a heightened comfort level in grasping the intricacies and market significance of their organization's technologies. Both sides of this multitasking relationship were in evidence on Pathfinder.

The third aspect is what Cisco CEO John Chambers describes as relying on *customers,* not the executives, for setting a company's strategic direction. When two major accounts were about to walk out the door a few years ago because Cisco didn't appear able to meet their upcoming needs, Chambers solved the problem by buying a company offering products that filled the gap, and kept both accounts.

Another trend is the growth of interdependence between organizations, in which traditional supplier relationships and partner relationships move to a higher level. We're learning about interdependence on my new project, teaming with the other projects within JPL for hardware and software and with the French space agency for engineering and scientific hardware. In both cases the "partners" are using their own money to develop and deliver flight-ready systems.

Yet interdependence brings major challenges, to the point that I sometimes consider it a necessary evil. I believe the success of interdependencies depends on all parties being fully competent to carry out their roles (not always a foregone conclusion), and sharing the commitment to the success of the project. Since management is no longer in full control of the project's fate, without both competency and commitment, interdependent relationships can dwindle downward to disaster.

I've been asked many times, "Is there anything you'd do differently?" My answer is, "No, the problem is trying to do it again." The conditions today have changed. On Pathfinder we were masters of our own fate. With today's interdependencies, that's no longer the case.

Despite these factors, I reluctantly concur with Cisco's John Chambers that partnerships and strategic alliances will be key to "the new world strategies of the twenty-first century." But I would add that the challenge is making them work. This may be where the Fifth Level of Change will come into its own.

In any period of great change, whether revolutionary or evolutionary, there comes a time of crisis that causes serious rethinking. In today's world of intense and rapid shifts, the Fifth Level of Change will likely offer powerful new ways to deal with countercurrents that stifle workers from performing at their best. When this happens, it will require a Fifth Level of *leadership*, where leaders will continue to push the envelope despite the failures that will inevitably occur.

But the drivers of change are very much set, and will take us places we can currently only guess at through the fog. Pritchett's advice: Don't become married to what works at Level Four—even the nature of change is changing.

THE DARK SIDE OF FBC

Mars Pathfinder provided extravagant proof that Faster, Better, Cheaper can work, yet it would be dangerous to suggest it should be the answer to every situation. And when misused or misapplied, FBC can be more harmful than beneficial. A few caveats are in order.

At its peak around the time that assembly and testing began, about 250 people were working full-time on Pathfinder, plus another 150 dividing their time between our project and others. No one yet knows what the maximum size is for an FBC project, but it's clear there *is* a maximum. It would be particularly foolhardy for an organization of 10,000 people to think of trying to perform an enterprise-wide Faster, Better, Cheaper project—the group is simply too large for rapid, nimble movement.

But certainly even large companies can put FBC to work within individual units or departments, or on individual projects. A good rule of thumb for the time being: a Faster, Better, Cheaper effort should be of a scope that can be within the span of control of a single leader or tight-knit leadership team (but recognizing that span of control is a function of the people themselves—some can handle a broader span than others). If the leadership can stay hands-on with most activities, and the decision-making process is fast enough to meet the project or task goals, then FBC should be viable. And once the lessons of FBC are learned on a small scale, those lessons can begin to infiltrate the larger organization. Efficiencies identified, applied and validated by an FBC team can be adopted by larger groups.

Yet one of the troublesome problems organizations face today, and JPL is a case in point, is the shortage of experienced leaders. That leaves the temptation for upper management to put an inexperienced person in charge of an FBC team. This does an enormous disservice to the team, particularly the people right below the leader.

There's a caution here for managers as well: someday you will likely be invited to lead an FBC mission within your organization. First take a hard look at the resources, scope, and degrees of freedom. If your upper management is eyeing FBC as a way to increase market share or some such motive, but has no experience with what a project of this kind really means, it will likely saddle the project with truly impossible constraints or unreachable goals. When the parameters don't fit the pattern for Faster, Better, Cheaper, have the guts to say No. Taking on a project labeled Faster, Better, Cheaper but without the resources and the freedom needed to succeed is not a sound career decision.

Every organizational leader knows that growing earnings at double-digit rates for consecutive years is difficult, and harder still after downsizing, when those who are left are expected to do more with fewer assets. In situations like that, any next great management scheme can look like manna from heaven, the best solution to all problems. Beware: there will be organizations tempted to embrace FBC for all the wrong reasons.

The *right* reasons to adopt FBC have to do with a stretch goal that represents an urgent or enterprise-critical effort, important enough that the project leaders will be given the latitude to recruit from other parts of the organization, operate in a more freewheeling manner than would otherwise be acceptable, and have the authority, responsibility and license to invent processes that offer the opportunity of grasping success. If the organization isn't willing to bestow that kind of latitude on the project leaders, then it isn't serious about doing things Faster, Better, Cheaper.

FBC is about doing things differently, doing things smarter. Face it, if the leadership isn't willing to do what *it* must do, any attempt at FBC will likely be doomed from the outset.

THE FUTURE OF FASTER, BETTER, CHEAPER FOR SPACE PROJECTS

Early on, James Martin, the chairman of our formal review panels and until Pathfinder the only man on Earth who had successfully led a team to land a spacecraft on Mars, had figured we didn't have a chance in hell of accomplishing our mission in half the time and one-twentieth the budget he had used. Martin thought we couldn't do it and said so. But as we progressed through the development, he became our ally. Jim remained constructively critical but defended our efforts when others, convinced we were going to blow the budget, sought to kill the project.

One of my nagging fears was that if Pathfinder had indeed failed, there would have been a huge backlash against the principles of Faster, Better, Cheaper. Some people would have used the failure to rail against the concept, those same people who were actually disappointed by our success. In today's society, as in today's stock market, a little bad news can create an irrational avalanche of negativity that undermines the basically healthy fundamentals and inflicts its own brand of harm.

In one respect, being the first to do a Faster, Better, Cheaper deep space project made our job easier. We proved that a planetary mission was possible for a fraction of the cost, but in the process we set the bar demandingly high, and that bar keeps getting raised. For all those missions coming after ours, it grows tougher. Pathfinder has now become the standard by which other projects are judged, and being faster, better or cheaper than Pathfinder won't be easy.

There is no universal definition of FBC and like so many things its meaning lies in the eye of the beholder, but it is and always will be a *relative* concept. The first FBC project in an organization will, if effectively managed, be groundbreaking. It will inevitably be in some ways revolutionary, defying and at the same time defining procedures, structures, relationships and traditional ways of doing things.

But what about the next one, and the next? It would be a mistake to think Faster, Better, Cheaper means that every project in the organization has to be revolutionary in being accomplished faster, producing better results, and at a significantly lower budget, than the preceding one. That way lies failure sooner or later.

Rather, I see FBC as a way of operating. The early efforts will set new patterns for carrying out projects in the organization. Subsequent projects will adopt these new patterns, these new ways of organizational behavior. The goal will not be the clearly impossible one of always setting new records for lower budget, shorter time, better results; instead, success will be measured by how well the project applies the practices of FBC as defined within the organization.

Along the way, there's a particularly hazardous pitfall to avoid. It's the natural inclination of leaders to see something that works well and try to bottle it—capture it, codify it—and require everyone to apply the process. But this is the antithesis of Faster, Better, Cheaper, which at root is the opposite of formulaic. What is inherently a dynamic, creative process dies when an organization or a manager attempts to codify and forcibly apply it.

Within the organization I belong to, the Jet Propulsion Lab, while there is a commitment to the principle of Faster, Better, Cheaper, we're still struggling to understand what it means for the diverse environment in which we work. One FBC project does not an organization make; it will only be through a series of projects that we finally grasp what FBC means to JPL.

But changing our ways of doing business, adopting FBC, is necessary to keep JPL alive and thriving.

The key to JPL's success, as I've said many times to the Lab's management, is in its hands-on people—so many people trained and developed through being personally involved in the design, building, testing and flying of real spacecraft on challenging missions.

The people of JPL are committed to conducting missions like Pathfinder Space Technology 4/Champollion, so that JPL will continue to grow and remain the preeminent leader in deep space exploration. The Lab has a rich legacy in space, and I continue to be dedicated to playing whatever role I can to ensure that the legacy will continue.

THE END OF PATHFINDER

NASA and military aerospace have had a long history of budget overruns—out of hundreds of missions, I suspect only a handful of projects were ever completed at their originally estimated cost. In that sense, Pathfinder introduced a new era. As for the Jet Propulsion Lab, the mission served as proof that the Lab could surely operate in this new mode, answering critics whose words predicted the Lab's demise. Cost growth and overruns have not been banished forever, but the tolerance for them has become very low.

The Pathfinder team, given the freedom to innovate, did just that, to an extent I hadn't realized until someone asked after the landing, "From an engineering point of view, what did the mission accomplish?" When tallied, the answer was that we pioneered twenty-five new or significantly reinvented technologies—things like the airbags, actuators, antennas, altimeter, deceleration rockets, computer (which has already become the standard for other planetary missions) and the ingenious rocker bogie suspension that allowed the rover to be so mobile. Despite more than the usual headaches and panics in development, every one of the new items did its job. We also delivered on many first-of-a-kind events including direct entry to Mars, mobility of a semiautonomous robot on another planet and rapid, nearly instantaneous mosaic image processing.

The lander and rover broke records, too. The design life expectancy for the rover had been put at about seven days. Early August came and went, and the rover was still trundling around sites like Rock Garden and Mermaid Dune. It began to look as if it might outlive the lander, though an occasional miscue by the drivers now and then caught the rover perched atop a rock or with one wheel hanging out in space. Luckily for her drivers, Sojourner was designed smart enough to keep herself out of trouble.

Based on a reasonable life span of its rechargeable batteries, we had estimated the lander could operate for at least thirty days. Eighty days after arriving, the lander was sending data and relaying messages to and from the rover as well as it had on its first Martian day, sol 1.

On September 27, 1997, sol 84, we were set up as usual waiting for Pathfinder to come into view of Earth and start its daily transmission. The time came, but no signal. It's all too easy to make mistakes in the complicated setup for communications; it had happened before. This time it was up to Jennifer Harris, who was serving as acting mission manager while Richard Cook, finally taking a long-needed vacation, was in Italy; possibly fearing just such a situation could ruin his much deserved getaway, Richard had decided to travel totally incommunicado. So, assisted by her number two, Dave Gruel, Jennifer led the controllers through the setup step by step. But they could find nothing wrong.

Though it was nearing midnight, phone calls went out to pull in the full team. We began trying all the usual suspects, starting with what the spacecraft had been doing the previous day—hunting for something we had told the spacecraft to do that was different from before. It had been woken up in the middle of the Martian night and asked to take wind and temperature measurements and photos of one of the Martian moons—I forget whether Phobos ("fear") or Deimos ("death"); if I believed in omens, I would be sure it was the latter.

We did determine that the lander had been woken up before on similar tasks, but had never had a problem. Did last night's assignment use too much power? Was the battery too weak? Or was there some command error, inadvertently telling it to do something wrong? The whole team worked for hours, trying to wake up Pathfinder and at the same time figure out what might be wrong. Jennifer finally let the rest of the team go, with firm instructions to return late the next day, in time for the next communications cycle.

Soon we declared a "spacecraft emergency." Something like clearing the skies and runways when a pilot declares an in-flight emergency, this status gave us a priority over other missions for using the giant antennas of the deep space network. Jennifer and the team, unwilling to give up, kept trying day after day to reestablish contact.

Typical of Jennifer, she remarked, only half joking, "The mission manager goes on vacation and I lose the spacecraft."

Four miserable days later, on October 1, the team decided to try switching to the backup transmitter, that "half a radio" Sam Vallas had built. Miracle of miracles, it worked—a weak carrier signal came through. We were in business once again; the team was ecstatic.

But at the time for next contact, Pathfinder's voice was again silent. The frantic messages from our control room went unanswered. Our hopes were raised by another brief, feeble signal a few days later, on October 7. After that, nothing further.

We continued to try to revive contact, but by the beginning of November accepted the fact that further efforts would be fruitless. On November 4, exactly four months after landing on Mars, we held a press conference to announce that the Pathfinder extended mission had officially come to an end. Chief scientist Matt Golombeck reviewed the impressive scientific achievements, and I gave what amounted to a eulogy.

People who had been part of the Pathfinder team gathered to say farewell, an event that, with self-mocking, we referred to as a wake. The lander's expected one-month life span had stretched out to nearly three; the rover, with its predicted life of seven days, had, incredibly, still been going strong when last able to transmit to the lander. So while there was indeed a foggy atmosphere of sadness, we chose to reflect on the upbeat aspects, the incredible success. Pathfinder had returned so much more data than we had counted on, and data of so much higher quality, that the inevitable loss was easily tempered by the sense we had accomplished far beyond what anyone had expected.

A few days later, on *Good Morning, America*, I described the loss as similar to losing a friend—an old friend who had lived a valuable and productive life. Perhaps it rationalizes away the pain, but it has a ring of truth: a time to live and a time to die. Pathfinder had passed away and we would remember our friend with smiles and tears.

ENVOI

Years before, as a young job applicant filling out a JPL questionnaire, in the space left for the answer to "What is your career objective?" I had responded with sincere honesty sprinkled with a generous lack of humility, "To make a contribution to the body of human knowledge." I couldn't have known that I might actually find a line of work that has, to my enduring surprise and satisfaction, made my presumptuous and unrealistic fantasy come true.

When I give talks on Pathfinder, people often ask, "What are you going to do next?" My one-sentence answer makes eyes go wide and mouths drop open when I describe Space Technology 4/Champollion. "I'm now working on a project that will attempt to land a spacecraft on an active comet and analyze what it's made of." The goals do indeed sound lifted from the pages of science fiction, yet we consider them feasible because Pathfinder demonstrated to NASA and to the world that the incredible of last year can become the reality of the next.

The Mars Pathfinder mission achievements are measured on a scale of space science. Yet it was most satisfying to all members of the team that people around the world experienced Pathfinder also as a success on the human level—as a cosmic adventure with what felt like very personal elements. It came as a surprise, something I still don't adequately grasp, that so many people reacted as if they themselves had been involved. It felt to them like a *universal* accomplishment. Many have said to me, "I will remember where I was on July 4, 1997." Clearly, so will I.

For the team, many felt it was the best job of their careers.

For the world, we engaged people in the spirit and adventure of exploration.

For the children, we introduced a new generation of youngsters to the excitement of space and a sense of what individuals who gain an education and apply themselves are capable of achieving.

Perhaps even more important, Pathfinder stands as a testimonial to what Bill Simon and I call "high velocity leadership": a real-world demonstration of leadership as the driving force that makes Faster, Better, Cheaper a workable business concept as we enter a new century.

I'm thankful I could be a part of it.

ACKNOWLEDGMENTS

Back-of-the-book acknowledgments to my wife are neither automatic nor trite, for she is the antithesis of anything trite, obvious or ordinary. As a result, I enjoy this chance, as each new book is completed, to admire Arynne's singular ability to comfortably and expertly combine so many roles. Her personal insistence that all work extend far beyond the ordinary has become a driving source of inspiration to me. And Arynne's youthful delight in everyday things has the power to lift what elsewhere too often become mundane—like cooking and conversation—to the heights of art. And yet many tell me she also has one of the best minds for both business and human behavior.

Her rare combinations of talents have been widely acknowledged by business leaders around the globe; as a result she travels to clients much of every week, though she knows how much I miss her when she's away. But I respect her needs for space and the freedom to be who she is; we both agree that giving each other the freedom to be who we are is the source of our many years of happiness. I consider Arynne's positive input on my work and my moods incomparably valuable. Our children, Victoria and Sheldon, would want me to include that she has become for us and for so many people a super model of skills, ethics and values.

This book, the story of a renowned spacecraft mission, is also about the driving force of the man behind that mission, Brian Muirhead. Exacting and demanding in the lab, he brought those same intense qualities to the collaborative process and this book is the better for it; in a sense we launched some lessons and landed a book. Each bringing our own demanding standards to the task of writing together, we drove each other nuts at times, but I believe will remain friends for a lifetime. Which is, after all, a real win in any effort.

Adrian Zackheim, publisher of HarperBusiness and the editor of this book, took me to lunch one day at La Côte Basque and said, "I think I may have a project for you." A fascinating subject I couldn't possibly have turned down. And then he fed enough praise to make sure I kept energized throughout the writing. Adrian, this one will be tough to beat.

Behind it all, with a graceful power of his own, is my agent Bill Gladstone, head of Waterside Productions; to him and agent David Fugate, these words of thanks are heartfelt.

How does one express appreciation to a copy editor who has the sophistication and good sense to respect the individuality of my sometimes quirky, often idiosyncratic punctuation? Thank you, Elenor Mikucki, and every other copy editor out there who understands how important matters of style are to a writer.

I couldn't possibly overlook Sue Baxter, my wife's associate, who also runs the office for us. Sue has somehow survived the pressure of making, breaking and remaking travel arrangements, schedules and phone interviews. It's been said that "God is in the details"; an office like Simon and Simon has to thank God for a Sue Baxter.

—Bill Simon

Writing a book about the Mars Pathfinder mission became a fire in my mind about two weeks after the landing on Mars. It seemed important to tell the inside, behind-the-scenes story of how a small group of unique people had pulled off this complex and seemingly impossible mission.

How can I ever thank my friend Pat McMahon, then Orange County editor for the *Los Angeles Times*, who gave me the confidence to "just do it" and then introduced me to Adrian Zackheim of HarperCollins. While on a trip to the West Coast, Adrian visited me at the Jet Propulsion Laboratory. I showed him around the

Pathfinder mission operations center and described some book ideas; he was immediately enthused about the business concepts behind the Pathfinder story and a project began to take shape.

It's also a pleasure to acknowledge consultant Price Pritchett, who quickly saw the value in the management lessons of Mars Pathfinder, and whose vision about this was another push forward. To Price, who wrote the preface to this book, and to Stephanie Snyder of his organization, I offer my warmest thanks.

I realize now how very much the time spent with Adrian, Price and Stephanie helped my thoughts and goals to mesh. Their encouragement was essential. And they forthrightly warned me about the painfully hard work ahead as a "content author" who was also holding down a full-time position with JPL. Then Adrian wisely got me together with writer Bill Simon, whose positive attitude for this particular project brought renewed vigor to my objectives.

Thank you to my wonderful daughters, Alicia and Jenna, who put up with my crabbiness while I struggled to meet the demands of this book, a new house, and JPL.

A special thanks to the Muirhead family, especially my grandparents, who are gone but often remembered. They were not quite sure I'd make anything of myself but they loved me anyway.

To my significant other, whom you met in the pages of this book: you are more than a wife, best friend and lover, thank you for believing in me, it has helped more than you will ever know.

It's appropriate that a major acknowledgment goes to my coauthor Bill Simon, whose skill, patience, tenacity and long hours made this work possible. Like me, Bill is not afraid of any challenge. Undaunted, we set out to do what would be best for the reader—no matter what it would take.

Bill has also contributed to the publishing world an idea that I expect will become a historical milestone: this book is the first to expand the text with video clips on the Web—"VideoNotes"—so that readers can get a complete and accurate picture of what took place by seeing Pathfinder in action.

I'd like to thank members of the Pathfinder team David Gruel, Richard Cook, Tom Rivellini, and Leslie Livesay, who graciously provided a review of the early manuscript to make sure I got the myriad facts straight.

And yet again I thank the entire Mars Pathfinder team, at JPL, at NASA, in academia, in industry and in Europe. As I've said before and will never grow tired of saying, your skill, spirit and commitment made history. This book from the start was intended as a tribute to the extraordinary people who made Pathfinder happen.

—Brian Muirhead